1990

HENRY V

The Practice of Kingship

HENRY V

THE PRACTICE OF KINGSHIP

———

Edited by
G. L. HARRISS

OXFORD UNIVERSITY PRESS

Oxford University Press, Walton Street, Oxford OX2 6DP
Oxford New York Toronto
Delhi Bombay Calcutta Madras Karachi
Kuala Lumpur Singapore Hong Kong Tokyo
Nairobi Dar es Salaam Cape Town
Melbourne Auckland
and associated companies in
Beirut Berlin Ibadan Nicosia

Oxford is a trade mark of Oxford University Press

Published in the United States
by Oxford University Press, New York

First Published 1985
Reprinted (new as paperback) 1985

British Library Cataloguing in Publication Data
Henry V: the practice of kingship.
1. Henry V, King of England
2. Great Britain — Kings and rulers — Biography
I. Harriss, G.L.
942.04'2'0924   DA256
ISBN 0-19-873080-2
ISBN 0-19-873079-9 Pb

Library of Congress Catalouing in Publication Data
Main entry under title:
Henry V: the practice of kingship.
Consists of lectures delivered to undergraduates in
the Modern History School at Oxford in 1982 and 1983.
Bibliography: p.
Includes index.
1. Great Britain — Politics and government — 1399–
1485 — Addresses, essays, lectures.   2. Henry V,
King of England, 1387-1422 — Addresses, essays, lectures.
I. Harriss, G. L.
DA256.H46 1984   942.04'2   84-19078
ISBN 0-19-873080-2
ISBN 0-19-873079-9 Pb

Set by Hope Services, Abingdon
Printed in Great Britain
at the University Press, Oxford
by David Stanford
Printer to the University

Preface

Henry V is the only fifteenth-century King of England not to have been the subject of a recent scholarly biography; indeed the standard work on the reign is still that of J. H. Wylie, whose first volume appeared seventy years ago. This present book, consisting of lectures delivered to undergraduates in the Modern History School at Oxford in 1982 and 1983, brings to a wider audience the fruits of the study of the reign in seminars at Oxford and Liverpool over the previous decade. The contributors wish to acknowledge their indebtedness to all who have joined in these discussions. The volume seeks to present a picture of Henry V as a ruler. It discusses the tasks that faced him at his accession and his achievements in domestic government, religion, war, and diplomacy. Each of the contributors makes his own judgement on the king, but their common aim has been to deepen an appreciation both of Henry's abilities as King and of the nature of late medieval kingship. The editor's conclusion offers a general assessment in these terms. The lectures are here printed as delivered, with only minor modifications. The photograph on the cover of this volume of the figure of Henry V on the screen at York Minster was made by Mr D. A. Whiteley and is reproduced by kind permission of the Dean and Chapter of York.

Contents

Abbreviations

All works cited in the footnotes more than once appear in the abbreviated forms listed here.

Allmand, *Lancastrian Normandy*	C. T. Allmand, *Lancastrian Normandy, 1415-1450. The History of a Medieval Occupation* (Oxford, 1983).
BIHR	*Bulletin of the Institute of Historical Research.*
BJRL	*Bulletin of the John Rylands Library.*
The Brut	*The Brut*, ed. F. W. D. Brie, 2 vols., EETS Original Series 131, 136 (1906, 1908).
Bourgeois	*Journal d'un Bourgeois de Paris, 1405-1449*, ed. A. Tuetey (Paris, 1881).
CCR	*Calendar of the Close Rolls, Henry V*, 2 vols. (HMSO, 1929-32).
CFR	*Calendar of the Fine Rolls, XIV 1413-22*, (HMSO, 1934).
CPR	*Calendar of the Patent Rolls, Henry V* 2 vols. (HMSO, 1910-11).
Cal. Signet Letters	*Calendar of Signet Letters of Henry IV and Henry V*, ed. J. L. Kirby (HMSO, 1978).
Chrimes, *Eng. Const. Ideas*	S. B. Chrimes, *English Constitutional Ideas in the Fifteenth Century* (Cambridge, 1936).
Complete Peerage	G. E. Cockayne, *The Complete Peerage*, ed. V. Gibbs and others, 12 vols. (London, 1910-59).

EHR	*English Historical Review.*
Ec. HR	*Economic History Review.*
English Court Culture	*English Court Culture in the Later Middle Ages*, ed. V. J. Scattergood and J. W. Sherborne (London, 1983).
English Parliament, ed. Davies and Denton	*The English Parliament in the Middle Ages*, ed. R. G. Davies and J. H. Denton (Manchester, 1981).
Fagan, 'Household of Henry V'	E. H. de L. Fagan, 'Some Aspects of the King's Household in the Reign of Henry V, 1413-22', unpublished MA thesis (London, 1935).
First English Life	*The First English Life of King Henry the Fifth*, ed. C. L. Kingsford (Oxford, 1911).
Foedera	*Foedera, Conventiones et Litterae*, ed. T. Rymer, 2nd edn., 20 vols. (London, 1727–35).
Fusoris	*Le Proces de Maitre Jean Fusoris*, ed. L. Mirot (Mémoires de la Société de l'Histoire de Paris, xxvii, Paris, 1901).
Gesta	*Gesta Henrici Quinti*, ed. F. Taylor and J. S. Roskell (Oxford, 1975).
Gower, *Works*	*The Complete Works of John Gower*, ed. G. C. Macaulay, 4 vols. (Oxford, 1899–1902).
Gray, *Influence of the Commons*	H. L. Gray, *The Influence of the Commons on Early Legislation* (Cambridge, Mass., 1932).
Griffiths, 'Henry, Prince of Wales'	W. R. M. Griffiths, 'The Military Career and Affinity of Henry, Prince of Wales, 1399–1413', unpublished M.Litt. thesis (Oxford, 1980).

Haines, 'Contemporary Preacher's View'	R. M. Haines, '"Our Master Mariner, Our Sovereign Lord": a Contemporary Preacher's View of Henry V', *Medieval Studies*, xxxviii (1976), 85-96.
Hist. Jnl.	*The Historical Journal.*
Hoccleve, *Minor Poems*	*Hoccleve's Works, The Minor Poems*, vol. i ed. F. J. Furnivall, EETS Extra Series, lxi (1892); vol. ii ed. I. Gollancz, EETS Extra Series, lxxiii (1925).
Hoccleve, *Regement*	*Hoccleve's Works, The Regement of Princes*, ed. F. J. Furnivall, EETS Extra Series, lxxii (1897).
Jacob, *Henry V and France*	E. F. Jacob, *Henry V and the Invasion of France* (London, 1947).
Jacob, *Fifteenth Century*	E. F. Jacob, *The Fifteenth Century, 1399-1485* (Oxford, 1961).
Jacob, *Chichele*	E. F. Jacob, *Archbishop Henry Chichele* (London, 1967).
Kirby, 'Financing of Calais'	J. L. Kirby, 'The Financing of Calais under Henry V', *BIHR*, xxiii (1950), 165-77.
Lydgate, *Minor Poems*	*Lydgate, The Minor Poems*, ed. H. N. MacCracken, 2 vols. EETS Extra Series, cvii (1911), Original Series, cxcii (1934).
Lydgate, *Siege of Thebes*	*Lydgate's Siege of Thebes*, ed. A. Erdmann, EETS Extra Series, cviii (1911).
Lydgate, *Troy Book*	*Lydgate's Troy Book*, ed. H. Bergen, 4 vols., EETS Extra Series, xcvii-cvi (1906-12).
McFarlane, 'Henry V, Beaufort and the Red Hat'	K. B. McFarlane, 'Henry V, Bishop Beaufort and the Red Hat', *EHR*, lx (1945), 316-48; reprinted in *England in the Fifteenth Century* (London, 1981), pp. 79-114.

McFarlane, *Lancastrian Kings*	K. B. McFarlane, *Lancastrian Kings and Lollard Knights* (Oxford, 1972).
McFarlane, *Nobility*	K. B. McFarlane, *The Nobility of Later Medieval England* (Oxford, 1973).
Monstrelet, *Chronique*	*La Chronique d'Enguerran de Monstrelet*, ed. L. Douët-d'Arcq, 6 vols., Société de l'Histoire de France (Paris, 1857-62).
Mum and the Sothsegger	*Mum and the Sothsegger*, ed. M. Day and R. Steele, EETS Original Series, cxcix (1936).
Newhall, *Normandy*	R. A. Newhall, *The English Conquest of Normandy, 1416-1424* (New York, 1924; reissue 1971).
Nicolas, *Agincourt*	Sir Harris Nicolas, *History of the Battle of Agincourt* (London, 1833).
PMLA	*Proceedings of the Modern Language Association of America.*
PRO	Public Record Office.
Proc. PC	*Proceedings and Ordinances of the Privy Council of England*, ed. N. H. Nicolas, 7 vols. (Record Comm., 1834-7).
Reg. Chichele	*Register of Henry Chichele, Archbishop of Canterbury, 1414-1443*, ed. E. F. Jacob and H. C. Johnson, 4 vols. (Canterbury and York Soc., 1938-47).
Roskell, *Speakers*	J. S. Roskell, *The Commons and their Speakers in English Parliaments, 1376-1523* (Manchester, 1965).
Rot. Parl.	*Rotuli Parliamentorum*, 6 vols. (London, 1767-77).
SHF	Société de l'Histoire de France.

Somerville, *Duchy of Lancaster*

R. Somerville, *History of the Duchy of Lancaster, i, 1265–1603* (London, 1953).

St Albans Chronicle

The St Albans Chronicle, 1406–1420, ed. V. H. Galbraith (Oxford, 1937).

Steel, *Exchequer*

A. Steel, *The Receipt of the Exchequer, 1377–1485* (Cambridge, 1954).

Taylor, 'Chronicle of John Strecche'

F. Taylor, 'The Chronicle of John Strecche for the Reign of Henry V', *BJRL*, xvi (1932).

Titi Livii Vita

Titi Livii Foro Juliensis, Vita Henrici Quinti, Regis Angliae, ed. T. Hearne (Oxford, 1716).

TRHS

Transactions of the Royal Historical Society.

Twenty-Six Poems

Twenty-Six Political and other Poems, ed. J. Kail, EETS Original Series, cxxiv (1904).

Usk, *Chronicon*

Chronicon Adae de Usk, 1377–1421, ed. E. M. Thompson (Oxford, 1904).

Waurin, *Croniques . . . 1399–1422*

Jean de Waurin, *Recueil des Croniques et anchiennes istories de la Grant Bretaigne a present nommé Engleterre, 1399–1422*, ed. W. Hardy (Rolls Ser., 1868).

Wylie (and Waugh), *Henry the Fifth*

J. H. Wylie, *The Reign of Henry the Fifth* vols. i, ii (Cambridge, 1914, 1919), vol. iii with W. T. Waugh (Cambridge, 1929).

I

Introduction: the Exemplar of Kingship

G. L. HARRISS

Henry V's historical image and reputation is that of a soldier: the victor of Agincourt, and the one English king to make good the claim to the crown of France. His military triumphs undoubtedly served to transform the prestige and authority of the English crown at home and abroad; but Henry V was more than the 'myghti conquerour', or even the 'flour of chivalrie', celebrated by the poets.[1] Contemporaries praised his governance as much as his feats of arms, and when he embarked for France in 1415 he already commanded greater respect than any English king since Edward III. Many of the contributions to the present volume explore the renewal of royal authority that he accomplished in the first years of the reign. In one sense this was merely the preparation and prerequisite for his greater designs in France, for the Lancastrian double monarchy of France and England stood in logical succession to the Lancastrian renewal of kingship in England. Henry V presented himself not as the conqueror but as the heir and saviour of France, the very terms in which his father had claimed the crown of England. An examination of his practice of kingship in England may thus suggest how he envisaged his prospective status and charge as ruler of both realms. Further, Henry's practice of kingship not only underlies and links his military and political ambitions but enables us to see him not in heroic isolation, but in relation to his subjects. Their expectations of kingship had been sharpened by the crisis of the monarchy under Richard II, so that when Henry commenced his thirteen-year apprenticeship as Prince of Wales, he entered a world where political debate was more heightened and criticism of royal government more widely

[1] Lydgate, *Troy Book*, iii, 875; Hoccleve, *Minor Poems*, i, 41.

disseminated than at any previous point in English history.

To his seniors and mentors the recent past had been a nightmare. The scandals and military defeats of Edward III's dotage, the great uprising of 1381, the spread of Lollardy, the feuds which had divided the nobility and culminated in Richard II's deposition, had all seemed to portend the dissolution of society into chaos. In 1399 Henry IV was hailed as a saviour, but the crisis merely deepened. The battle of Shrewsbury appeared to mark the onset of civil war, Glyndwr's rebellion the dismemberment of the realm; the spectre of French invasion reappeared, while internally Henry IV's government looked like collapsing into insolvency and disorder. This unnerving and inexplicable sequence of social, religious, and political crises was still vividly present to the mind of a preacher at parliament in 1421 who likened it to an uncontrollable storm in which the ship of state had all but perished.[2] Gower had used the same symbolism to denote the impact of the Peasants' Revolt, while for thirty years following the Good Parliament of 1376 the Commons' bitter criticisms, unparalleled pretensions, and repeated demands for 'good and abundant governance' only thinly concealed their own bewilderment and lack of effective remedies. Of all the Ricardian poets Gower is most representative of the middle and 'professional' stratum of free society which in the late fourteenth century had become alienated from royal government, and impotently voiced its grievances and remedies in a wide range of the surviving literature.

In the *Mirroir de l'Omme* he had categorized the sins of each estate which lay at the root of the social malaise, and in *Vox Clamantis* he developed the same theme with greater emphasis on the dread consequence of an overthrow of ordered society from below. The laxity of the clergy, the indolence of the nobility, the corruption of the lawkeepers, and the quarrelsomeness of the merchants were matched by the discords of heresy and the stirrings of the plebs. No anchor secured the ship of state. The voice of a people crying out was God's warning to unjust rulers. But, Gower insisted, neither the overthrow of kingdoms nor the fall of princes

[2] Haines, 'Contemporary Preacher's View', p. 90.

was the result of Fate or Fortune; both were the consequence of man's sin, which it lay in himself to correct and thus to restore his moral and political health. Gower saw good governance by the king as providing a framework for Christian virtue, and his political ideals were centred on order, stability, and honesty.

It has recently been suggested that far from being 'courtier' poets, Chaucer and Gower found their circle and audience among the 'household knights, and officials, career diplomats, and civil servants', representative of 'the national administration and its metropolitan milieu'. With one or two specific exceptions their works were neither commissioned nor owned by the courtier nobility, who still favoured traditional romances and epic and chivalric themes.[3] Further, the tone of Ricardian poetry has been described as private and civilian: its image of man was consciously unheroic, its preoccupations were the dilemmas of everyday living rather than epic struggles or grandiose visions. Its basic moral earnestness was tempered by irony and good-natured tolerance and its ideal was not that of knightly prowess but of balance, maturity and practical wisdom.[4] This contrast extended to language, for whereas the books read and owned by the aristocratic and chivalric class were virtually all in Latin or French, which was still the language of the court, the Ricardian poets, though professionally trilingual, increasingly and consciously favoured English. Gower explained with a note of apologetic defiance that he had chosen this for his great anatomy of courtly love:

> And for that fewe men endite
> In oure englissh, I thenke make
> A bok for Engelondes sake.[5]

Finally, we find in this poetry for the first time not merely

[3] D. Pearsall, 'The Troilus Frontispiece and Chaucer's Audience', *Yearbook of English Studies*, vii (1977), 68–74; V. J. Scattergood, 'Literary Culture at the Court of Richard II', and A. I. Doyle, 'English Books in and out of Court from Edward III to Henry VII', both in *English Court Culture*, pp. 38, 168–9. Dr Catto surveys this group in chapter iv, below.

[4] J. A. Burrow, *Ricardian Poetry: Chaucer, Gower, Langland, and the Gawain Poet* (Oxford, 1971), ch. 3.

[5] Gower, *Works*, ii, 2.

a nationalistic but a patriotic note, celebrating a love of England, pride in her achievements, and sorrow at her current misfortunes. Gower is notable for this and for his consequent search for political as well as moral regeneration.

But much as these 'professional' classes were inclined to see themselves as the salt of society, their strictly defined role in the political hierarchy restricted their own capacity to effect reform. It was to the king that they looked, and it was to the duties of kingship that Gower devoted Book VII of *Confessio Amantis*. Drawing on the 'Mirror of Princes' tradition, it presented the canons of good kingship in direct, forceful, and heartfelt English, and was intended as a tract for the times. For it is clear that Gower became increasingly disturbed and disillusioned with Richard II's rule and deliberately cast himself as the apologist of Lancastrian regeneration. In 'O Deus Immense' he blamed Richard's destruction on his obduracy in neglecting to listen to the voice of his subjects, attend to their complaints, and win their love, while in the *Chronica Tripertita* he retold the events of 1388-1400 from the Appellants' point of view, paraphrasing the articles of deposition in the 1399 parliament, and concluding with a sustained characterization of Richard and Henry as epitomes of bad and good kingship.[6] He hailed Henry IV as the saviour of society:

> God hath the chose in comfort of ous alle:
> The worschipe of this lond, which was doun falle,
> Now stant upriht thurgh grace of thi goodnesse.[7]

Gower never voiced his disillusionment with Henry IV's rule and his last poem, 'In Praise of Peace' urged the king to complement his restoration of internal tranquillity with the establishment of peace abroad. Although Gower accepted the traditional English claim to the French crown and affirmed that a king might legitimately wage war

---

[6] G. R. Coffman, 'John Gower, Mentor for Royalty: Richard II', *PMLA*, lxix (1954), pp. 953-64; *The Major Latin Works of John Gower*, translated by E. W. Stockton (Seattle, 1962), pp. 290-326.

[7] Gower, *Works*, iii, 481.

> To cleime and axe his rightful heritage
> In alle places wher it is witholde,[8]

peace alone was pleasing to God and the mark of true kingship:

> What kyng that wolde be the worthieste,
> The more he myghte our dedly werre cesse,
> The more he schulde his worthinesse encresse.[9]

He urged Henry IV:

> Ley to this olde sore a new salve,
> And do the werre awei, what so betide.[10]

Gower's dislike of war was probably broadly representative of the interests and attitudes of his class. Finally, with peace and unity restored among nations, kings should strive to bring the same to the church, ending the schism in the papacy and uniting all Christendom in a crusade against heathendom. But these were far distant visions, and Gower's main concern was for the regeneration of his native land: 'I, John Gower, conclude my counsel: the king and his people are like the head and the body. Where the head is infirm the body is infirm. Where a virtuous king does not rule, the people are unsound and lack good morals.'[11] All hopes for political and moral regeneration were thus centred on the king.

It is scarcely to be doubted that the one circle among the aristocracy where Gower was read and welcomed was in the Lancastrian *familia*. He himself wore the Lancastrian collar, and copies of *Confessio Amantis* were owned by Henry IV's sons.[12] With Henry IV's accession the character of the court changed, becoming more attuned to the interests, expectations, and culture of metropolitan opinion. The use of English began to be consciously promoted, while parliament again voiced its concern for honest and economical administration and financial accountability. Whatever the other deficiencies of his government, Henry IV could not be accused

[8] Ibid. 483.
[9] Ibid. 485.
[10] Ibid.
[11] Coffman, op. cit., p. 961, freely translating from *Works*, iv, 364, ll. 83–6.
[12] Doyle, 'English Books', p. 170.

of failing to heed the voice of his subjects, and the serious-
ness with which both he and they viewed the duties and
obligations of kingship must have had a profound effect on
Prince Henry.

Gower had no immediate successor as a Lancastrian
apologist, and the continuing crisis of disorder, insolvency,
and parliamentary complaint in the first part of the reign
produced the first great age of English political verse which
criticizes, lampoons, warns, and advises the ruler and his
ministers. These occasional pieces are more topical, and
often more directly related to matters of parliamentary
debate, than the great narrative poems of the Ricardian
poets. Their context is, of course, the political divisions
which still continued to rend the State. In *Mum and the
Sothsegger* the 'eager envy' of lords in their scramble for
royal patronage is discerned as the principal cause of civil
war and political murder over the past forty years; or, as the
poem 'Wit and Will' succinctly puts it:

> In kyngdom, what maketh debate,
> Riche and pore both anoyed?
> Yong counseil and prevey hate,
> And syngulere profit ys aspied.[13]

Richard the Redeles blames Richard's alienation from his
subjects on the swarms of liveried retainers whose demands
on royal patronage could only be satisfied by imposing
burdens on the realm. Henry IV's denunciation of Richard II
on this score rebounded on him, and the parliaments of
1401-6 were full of bitter criticism of the costs of the royal
household, of excessive annuities, and taxes misspent. These
attempts by the Commons to impose remedies and restraints
on the crown are reflected in *Mum and the Sothsegger*, in
which a resumption of royal grants is advocated as the only
remedy for the courtiers' greed for patronage and their
purloining of taxation for their own gain.[14]

The audience for this verse was essentially those whose
interests were represented in parliament, on which their
hopes for reform of government centred:

[13] *Twenty-Six Poems*, p. 23.
[14] *Mum and the Sothsegger*, pp. 74-5.

Whanne alle a kyngdom gadrid ysse
In goddis lawe, by on assent,
For to amende that was mysse,
Therefore is ordayned a parlement[15]

The duties of representatives were conceived in the same sense:

When knight for the comune been come for that deede,
And semblid forto shewe the sores of the royaulme
And spare no speche though thay spille shuld,
But berste oute alle the boicches and blaynes of the hert
And let the rancune renne oute a-russhe al at oones.[16]

The bitter satire with which *Richard the Redeles* castigates the knights of the shire who kept silent from cowardice, sloth, or self-interest showed how much the parliamentary classes valued their role as critics and reformers of government.[17] For in their own eyes they were the guardians and saviours of the kingdom from the very danger of which Gower had warned, the destructiveness of the mob; and their duty in parliament was to lance the sores of the realm lest these fester into rebellion.

They believed further, that on their administrative and judicial expertise, as well as on their military experience and wealth, royal prestige and national prosperity rested:

For comons mayntene lordis honour,
Holy chirche, and religyoun,
For comouns is the fayrest flour
That evere god sette on erthley crown.[18]

In consequence they were ready to accept that the crown had to be kept solvent, if necessary by taxation:

For nedis moste oure liege lord like his estat
Have for his houshold and for his haynous werres
To maynteyne his manhoode, there may no man seye other[19]

and Gower consciously distanced himself from the plebs, whose reaction to all and any taxation was merely to grouse and complain:

---

[15] *Twenty-Six Poems*, p. 55.
[16] *Mum and the Sothsegger*, p. 59.
[17] Ibid., pp. 24–6.
[18] *Twenty-Six Poems*, p. 55, and similarly p. 12.
[19] *Mum and the Sothsegger*, p. 75.

> And ek his kinges realte
> Mot every liege man conforte,
> With good and bodi to supporte
> Whan thei se cause resonable.[20]

But at the same time the king must meet his obligations to uphold and govern by law, since 'for fawte of law the commons rise'. Indeed the whole social and political order rested on respect of the law by the king and obedience and co-operation by his subjects.

I have chosen to illustrate this concern with the practice of government from poetry rather than from the more specific record of the parliament rolls and chronicles, partly to emphasize its diffusion among the literate class, and partly because such poetry delineates the faults of government by restating the ideal. Indeed at the beginning of *Richard the Redeles* the poet claims that his work would teach good government to every king in Christendom, and it is important not to lose sight of the 'Mirror of Princes' strain even in this more racy and topical verse, addressed primarily to an urban and political class. For it is precisely from this background that Hoccleve comes, and his *Regement of Princes* continues the tradition of Lancastrian patronage for a work of political advice. It was less the novelty of his matter than Hoccleve's direct and fresh language, topical allusions, and tone of optimism that gave the *Regement* immediate and enduring popularity, as the forty-five existing manuscripts show. It is also indicative of the stimulus given under Lancastrian government to the use of English for serious political and philosophical themes, not least by Prince Henry himself. Hoccleve credits the prince with knowledge of his three sources:

> I am sure that the bookes alle thre,
> Redde hath and seen your Innat sapience,
> And, as I hope, her vertues folwen ye;[21]

[20] Gower, *Works*, iii, 291.
[21] Hoccleve, *Regement*, pp. 77-8. Hoccleve says that his sources were the *Secreta Secretorum*, Giles of Rome's *De Regimine Principum*, and the *De Ludo Scaccorum* of Jacobus de Cessolis. For the influence of this tradition, see A. H. Gilbert, 'Notes on the Influence of the *Secreta Secretorum*', *Speculum*, iii (1928), 84-98; L. K. Born, 'The Perfect Prince: A Study in Thirteenth and Fourteenth Century Ideals', ibid. 470-504.

He expects that Henry will read his stories 'When that ye ben in Chambre at eve', and trusts in his critical judgement:

> His hye prudence hath insight verray
> To judge if it be wel y-made or nay.[22]

Lydgate likewise tells us that the reason why Henry commissioned him to translate the Troy legends was

> Bycause he wolde that to hyghe and lowe
> The noble story openly were knowe
> In oure tonge, aboute in every age
> And y-writen as wel in oure langage
> As in latyn and frensche it is.[23]

The date of these compositions was important. Lydgate records that the *Troy Book* was commissioned on 31 October 1412. The *Regement*, completed in 1411, was probably commenced two years earlier. These two years were precisely those in which the prince, at the head of a council of his own choosing and virtually without reference to his father, was carrying through a sustained programme of 'bone governance' to which he had pledged himself in the parliament of January 1410. The council minutes bear witness to its close surveillance of government, exercised in frequent meetings which, as Hoccleve deplored, encroached on Holy Days. Its work, in bringing order into the royal finances and in regaining the confidence of parliament, formed the prelude to Henry V's own reign. The prince's brief period of rule thus furnished a solid expectation of an effective and reinvigorated kingship very different from the pious hope which Gower had expressed in Richard II's youth. As Prince Henry prepared to ascend his father's throne in March 1413 he was to an unusual degree the focus of the hopes and apprehensions of his subjects. Could the forty years of defeat and discord, of spiritual and social malaise, be brought to an end? If some doubted, all were probably agreed that it rested with the king. Even though power and wealth were becoming more widely diffused and political responses more sophisticated, the political class was still sufficiently restricted and cohesive

---

[22] Hoccleve, *Regement*, p. 69.
[23] Lydgate, *Troy Book*, i, 4.

to stand in a personal relationship to the king and to believe that, next to God, a nation's salvation or destruction rested with its monarch. It is quite certain that Henry felt the same, and the stories of his conversion and his visit to the recluse of Westminster underline his messianic approach to the duties of kingship.

What, then, were the ideals of kingship which he and his subjects shared?

The role of the king

The king stood at the apex of human society, looking to God immediately above and to his subjects below him. To God he should be humble and obedient, for only thus could he expect the obedience of his subjects. To his subjects he should appear magnificent, just, and benevolent, representing to them the qualities of the Godhead. As Hoccleve reminded Henry:

> a kyng, by wey of his office
> To god I—likened is,[24]

and most evidently his power to deliver judgement on them was godlike. The Digby MS says:

> Eche a kyng hath goddis power,
> Of lyf and leme to save and spille.[25]

More generally, because his virtues and vices would be reflected in his rule, a king had power 'to save or spille' his whole people. The *Secreta Secretorum* likened a just king to rain on the earth, Gower to the tiller of the soil which was his people. Both Gower and the Digby poet emphasize that he is the head of the body politic, the seat of reason and wisdom which directs and guides the limbs, his subjects.[26] They could not correct his misrule for, as Gower affirmed, 'his estate is free towards all other than God'; only the king could release himself and his subjects from the coronation oath, acknowledging his errors, as had Richard II, with the cheerful countenance of a repentant sinner. The observance of that oath was the formal test of true kingship. Hoccleve

---

[24] Hoccleve, *Regement*, p. 87.
[25] Twenty-Six Poems, p. 55.
[26] Ibid., pp. 64–9.

cautioned Henry V:

> Tho othes that at your creacioun
> Shul thurgh your tonge passe, hem wel observe;
> .   .   .   .
> It is nat knyghtly from an oth to varie;
> A kyng of trouth, oweth bene exemplarie.[27]

Henry remained highly conscious of his coronation oath and when, three and a half years and six parliaments later, the chancellor Henry Beaufort likened the king's labours on his people's behalf, and in fulfilment of his oath, to those of the Holy Spirit which in six days created the world and ⊄— rested on the seventh, it was an affirmation that Henry had discharged his responsibility for the salvation of his subjects and kingdom.[28]

Justice

As we have seen, the most conspicuously divine attribute of kingship was the power to render justice, and for this the king was set above the law in order to enforce it impartially:

> Prince excellent, have your lawes chere;
> Observe them, and offende hem by no wey!
> Bi oth to kepe it, bounde is the powere
> Of kyng; and by it is kynges nobley
> Sustened; law is both lokke and key
> Of suerte; while lawe is kept in londe,
> A prince in his estate may sikir stonde.[29]

The maintenance of law was the very basis and essence of ordered society and the exercise of royal authority, and a king who flouted the law lost all title to rule:

> What king of lawe taketh no kepe,
> Be lawe he mai no regne kepe.
> Do lawe awey, what is a king?
> Wher is the riht of eny thing,
> If that ther be no lawe in londe?[30]

[27] Hoccleve, *Regement*, p. 80.
[28] *Rot. Parl.* iv, 94.
[29] Hoccleve, *Regement*, p. 100.
[30] Gower, *Works*, iii, 317.

The king ministered justice both on an individual and a social basis. For treason and premeditated murder punishment should be inexorable, and to spare the guilty was a sign of weakness and a failure of justice. Gower, with the story of Saul's sparing of Agag in mind, was uncompromising in demanding the death penalty:

> For in the handes of a king
> The deth and lif is al o thing
> After the lawes of justice
> To slen it is a deadly vice
> Bot if a man the deth deserve,
> And if a king the lif preserve
> Of him which oghte forto dye
> He suieth noght thensaumplerie
> Which in the bible is evident.[31]

Henry V's punishment for treason was swift and stern, even embracing his much-loved companion Henry, Lord Scrope. But mercy or pity was equally requisite in a king; Gower recommended that justice be 'medled with pity' and Hoccleve praised Henry V for seeking to persuade the tailor John Badby to recant his heresy before the stake. Henry was similarly to plead with his friend Sir John Oldcastle before treason put him outside the law. But it was a king's maintenance of law and order in the realm that gave the full measure of his kingly duty. The endemic problem of public order had reached acute proportions in some areas at the end of Henry IV's reign, producing complaints in the parliaments of 1410, 1411, and 1413 of major disorders in the western shires. In a long section of the *Regement* on law observance Hoccleve asked:

> Whi soffrest thou so many an assemble
> Of armed folk? wel ny in every shire,
> Partye is made to venge her cruel ire.

Neither a new statute of riots nor the issue of an oyer and terminer commission had any effect, since as Hoccleve explained:

---

[31] Ibid. iii, 343.

And al such mayntenance, as men wel knowe,
Sustened is naght by persones lowe,
But Cobbes grete this ryot sustene.[32]

Shortly after his accession Henry acted decisively to curb the worst disorders amongst the nobility. Dr Powell's investigation of the proceedings before the court of king's bench in the summer of 1414 suggests that Henry's principal aim was to restore the social peace, rather than to punish crime.[33] The crown itself lacked the machinery to apply a penal code on any scale, and was heavily dependent on the local nobility in securing respect for and enforcement of the law. It had to proceed by example and encouragement and apply direct pressure on the county élite either by intimidation or by way of arbitration. Later, on his last visit to England, Henry settled a number of magnate disputes, some of them violent, in this way. His continual concern for order, justice, and 'good governance' is revealed in a letter to the Duke of Gloucester from the siege of Melun in 1420 charging him to ensure that justices, sheriffs, escheators, coroners, and the like 'been no troublers in their countries and that they be chosen without brokage or favour of persons, or other unleeful means'.[34] At his death Henry V was widely acknowledged even by his enemies to be 'the prince of justice'.

Counsel

The root of all kingly rule was wisdom—Solomon's preferred gift from God—and this manifested itself in the choice of wise councillors. In Gower's words:

> . . . for ther is nothing
> Which mai be betre aboute a king,
> Than conseil, which is the substance
> Of all a kinges governance.[35]

The *Secreta Secretorum* offered many tests of how to distinguish between good and evil counsel and the lesson of Rehoboam was frequently held up to medieval kings. Much

---

[32] Hoccleve, *Regement*, p. 101. 'Cobbes' = lords.
[33] Below, chapter iii.
[34] PRO, C 81/1543, no. 21.
[35] Gower, *Works*, iii, 344.

of the blame for Richard II's tyranny was placed on his young and covetous councillors and the Commons' demands for a 'sad and substantial' council formed their principal remedy for misgovernment in Henry IV's early years. It was as the head of a reforming and aristocratic council that Prince Henry made his political début, and the chancellor's text for the first parliament of his reign was 'Ante omnem actum consilium stabile'. Hoccleve repeated these shibboleths. In making his council, the wise king

> Chesith men eke of olde experience;
> Hir wit and intellect is gloriouse;
> Of hir conseil, holsome is the sentence;
> The old mannes rede is fructuouse;
> Ware of yong conseyl, it is perilouse.[36]

Henry chose his council from the known and tried servants of the house of Lancaster: whether from the nobility or the knightly class, all were old in experience though some, like the king himself, still young in years.[37] In parliament the king took the wider counsel of the realm. The preceding forty years had seen a 'crisis of parliaments' in many respects similar to that of the seventeenth century. King and parliament had been at loggerheads and their frustrations had produced constitutional conflicts but little effective government. Men had come to see parliament as a place in which to 'shewe the sores of the royaulme', as the Commons had in their marathon petition in the Good Parliament. But in Henry V's reign its function was different. Its short frequent sessions had a more businesslike character, and his parliaments marked successive stages in the fulfilment of a programme of good governance in establishing order, enacting good and necessary laws, and winning agreement for the pursuit of the king's claim to France. Henry worked through parliament, using it to implement his policies and secure the support of the political nation for them. That the character of its proceedings changed so swiftly and completely after forty turbulent years shows that Henry's use of it met the expectations of the political community it represented.

[36] Hoccleve, *Regement*, p. 178.
[37] Cf. *Gesta*, p. 2.

Finance

The contrast is particularly marked in the total cessation of financial grievances which had continued so persistently throughout the previous two reigns. In many ways financial rectitude was the paradigm of good kingship, for both profligacy and avarice would impel a king to tyranny as he sought to live at the expense of his people. Profligacy was the characteristic sin of a young monarch and Hoccleve, repeating the *Secreta Secretorum* almost verbatim, warned:

> What kyng that dooth more excessif despenses
> Than his land may to suffice or atteyne,
> Schal be destrued, after the sentences
> Of Aristotle; he schal naght fle the peyne
>
> .   .   .   .   .
>
> Foole largesse geveth so moche a-way,
> That it the kynges cofres maketh bare.[38]

Yet Bacon's praise of the 'felicity of full coffers' was not shared by medieval writers, for that betokened avarice in a king, whose heart should be set on his people's wellbeing more than his own.

> For whan his herte lurketh in his cofre,
> His body to batayle he dar not profre,
> If that a kyng sette his felicite,
> Principally on rychesse and moneye,
> His peple it torneth to adversite,
> For he ne rekketh in what wise or weye
> He pile hem; allas that kynges nobleye
> Turne schulde into style of tirannye![39]

Good kingship consisted in the conservation of the crown's rights and revenues, so that these should bear a large part of his expenses, and a careful control of expenditure. This was the recommendation of *Mum and the Sothsegger*, and Hoccleve likewise urges the king to live of his own:

> By wise conseil, settith your hy estat
> In swhiche an ordre as ye lyve may
> Of your good propre, in reule moderat.[40]

---

[38] Hoccleve, *Regement*, p. 159.
[39] Ibid., p. 145.
[40] Ibid., p. 174.

Yet, like the responsible leaders of the Commons, he acknowledges the need for taxation for the common good:

> Naght speke I ageyn eides uttirly,
> In sum cas they ben good and necessarie;
> But whan they goon to custumablely,
> The peple it makith for to curse and warie;
> And if they ben despended in contrarie
> Of that they graunted of the peple were,
> The more grucchen they the cost to bere.[41]

Men still remembered that it was the 'grucchyng' against taxation that had precipitated the rising of 1381, and for a whole generation thereafter parliament had granted taxation fearfully and reluctantly, imposing conditions and restrictions on its use and expenditure. But under Henry V parliament not only sanctioned an even heavier incidence of taxation than in the years 1377-81, but did so without arousing complaint, criticism, conditions, or demands. The Commons seem to have regained confidence in their own power to tax and in the king's proper use of their money. The reasons for this go to the heart of the king's financial policy, discussed in chapter viii. Henry coupled strict financial discipline with a well-publicized determination to exploit his own—the crown revenues—to the full and to check waste and embezzlement, thereby rendering the Commons' habitual complaints about taxation and demands for resumption superfluous.

Political harmony

As well as disorder, insolvency, and the role of parliament, the theme of civil strife is prominent in post-Ricardian poetry. Lydgate in the *Troy Book* exclaims:

> Lo, what meschef lyth in variaunce
> Amonge lordis, whan thei not accorde[42]

and Hoccleve was bitterly aware that

> The ryot that hath ben within this lande,
> Among our-self, many a wyntres space,
> Hath to the swerd put many a thousand:

·   ·   ·   ·   ·   ·

---

[41] Ibid., p. 159.
[42] Lydgate, *Troy Book*, ii, 461.

> Werre within our-Iself is most harmful
> And perillous, and most is agayn kynde.
> Ther-with this land hath wrastled many a pul;
> The smert is swich, it may not out of mynde,
> For it hath cast our welthe far be-hynde,
> And ferther wole, but thoo werres stynt.[43]

Henry V scarcely needed to be reminded of that. His father had faced conspiracy and treachery from the Ricardian nobility and the Percies for two-thirds of his reign, while at the battle of Shrewsbury he himself had barely escaped with his life. His own succession had been in question and within two years of it he twice experienced treachery from within his own household and faced the danger of armed rebellion. The author of the poem 'God Save the King and Keep the Crown' probably written on the occasion of Henry's coronation, was alive to the danger:

> Yif we among oure self debate,
> Than endeth floure of chivalrie.
> All other londis that doth us hate,
> Our feblenes wol aspye;
> On every syde they wole in hye
> The stalworthe cast the feble adoun.
> Yif they with myght have maystrye
> Fro the right heire wolde take the crowne.[44]

Henry's reaction to this tells us much about his own character and that of his kingship. To choose the path of magnanimity and reconciliation, as the poets urged, demanded political courage and vision of a high order. Yet the bringing of love out of hate, a major theme of *Confessio Amantis* and of Lydgate's *Siege of Thebes*, was the role of an earthly as well as the heavenly King, and though he had to wield the sword against rebels, a king should strive to bring harmony out of discord. It is the figure of King David and his harp that is used by Bromyard and by Gower in the *Mirroir de l'Omme* to define the king's role, for he exercises the skill of the harpist in tuning the discordant strings—his subjects—into harmony.

[43] Hoccleve, *Regement*, pp. 188–9.
[44] *Twenty-Six Poems*, p. 51.

It was in this spirit that Henry V treated the heirs of those
who had rebelled against his father, offering them restoration
to their lands and dignities at the price of loyal and strenuous
service. The failure of the Earl of Cambridge to implicate
them in his conspiracy marked a victory for Henry's policy.
Nor was their loyalty purchased through bounty and bribery,
for his distribution of patronage, like his distribution of titles,
was extraordinarily restrained. If we ask how Henry commanded their loyalty and service, one answer very evidently
lies in his military qualities; but before passing to this let
us observe how in many other respects Henry's behaviour
conformed to the model of kingship. He was abstemious
in food and drink and chaste in body; as Hoccleve bade, he
was sparing of his words:

> A kyng from mochil speche him refreyne;
> It sitte him ben of words mesurable.[45]

Yet it is also important that his behaviour to his lieges should
be open, gracious, and benign, giving no cause for fear,
resentment, or suspicion. Lydgate advises:

> Her may ye see how myche may avaylle
> The goodlihed and lownesse of a kyng,
> And specealy in cher and in spekyng,
> To his lyeges and to bern him fayre
> In his apport and shew hym debonayre,
> And nat to bene to straunge ne soleyn
> In contenaunce outward be disdeyn,
> Whiche causeth ofte, who that can adverte,
> Grete hatred in the puples herte.[46]

Richard II's reputation was one of arrogance and disdain
and he was widely accused of speaking fair words to his
magnates while plotting their destruction in his heart. For a
king above all others needed to keep faith and practise no
deceit, so that his subjects could trust his word. Henry's
magnanimity and good faith goes far to explain how he
won the confidence of his magnates.

---

[45] Hoccleve, *Regement*, p. 88.
[46] Lydgate, *Siege of Thebes*, i, 12–13.

Chivalry

Fidelity to his word was essential in a knight:

> Amonges alle thinges in a knyght,
> Trouthe is a thing that he ne lakke may[47]

and Henry V as the exemplar of knighthood, the recipient of Ullerston's *De Officio Militari*, and hero of the *Gesta* and the *Ballad of Agincourt*, is so familiar a figure that we need not elaborate upon it. Yet we must note two points relevant to our theme of Henry as the embodiment of the ideal of kingship. The first is that kingship was perhaps becoming distanced—divorced would be too strong—from knighthood. In *Vox Clamantis* for instance, Gower groups the king with the lawyers rather than the knights and sets him the role of regulating the machinery of government. Secondly, the chivalric ideal was itself in crisis, brought about by the excesses of the mercenaries and routiers on the one hand and those of the courtier knights of love on the other. The contrast between these false knights and the true knight performing his traditional function of defending the realm from its enemies, the poor from their oppressors, and the true faith against the infidel, and enduring hardship and danger without complaint, is the theme of one of the Digby MS poems, 'Mede and Much Thanks'. There is no doubt which type of knighthood Henry V exemplified, nor that in so doing he restored the traditional identity between knighthood and governance:

> Eche kyng is sworn to governaunce
> To governe goddis puple in right.
> Eche kyng bereth sword of goddis vengeaunce
> To felle goddis foon in fight.
> And so doth everons honest knyght
> That bereth the ordre as it wes.[48]

We can barely pause on Henry as the epitome of knighthood: Lydgate's celebration of him as

> of knythod loodesterr,
> Wis and riht manly, pleynly to termyne,
> Riht fortunat preevid in pes & werr,

---

[47] Hoccleve, *Regement*, p. 83.
[48] *Twenty-Six Poems*, pp. 6–9, 13.

> Gretly expert in marcial disciplyne,
> Able to stonde among the Worthi Nyne[49]

summarizes his abiding reputation. As C. T. Allmand notes,
Henry was renowned for his discipline, the key to his success
both in field and siege warfare. Prowess in arms, fortitude
in adversity, generosity in victory were other qualities of
knighthood he displayed in good measure. But victory in
battle was more a matter of mind than of muscle, or even
courage. There was no virtue in foolhardiness; indeed true
'hardiness' lay not in heroic sacrifice but in perceiving the
military advantage and fighting hard to secure victory for
the just cause. Judgement—sapience—was as necessary for a
knight as for a king; as well as fighting bravely, Henry had
thought about war.[50] Some held that a king should not risk
his life in battle, but Hoccleve praised the Athenian king
Codrus who chose death for himself rather than see his men
discomfited, and Henry V's boast that 'as I am trew kynge
and knyght for me this day schalle never Inglond rawnsome
pay' shows that he obviously agreed.[51] Yet if his cause *were*
just, and he were assured of God's support, a king need fear
no odds. He could, as Gower emphasizes in retelling the
story of Gideon, fight with the remnant of a remnant and
still secure victory. Gideon, surely, was in Henry's mind on
St Crispin's Day, as in the mind of the chaplain waiting and
watching from the rear.[52]

War and peace

Stemming from a family renowned for its feats of arms,
Henry V naturally aroused similar expectations, expressed
by Hoccleve:

> O worthi Prince! I truste in your manhode,
> Medlid with prudence and discrecioun
> That ye shal make many a knightly rode,
> And the pride of oure foos thristen adoun.[53]

[49] Lydgate, *Minor Poems*, ii, 716.
[50] Below, chapter vi.
[51] Hoccleve, *Regement*, pp. 142-3; *Political Poems and Songs*, ed. T. Wright
2 vols. (Rolls Ser., 1861), ii, 124.
[52] Gower, *Works*, iii, 337-42; *Gesta*, p. 121.
[53] Hoccleve, *Regement*, p. 143.

Yet at the same time Gower, Hoccleve, and Lydgate are at one in condemning the brutality and waste of war and the scandal of conflict between Christians. They have no illusions about the motive and consequences of war. It is undertaken, says Hoccleve, 'to win worldly wealth', and Lydgate concurs:

> And ground and cause why that men so stryve
> Is coveytise and fals Ambicioun,
> That everich wold han domynacioun
> Over other, and trede hym undyr foote.[54]

Lydgate, who had begun the *Troy Book* to encourage Henry and England to deeds of arms, in the *Siege of Thebes*, written in 1421, depicts at length the unpredictable consequences of war: commenced lightly, it consumes the wealth of kingdoms and brings destruction to both sides and to men of high and low estate. Hoccleve, likewise, details the sufferings of non-combatants and the destruction of their property, and points to the inherent folly of war in inflicting loss in order to achieve a peace to which both sides could have agreed beforehand. The love and reconciliation with which true kings rule their subjects should govern their relations with each other, and Hoccleve urges Henry to 'purchase pees by way of marriage' according to the prophecies of St Bridget. Although the divisions in France excited the cupidity and adventurism of a few professionals, from Hoccleve and his circle, and perhaps from the majority of Englishmen, they evoked pity:

> I am an Englyssh-man, and am thi foo,
> For thou a foo art unto my lygeance;
> And yit myn herte stuffid is with woo
> To see thyn unkyndly disseveraunce.[55]

That was the authentic, but dying, echo of Ricardian poetry. For it was France's 'disseverance' that offered Henry both the opportunity and justification for realizing his claim to the crown of France. It is at this point that a gulf appears to open between the model of kingship urged upon Henry V by the poets and philosophers and his own martial ambitions. He had met the yearnings of his subjects for a restoration of

---

[54] Ibid., p. 193; Lydgate, *Siege of Thebes*, p. 191.
[55] Hoccleve, *Regement*, p. 191.

'bone governance' in England but could he win their unstinted support for a costly and prolonged war overseas? Henry did so by a conscious appeal to traditional theory. Gower and Lydgate, though they condemned war as the first choice of the adventurer, both acknowledged that it might be the last resort of the statesman. When all peaceful means had failed, a war fought for a rightful end was just and necessary, and out of victory a lasting peace might be born.

Henry V, therefore, needed to justify his cause to his people, and as he prepared for war in the year preceding the expedition to Harfleur, his diplomacy had two objects: to keep his enemies divided, and to demonstrate the insincerity and insufficiency of the French offers. In neither was he at first wholly successful. In the negotiations with the French in the summer of 1414 he pitched his claims too high and counted too heavily on Burgundy's need of his support; by the autumn, when Burgundy and Armagnac had patched up their quarrel, parliament advised Henry to negotiate further and moderate his claims. Accordingly the second embassy to Paris, in the spring of 1415, asked for little more than had been agreed under the Treaty of Brétigny, and it was the French refusal of these lands in sovereignty that provided the ground for Henry's resort to the 'way of justice' by the arbitrament of war. Henry sailed to France with the blessing of the church, but it was the victory of Agincourt that irrefutably delivered the judgement of God. It also changed the popular mood from caution and distrust to the euphoric patriotism displayed in the Agincourt Carol and Song. Henry's view of French duplicity, which the renewed negotiations during the siege of Harfleur in 1416 were exploited to confirm, was adopted by Sigismund and urged on the Council of Constance. At home, the anonymous poet of 'Dede is Worchyng' not merely exhorts the king to make good his claim to the crown of France in the assurance that the realm is united, but to spurn further negotiation with the French as being merely a trick to deprive him of his rights.[56] By 1416 Beaufort could confidently invoke the assent of all estates to the great enterprise on the ground that

[56] *Twenty-Six Poems*, p. 59.

war was necessary to secure a just peace: 'bella faciamus ut pacem habeamus'.[57]

Opinion thus swung to the king's side, and when that peace was finally achieved at Troyes it seemed to confound his faint-hearted critics. The two realms were now indeed united in the bonds of peace, love, and marriage. On Henry's return in 1421 Lydgate could at last present him with the completed *Troy Book* in the concluding lines of which he anticipated the golden age when war would cease, thanks to

> This worthi kyng of wisdam and resoun
> And of knyghthood shall so doon his peyne
> To maken oon that longe hath be tweyne;
> I mene thus, that Yngelond and Fraunce
> May be al oon, withoute variaunce,
> Out of hertis old rancour to enchase
> By influence of his myghti grace,
> That called is of clerkis, douteles
> The sovereyn lord and the prince of pes,[58]

while in a similar conclusion to the *Siege of Thebes* he cites almost verbatim the words of the Treaty of Troyes: 'There shall be from hens forth for ever more and shall follow Pees, Tranquillity, Good Accord and Commune Affection and stable friendship and steadfast between the same roialmes and her subjects before sayd.'[59] As M. H. Keen writes, 'peace was the most important thing Henry suggested he could deliver—and the most difficult of delivery'.[60] That Henry had not, in fact, brought peace, but an indefinite commitment to war, was half perceived by Adam of Usk and others and was underlined by the disaster at Baugé and Henry's recruitment of a new army for France. In retrospect the Treaty of Troyes appears an over-ambitious attempt to cut the Gordian Knot of Anglo-French enmity, and doomed to failure; but it was still possible before Henry V's death to believe that he might resolve the great dilemma he had posed: how to bring peace with justice out of the horrors of

[57] *Rot. Parl.* iv, 94.
[58] Lydgate, *Troy Book*, part iii, p. 870, and similarly in Hoccleve's 'Ballade to Henry V on his Last Coming from France' in *Minor Poems*, ii, 34–5.
[59] *Foedera*, ix, 919.
[60] Below, chapter ix.

war, and achieve the unity of Christendom by conflict
between Christian kings.

Religion

That unity, Philippe de Mézières had argued, was the necessary prelude to a crusade and, according to one report,
Henry died claiming that his intention had been to build
again the walls of Jerusalem. But there were more urgent
tasks for a Christian king in the first decades of the fifteenth
century, namely the ending of the papal schism and the
eradication of heresy. Gower had exhorted Henry IV to the
first, but it was only when, on Henry V's initiative, the
English claimed and won full representation as a separate
nation at the Council of Constance, that the northern mon-
archies took over control of the conciliar movement from the
college of cardinals. Acting first in alliance with Sigismund to
procure the resignation of the three rival popes, and subsequently in opposition to him to achieve the election of
Martin V, Henry's intervention was forceful and decisive.
Conciliar politics was a strand in Henry's anti-French diplomacy, but the conciliar programme of reform interested him
little. What did interest him was the reform of the church in
England.

Chaucer's satire, Langland's allegory, and Gower's denunciation all reflect the tide of disillusionment with, and alienation
from, the traditional ecclesiastical order, just as the growth
of lay piety and Lollardy revealed the desire for a more
puritanical and personal commitment. Henry's own piety
was of this kind, and closely allied to his messianic streak;
but it impelled him to a regeneration of the traditional
structures rather than to the initiation of a new order.
Whatever his political disagreements with Archbishop Arundel,
he was at one with him in seeing the church as a pillar of the
kingdom, and was ready to protect its rights and liberties
against anticlericals and Lollards. But the pillar must have
firm foundations in the life and example of its priests. Only
then would the church resume its traditional leadership in
faith and morals, and its prayers become effective. In the
Regement of Princes Hoccleve urged the use of papal provision

to advance men of probity, and the papal schism enabled the first Lancastrian kings to staff an episcopate whose academic attainments and personal integrity were applied, as J. I. Catto writes, to the 'coolly professional' exercise of their office.[61] Through a sensitive, authoritative, and above all practical restatement of traditional doctrine and liturgy they reclaimed the spiritual allegiance of the laity. In this they were undoubtedly sustained and encouraged by Henry V's own example. He chose Carmelites as his confessors, Carthusians for his new foundation at Sheen; on the Benedictines he urged reform. His concern with the music and ceremonial of his chapel and with wider liturgical innovation, his contribution to the nave at Westminster and perhaps to the screen at York, show his pervasive interest in the welfare of the church, while beyond and above all else he freed it once and for all from the threat of Lollardy. In his ballade on the reinterment of Richard II at Westminster Hoccleve had contemplated the possibility of a king who embraced or favoured Lollardy:

> A king set in that wrong opinioun,
> Mighte of our feith be the subversioun[62]

but in a later ballade addressed to the king and the knights of the Garter he can celebrate Henry in terms which were to be accorded to his later namesake, as a new Constantine and defender of the faith:

> O Lige Lord, that han eek the liknesse
> Of Constantyn, thensaumple and the mirour
> To Princes alle, in loue and Buxumnesse
> To holy chirche o verray sustenour
> And piler of our feith, and werreyour
> Ageyn the heresies bittir galle,
> Do foorth do foorth continue your succour!
> Holde vp Crystes Baner lat it nat falle!
> This yle, or this, had been but hethenesse,
> Nad been of your feith the force and vigour![63]

---

[61] Hoccleve, *Regement*, p. 105; below, chapter v.
[62] Hoccleve, *Minor Poems*, i, 48.
[63] Ibid. i, 41.

Conclusion

In the ballade which Hoccleve addressed to Henry V on the day when the lords rendered homage to him at Kennington in March 1413 he provided a synopsis of the ideal of kingship which we have reviewed:

> God dreede and ficche in him your trust verray;
> Be cleene in herte and loue chastitee;
> Be sobre, sad, just, trouthe obserue alway;
> Good conseil take, and aftir it do yee;
> Be humble in goost, of your tonge attempree,
> Pitous and merciable in special,
> Prudent, debonaire, in mesure free,
> Nat ouerlarge, ne vnto gold thral.
>
> Be to your liges also sheeld and wal;
> Keepe and deffende hem from aduersitee;
> Hir wele and wo in your grace lyth al;
> Gouerneth hem in lawe and equitee;
> Conquere hir loue and haue hem in cheertee;
> Be holy chirches champioun eek ay;
> Susteene hir right, souffre no thyng doon be
> In preiudice of hir, by no way.[64]

Even at this early stage it is doubtful whether Henry V needed instruction in his duty, or was unaware that on him were fixed the hopes of that numerous, influential, and critical middle stratum of the political nation which in poem and petition had voiced the demand for good governance over the preceding forty years. He and they had grown up to a spiritual, social, and political crisis which seemed to have no end or solution. The accepted diagnosis was that it sprang from a failure of all estates to fulfil honestly and scrupulously their appointed roles. Health and harmony would only be restored when they did; but regeneration must start from the head, by the king's example, exhortation, and authority. Henry V set himself to achieve this, to be the perfect king, the exemplar of kingship and the saviour of his realm and people. Perfect kingship indeed embraced perfect knighthood, so that Hoccleve could celebrate him as both

[64] Ibid. i, 40.

Swerd of Knyghthode and Flour of Sapience!

Similarly a contemporary genealogist memorialized him as outstanding 'tam in temporali policia quam in armis militaribus'.[65] His contribution to the practice of government which his contemporaries recognized has gone almost unnoticed by historians, largely because his methods, like his model, were entirely traditional. In law-keeping, finance, council, parliament, and the church, he avoided institutional innovation, preferring to breathe life and effectiveness into the old forms. In this sense the importance of his reign lies in demonstrating that the perfected system of medieval English government could be made to work. A revitalizing of traditional kingship was what men looked for; had he attempted a revolution in the character of government he would at worst have alienated the political classes, at best have needed far longer to re-educate them. As it was, precisely because his programme was restorative rather than innovatory, and fulfilled the demands of that widening and newly articulate middle class for good governance, it succeeded swiftly. The transformation effected by his short reign in the conduct of government and in the minds of the governed was dramatic. The sense of delivery from the prolonged crisis of the preceding reigns is vividly conveyed in the sermon in Bodley MS 649 where the king is seen as the mediator with God for his people's welfare. It is through Henry's love of God (and notably his war against heresy) that the realm has been blessed with wealth and victory. It is through the 'gracious and prudent regimen' of 'Our Master Mariner, Our Sovereign Lord' that the ship of state again sails forth, its breaches repaired.[66] In chronicles and verse there is a new and uninhibited pride in English achievements. The 'image of man' favoured by the Ricardian poets, anti-heroic, civilian, and focused on quotidian concerns has, like their preoccupation with the failings and evils of the age, faded away. Lydgate's themes and viewpoint are those of the court, and his more ambitious works are heroic in tone and epic in aspiration. The muted patriotism in Gower's lament for England under

---

[65] Ibid. ii, 34; Magd. Coll. Oxford MS Lat. 248.
[66] Haines, 'Contemporary Preacher's View'.

Richard's rule, now rings out with unrestrained excitement in the Agincourt Carol or in the less pleasing jingoism of Lydgate's

> Bi Bowe and arwis sith the werr began
> Have Ynglysshmen, as it is red in story,
> On here enmyes had many gret victory.[67]

The most conspicuous feature of this liberation of the national spirit was that it sprang from and was focused on the king himself. Henry V inspired it and himself became the symbol of national identity to a degree only later equalled by Elizabeth I. In this sense the myth of perfect kingship made a powerful and self-fulfilling contribution to the restoration of royal authority. In providing his subjects with order, efficient administration, and military glory, the king met their deepest yearnings and won their abiding loyalty. The aphorism that a king's greatest wealth lay in the love of his subjects became a reality, for they opened their purses for his ends in an un-exampled manner. His conquests brought them profit and his victories pride and renown, but as his wider visions unfolded and he and they were called to a political destiny in France, the earlier harmony of purpose faltered. The idea of a double monarchy was distrusted and its implications perhaps never fully understood, nor were Englishmen prepared for the financial and military effort still needed to make it secure. At the end of his life Henry's vision, or ambition, stretched beyond that of the majority of his subjects, from whom he may have been in danger of becoming isolated. As it was, his death produced not only a sense of loss but of disorientation, as if the ship of state again lacked a helmsman.[68] Whether or not, in these final years, Henry showed signs of harshness, obduracy, and pride, as some have claimed, the burden of kingship had certainly begun to take its toll. If his statue on the screen at York Minster conveys a true image of him on his return to England in 1421—and there is some ground for thinking that it may[69]—we can trace in the care-lined face

---

[67] Lydgate, *Minor Poems*, ii, 548.
[68] C. L. Kingsford, 'The First Version of Hardyng's Chronicle', *EHR*, xxvii (1912), p. 744.
[69] In his chapter 'Architectural History from 1291 to 1558' in *A History of York Minster*, ed. G. E. Aylmer and Reginald Cant (Oxford, 1977), pp. 181-6,

and furrowed brow, the firmly set lips, the piercing gaze, and the aggressive tilt of the head some of the characteristics we have learned to recognize in him as a ruler. For here he stands, every inch a king, as his subjects chose to remember him, and as Lydgate saw him in his mind's eye:

> And manly holdest in thin hondes two
> —Who can beholde by clere inspeccioun—
> The swerd of knyghthood and the scepter also:
> The ton to bring to subieccioun
> Hertes made proude by fals rebellioun
> And with the scepter to rewle at the beste
> Thi pore liges, that wolde live at reste.[70]

Dr J. H. Harvey has argued that the stone screen must have been designed and partly built before the death of Henry V in 1422, since the central arch was clearly intended to be flanked on either side by seven niches with the English kings from William I to Henry V. The subsequent addition of the figure of Henry VI unbalanced the whole design. Whether this design originated with Henry V's mason at York, William Colchester (d. 1420) or his successor John Long, sent by the king from Westminster, the king's interest in the project must have been underlined by his visit to York in April 1421 when he was on pilgrimage to shrines and raising a further army for his return to Normandy. Indeed the screen may have been designed to celebrate and symbolize the recovery of Normandy, the ancient heritage of the English crown, which was held by all the kings on the north of the archway until lost by John, the last represented, and was only repossessed by the last king on the south side, Henry V. The screen was thus a powerful statement of not only the success but the legitimacy of the Lancastrian dynasty, and its significance in facing down the nave of the cathedral in which the martyred Archbishop Scrope was still venerated is evident. As Dr Harvey suggests, it may well have been separately funded. The statues themselves were carved later, though their strongly characterized portrayal of a literary tradition may well have been part of the original conception. In particular that of Henry V (reproduced on the cover of this volume) is likely to have approximated to portraiture; interestingly it represents him with a small forked beard in the style of his Plantagenet predecessors.

[70] Lydgate, *Troy Book*, iii, 877.

II

The King and his Magnates

G. L. HARRISS

Henry V's relations with his magnates are largely the story of how the legacy of faction and feud engendered by Richard II's partisan rule was dispelled, and how confidence in the right exercise of royal authority was reborn. Richard II's revenge on the Appellants had brought ruin to his uncle, Thomas of Woodstock, and the Earls of Warwick and Arundel in 1397, and to the houses of Lancaster and Mowbray in 1398-9. The spoils had fallen to the families of Holland, Montague, Despenser, and York, all of whom had then opposed the Lancastrian usurpation, so powerfully underwritten by the Percies for their own gain. Henry IV's attempts to win acceptance for his rule had foundered on the fears and resentments of these displaced Ricardians and the far-reaching ambitions of the Percies. The first half of his reign was punctuated by plots, rebellions, and battles which, though they left Henry IV on the throne, deepened and embittered the feuds of the nobility. It was this problem which shaped Prince Henry's first political apprehensions; indeed from the moment when Richard II took him to Ireland as hostage for his exiled father, faction and treachery were never far from his experience.

From 1401 until the final siege of Aberystwyth in 1408 the prince spent part of every summer, and some winters, in long and unrewarding campaigns in the marches and mountains of Wales. Although his own campaigning was intermittent, his formal responsibility as Prince of Wales and, periodically, as the king's lieutenant in the marches, gave him direct command over some of the principal members of the English nobility. His first commission as king's lieutenant, in March 1403, may itself have contributed to the revolt of the Percies in July, for hitherto they themselves had exercised royal authority in Wales and had been the prince's governors. In the revolt the prince narrowly escaped seizure and death, and men from his own retinue and from his earldom of Chester fought against him at the battle of Shrewsbury. Two years later he took part in the suppression of the second Percy revolt in Yorkshire, which was abetted by the Earl Marshal, Lord Bardolph, and Archbishop Scrope of York. The Earl Marshal, Thomas Mowbray, held lands in South Wales and claimed Gower, which Henry IV had granted to the Earl of Warwick. Mowbray, still under age in 1405, was the son of Henry IV's old rival and enemy who had died in exile in 1399, but he had recently been promised his inheritance as the price of loyal service in Wales. Distrusting the king's proffer, he had been drawn into rebellion; his execution was a lesson to his brother and heir to tread a different path. Others among the great families of the Welsh march were also numbered among the traditional enemies of Lancaster. The heirs of two of Richard II's favourites, John Montague, Earl of Salisbury and Thomas, Lord Despenser, both of whom had risen on behalf of the deposed monarch in 1400 and had suffered execution and forfeiture, were under age, and their lands in Hawarden and Glamorgan were in the king's hands. Of greater importance were the Mortimer lordships in North Wales and the central march to which Edmund, Earl of March was heir. Although still a mere boy in 1400, his descent from the senior line of Lionel of Clarence, albeit through female succession, gave him a claim to the throne; the Percies ostensibly championed him in 1403 and he was the focus of plots in 1405 in which Edward, Duke of York was implicated. Thereafter he was kept in close custody by Henry IV until in 1409 he was placed in Prince Henry's household.

The custody of these heirs and their lands, together with its own Lancaster lordships and Bohun inheritance, gave the crown overwhelming predominance among the marcher lords. Although for the most part they were absentees from their lands, leaving the burden of defence against the Welsh to their officers and retainers, Prince Henry was made aware of the interests and attitudes of these great families, some of whose members became his comrades in arms. He could

certainly count on the active support of three great families
who were traditional Lancastrian supporters, namely the
Fitzalan Earls of Arundel who held the important lordships
of Clun and Chirk, the Earls of Stafford as lords of Newport
and Caus, and the Beauchamp Earls of Warwick who held
Elfael and Gower. Both Warwick and Stafford campaigned
with the prince and the latter was killed at the battle of
Shrewsbury. Arundel and Warwick became life retainers
of the Prince of Wales, with fees of 250 marks p.a., while
under his command were such resident lesser lords of the
marches, as Lords Grey of Ruthin, Charlton of Powys and
Grey of Codnor, along with numerous gentry from Hereford,
Shropshire, and Cheshire.[1] It was thus in the Welsh marches
that Henry V first learned to lead his nobility.

When, after 1408, the prince's career shifted decisively
from Wales to Westminster, he brought into the king's
council the Earls of Warwick and Arundel. These, with his
old mentor Bishop Henry Beaufort, Sir Thomas Beaufort,
later Earl of Dorset, and Lord Burnell, formed the core of
the council headed by Prince Henry which displaced Archbishop Arundel and governed, virtually without reference
to the king, from the beginning of 1410 to the end of 1411.
But the vigour of his rule, combined with the ambivalence
of his status as heir apparent, strained loyalties within the
royal family, and led to conflict with the king and rivalry
with his brother Clarence. The dismissal of the prince and his
chosen council at the end of 1411 almost precipitated him
into an open challenge for the crown, and awoke suspicions
that his enemies planned to supplant him in favour of Clarence.
When he found himself displaced from the leadership of the
expedition to Aquitaine in 1412 he marched to London in
strength to vindicate his position and seek a reconciliation
with his father.

Within months Henry IV was dead and Prince Henry
succeeded without opposition, but his position was full of
uncertainty. The young heirs of those families who had
opposed Henry IV and had suffered at his hands were now
coming of age. Would they see, in an untried king and the

[1] Henry's retainers and annuitants as Prince of Wales are listed by Griffiths,
'Henry, Prince of Wales', pp. 204–17.

recent divisions within the Lancastrian family, the opportunity to regain their forfeited inheritances through conspiracy, treachery, and force? How readily did they accept the verdict of 1399, and how anxious were they to give fresh impetus to the feuds that had rent the English nobility over the past fifteen years? The first months of the new reign gave no clear indications. One chronicler remarks that Henry was crowned 'with the agreement of the greater part of the lords of the realm', while to another the hail and snow which accompanied the coronation in April 1413 was indicative of the new king's icy temperament and future severity. In June the council advised him not to move far from London, so that he could make speedy reaction to the news from every coast.[2] Two years later a member of a French embassy could report that a large part of the country still favoured the Earl of March or the Duke of Clarence, and within those two years Henry V had yet again experienced treachery from the most intimate members of his household. Sir John Oldcastle, one of his most trusted captains in Wales, led the Lollard revolt of 1414, and Henry Lord Scrope, who shared the king's bed-chamber, joined the Earl of Cambridge's conspiracy in 1415. Both plots involved the assassination of the king, and the chroniclers give significant hints that many more within the royal retinue and household were disaffected.[3]

What effect did the experience of treachery have on Henry's character? He had been inured to it from his youth and might have been expected to develop symptoms of paranoia, like John and Richard II or the first two Tudors, who suspected all save close favourites, and sought safety in vigilance and intimidation. In fact, Henry V's reaction was different. In the first place, plain treachery was punished with a measured, public, and inexorable justice; but after that there were no witch hunts, no suspended penalties, no cooked-up trials, or treason charges on imputed words. Henry was ready to credit professions of loyalty and await

---

[2] C. L. Kingsford, *English Historical Literature in the Fifteenth Century* (Oxford, 1913), p. 284; Taylor, 'Chronicle of John Strecche', p. 13; *Proc. PC*, ii, 125.

[3] Wylie, *Henry the Fifth*, i, 507; *St Albans Chronicle*, p. 78; *Rot. Parl.* iv, 65.

the deeds to prove them. That is the tenor of his reputed answer to his dying father's warning that Clarence might attempt to usurp his throne: the prince vowed that he would love and honour his brothers 'as long as they be to me true, faithful, and obedient as to their sovereign lord. But if any of them fortune to conspire or rebel against me, I assure you I shall as soon execute justice upon any one of them as I shall upon the worst and simplest person within this your realm'.[4] That provides the key to his treatment of the magnates, which I want to examine under three headings: first, how Henry sought to reconcile those families who had opposed the Lancastrian usurpation; secondly, how he offered his nobility opportunities for service and reward; thirdly, how he ruled the nobility in those matters where the crown's authority and its own interests conflicted with theirs.

The policy of reconciliation had begun even before Henry V ascended the throne. It had two features: it sought to create personal ties between the heirs of the dissident nobility and loyal Lancastrian families; and it offered a stage-by-stage restoration of their inheritances. We have already noted how the young Earl of March had in 1409 been released from strict custody and placed in Prince Henry's household; in 1413 he was given his estates, allowed to purchase his right to marry, and to choose Anne Stafford as his bride. Thomas Montague, the son of the rebel of 1400, came of age in 1409. His family had long-standing ties with that of Lancaster and his loyalty was not suspect; he was allowed to recover his entailed estates (his lands in fee simple remained in the king's hands) and he was summoned to parliament as Earl of Salisbury.[5] John Mowbray, brother of the rebel of 1405, had been kept first in the household of Henry IV's mother and then in that of the king, until in 1411 his marriage was granted to the Earl of Westmorland, who made him his son-in-law and at the same time restored to him the office of Marshal of England which Mowbray's father had lost. On coming of age in 1413, he was summoned to parliament and received the estates of his brother, which had escaped

[4] *First English Life*, p. 14.
[5] For these and other biographical details about members of the peerage, see appropriate entries in *Complete Peerage*.

forfeiture since he had been under age when executed. The young Holland heir, John, was still under age in 1413, living at Dartington under the care of his mother, Elisabeth of Lancaster, a daughter of John of Gaunt who had remarried Sir John Cornewaill, Prince Henry's principal retainer in the duchy of Cornwall. John Holland was to be restored as Earl of Huntingdon in 1416. Richard, the last of the Despensers, son of the rebel of 1400, was still a minor when he died in 1414. It had certainly been Henry V's intention to restore him for, like John Mowbray, he had been married to another of the Earl of Westmorland's daughters, Eleanor Neville, in 1412. Following the revolt of the Percies in 1403, the crown had relied on the family of Neville to hold the north loyal, and the Earl of Westmorland had been primarily responsible for the defeat of the revolt of 1405. His strong-minded and productive wife, Joan Beaufort, provided the link with the royal house and contributed to the growing influence of the Beauforts with Henry V.

Indeed, parallel to a policy of reconciling the old enemies of Lancaster, Henry V made a conscious attempt to knit together the Lancastrian family and its traditional allies. At the Leicester parliament of 1414 the king's brothers, John and Humphrey, were created Dukes of Bedford and Gloucester, and Clarence's title was confirmed. On the other side of the family Edward, Duke of York, was declared purged and free of all suspicions about his ambivalent conduct in the previous reign and the full name and honour of his title was confirmed. Moreover his brother Richard was allowed to revive the family title of Earl of Cambridge. By awarding recognition to the heirs of Edmund of Langley, Henry V hoped to prevent them from supporting the Mortimer claims against those of Lancaster. In this he was not wholly success-ful: Cambridge, the Earl of March's brother-in-law, was to organize the conspiracy of 1415, but York was no party to it, and March himself ultimately betrayed the plot to the king. The conspirators probably hoped for Clarence's support, but he was not involved. On the whole any revival of faction within the royal house had been prevented.

The conspiracy of 1415 was an attempt to activate the two dormant threats to the Lancastrian throne, from the

dynastic claims of the Earl of March and the military resources of the house of Percy. Hotspur's son, the young
Henry Percy, had been taken to Scotland by his grandfather
and was living under the guard of the regent, the Duke of
Albany. He seemed poised, with Scottish support, to resume
the long-standing quarrel with the houses of Neville and
Lancaster who now enjoyed his estates and offices in the
north of England. In view of Hotspur's treachery, it would
have been understandable if Henry V had regarded his
heir as a mortal enemy, whose perpetual exclusion and ruin
could now be accomplished. Few things, in fact, better
illustrate Henry V's capacity to see beyond his immediate
advantages than his plan to offer Percy restoration to his
estates and dignity, though at a price. Both the long-term
prospects for stability in the north and the immediate need
to secure the frontier against Scottish intervention when the
king went to France dictated this. None the less it was a bold
and risky initiative and probably unpopular with his Neville
allies. The first moves took place in the parliament of
November 1414 when, at the king's prompting, Percy,
though still in Scotland, was granted permission to sue for
his restoration and succession to the earldom of Northumberland. Negotiations were then set on foot for his exchange
with Albany's son whom the English held prisoner, Percy
undertaking to pay his ransom of £10,000. At the same
time he was married (by proxy) at Berwick-on-Tweed to
Eleanor Neville, the recent widow of Richard Despenser,
thereby forging a relationship with the Lancastrian family
and marking a reconciliation between the two great rival
houses of the north. At the last moment Henry V's plan to
secure Percy's restoration by royal authority was frustrated,
for the conspirators under the Earl of Cambridge kidnapped
Albany's son, hoping themselves to trade him for Percy
whom they could use to raise the north in revolt. But their
plans were bungled, the Percy affinity in the north had got
the royal message and did not rise, and the aborted attempt
unnerved and disorientated the conspirators. After some
hesitation the Earl of March disclosed the plot to the king.
His action saved his head, but brought inexorable execution
on those he implicated: the Earl of Cambridge, Lord Scrope,

and Sir Thomas Grey. All were tried and convicted by a panel of peers on which the Earl of March himself sat, and the full penalties of treason were exacted.[6]

These events, speedily followed by Henry's victory at Agincourt, removed all further danger of conspiracies or attempts to challenge Henry's throne. Because the conspirators, except for Cambridge, were faint-willed and inept, and lacked widespread support, it is tempting to dismiss the danger they posed. Yet the structure of their planned insurrection in Wales and the north, and their intention to assassinate the king and his brothers during embarkation at Southampton, were clearly modelled on the far more serious conspiracies and risings against Henry IV. There is no doubt that there were many who were ready to lend at least half an ear to a revival of such schemes, to see what mileage there might be in them for their own particular ambitions. It was by demonstrating that all who meddled in them forfeited his mercy, and at the same time by offering an honourable restoration to all who earned it by loyal service, that Henry finally dissolved the legacy of faction bequeathed by Richard II.

The suppression of the plot was sufficient to forestall Scottish intervention but Percy's own restoration was delayed until Henry's return from Agincourt. When he was finally released in 1416 Henry pointedly *created* him Earl of Northumberland thereby confirming the justice of his grandfather's forfeiture for treason and the king's own authority to restore him as a matter of grace. The importance which Henry attached to this principle had already been shown in the Leicester parliament of 1414 when the Earl of Salisbury brought a test case alleging that the attainder of his father in the parliament of 1401, after the rising, was invalid on technical grounds, and claiming his own restoration in blood, estate, and dignity as of right. Whatever the legal arguments, it was highly unwelcome to Henry V to have the judgements of his father's reign set aside, and Salisbury's plea was dismissed. Not until 1421 at the peak of his distinguished career in France when, in the king's absence, he

[6] The best account of the plot is in Wylie, *Henry the Fifth*, i, ch. 27.

held Normandy firm after the defeat at Baugé, was Salisbury declared to be heir in blood fully entitled to inherit the honour, estate, and lands of his father. This legal doctrine, that treason corrupted the blood of succeeding generations, was introduced in Henry IV's reign. It invalidated all normal rights of inheritance and title for this most heinous of crimes, and made restoration solely dependent on the king's grace and will. (Only the royal grace and pardon could wash away the guilt that had infected the family blood.) Henry V made good use of it not only in the cases of Percy, Montague, Despenser, and even York, but also in that of John Holland. In the parliament of November 1416, Holland asked for restoration to the fame, honour, and dignity of his father, Earl of Huntingdon, when he should come of age next spring, and for the recovery of his entailed estates. As the king's ward he had already served at Agincourt, and his request was granted. But such restorations were still only the first step towards the recovery of all that had been forfeited. Salisbury, Northumberland, and Huntingdon had all been restored to their entailed lands, but in each case the lands their fathers held in fee simple were still in the hands of the king or one of his brothers to whom they had been given as reward.[7] Not until John, Duke of Bedford's death in 1435 did Percy finally recover all his family's estates. Beyond this some might even look to recover the titles and dignities their families had received from Richard II —for the Hollands the dukedom of Exeter, for the Mowbrays that of Norfolk. It was an indication of the unchallengeable authority he wielded by 1416 that Henry V could bestow on his uncle, Thomas Beaufort, the dukedom of Exeter which the Hollands coveted as theirs. In fact the Hollands and the Mowbrays had to wait until the minority of Henry VI to recover their ducal titles. Thus the full restoration of families who had rebelled, in blood, lands, and title, was a long process, each stage of which had to be earned by loyalty and received through royal grace and authority. As such, it might have precipitated impatient and resentful spirits into

[7] The parliamentary proceedings relating to these lords will be found in *Rot. Parl.* iv, 17, 35, 37, 71, 100, 110, 141. For the Percy estates see J. M. W. Bean, *The Estates of the Percy Family, 1416–1537* (Oxford, 1958), pp. 69–75.

revolt, but in Henry V's hands it ensured continued fidelity and service. That service was rendered mainly in war.

Henry was well fitted to lead his nobility in war, not only by reason of his military genius and the devotion he commanded but because, like Edward I and Edward III, he headed a nobility of his own age. Of the seventeen members of the upper nobility in 1413, eleven were within the age-bracket 18–32, the age when the fighting man was at his peak. Henry himself was 26—exactly in the middle. The fact that they were broadly the same generation made an enormous contribution to Henry's hold over them. As we have seen, it helped them to put behind the sins and mistakes of their fathers and look to the future. After Agincourt they could have confidence in the prospects of service under the king; and they could be sure that his promises of reward for loyal service would be fulfilled. Triumphs in arms, as well as bringing profit, restored honour to families tainted with treason. The eagerness of a new generation to revive the glories of Edward III's reign is sufficiently explained by the profit and the honour this could bring. But the almost universal involvement of the upper nobility in the French wars also reflected the king's own belief that the nobility were his natural companions in arms and his insistence that they fulfil their role.

War held out exciting prospects but it also imposed legal and financial disciplines on the nobility. Their obligations to the king were defined by indenture, and the stipulation that they should muster at a particular time and place, with a specified contingent, imposed an obedience to royal requirements which was rarely matched in other aspects of their relationship with the crown. Henry V's two expeditions of 1415 and 1417 included larger numbers of the upper nobility than any that had sailed since the reign of Edward III. Their assembly was governed by a specific timetable which involved each noble retinue in elaborate planning for the mustering of its equipment, men, supplies, and shipping. Henry V was insistent that his requirements be met. Towards the end of his life his brother Humphrey, Duke of Gloucester, recalled that simply because he lacked two of his men-at-arms at his muster, he had been made to bear the cost of shipping his retinue to France and received no pay until he had mustered his full complement at Dreux. In 1417 the king publicly voiced his anger at those lords who failed to muster on time, and in 1421 Sir Hugh Annesley, who mustered and drew his wages to go to France and then failed to set sail was clapped in irons in the Tower on the king's special command.[8] A nobility disciplined to obey the king in war was one which would more readily obey him in other matters.

War also imposed financial constraints on the nobility. Although the retinue served at the king's wages, the provision of horses, armour, tents, victuals, the prestigious trappings of harness, banners, pennants, and livery for the lord's retinue, together with the organization and transport of all these to the point of muster, were all expenses which the lord had to bear. An account of the Earl Marshal's preparations for the Agincourt campaign shows an expenditure of some £2,500 while the wages which he received from the crown for himself and his retinue totalled only £1,450. Mowbray borrowed from the Earl of Arundel while the Duke of York, who had recently refounded the collegiate church at Fotheringhay and was shortly to be buried there, mortgaged a number of his estates on the eve of sailing. Later, Duke Humphrey had to do likewise.[9] For the Agincourt campaign, moreover, the king had insufficient money to pay the wages of war due for the second period of three months' service, and the nobility high and low had to accept royal jewels as pledges of future payment. Many crown jewels were only redeemed, and the wages for war service paid, in Henry VI's reign: the Earl of Huntingdon in 1423 claimed no less than £8,158, while as late as 1427 the Duke of Gloucester and the Earl of Salisbury bargained to retain their jewels in lieu of wages still owed them. On the other hand the booty and prisoners taken at Agincourt undoubtedly replenished some noble coffers, though Henry's notorious order to kill the prisoners held after the first assault, when a fresh attack seemed likely, and his subsequent veto on the ransoming of all those who

[8] *Proc. PC*, ii, 303; iii, 303-4; *CCR, 1413-19*, pp. 433-4.
[9] I am indebted to Dr R. E. Archer for information on the Earl Marshal's expenditure and on the proportion of the Mowbray estates held in dower referred to below. *CPR, 1413-16*, p. 350; *CPR, 1416-22*, p. 129.

could be used as political pawns, certainly diminished the extent of the gains.[10]

Some of the nobility may also have looked to war to relieve and remedy their impoverishment. This was not, as was once assumed, the result of falling rents, higher wages, and deserted holdings. Such things had hardly more than marginal impact. Much more devastating was the existence of dowagers—mothers and even grandmothers—in whose hands one-third of the young lord's total patrimony (and even more if her former husband had made her a jointure to hold for life) remained until her death. One result of the untimely ends of those nobles who had rebelled against Henry IV was that they left young widows endowed with a proportion of their estates. The worst-hit of any was undoubtedly John Mowbray, the Earl Marshal, whose mother Elisabeth and sister-in-law Constance were both endowed from his patrimony and did not die until respectively 1425 and 1437. Until 1425 Mowbray had at his disposal only half of his estates. The Earl of Salisbury's case was almost as bad. The widow of his great uncle—the second earl, from whom his father had inherited—survived until 1415, and his own mother until 1424. The Earl of Huntingdon's mother, Elisabeth of Lancaster, lived until 1425. If, as she did, a widow remarried and bore issue, her second husband retained a life interest in his wife's estates: Elisabeth's husband, Sir John Cornewaill, died only in 1435. Richard Despenser, had he lived, would have faced the same problem, and some portions of Henry Percy's estates were in the hands of his mother (d. 1417) while others were retained by John, Duke of Bedford until his death in 1435. As heirs to run-down estates, fragmented by family settlements, with other parts still forfeit to the crown, the younger nobility of Henry V's reign were only too ready to accept the offer of reconciliation, the invitation to loyal service, and the prospect of restoration and reward which the king held out. It is significant that, to a man, the heirs of Henry IV's rebels steered clear of the Earl of Cambridge's conspiracy.

Even so it is clear that, at least at first, Henry did not

---

[10] *Rot. Parl.* iv, 247, 320; Nicolas, *Agincourt*, p. 61.

wholly trust them. Those whom he invested with the principal commands and offices at the beginning of the reign were the same small group with whom he had been previously associated as Prince. The Earl of Westmorland and John, Duke of Bedford guarded the north; the Earl of Warwick took over the captaincy of Calais which Henry had held as Prince (though as Captain of Guînes Clarence was the more obvious choice); the Earl of Arundel became constable of Dover and warden of the Cinque Ports and through his lieutenants kept a firm grip on the Welsh marches; while Sir John Stanley and John, Lord Talbot were successively lieutenants in Ireland, a post which Clarence had surrendered. In Aquitaine it was Thomas Beaufort, Earl of Dorset, rather than Edward of York, the senior in command, whom Henry ordered to remain as lieutenant on Clarence's return from the expedition of 1412. It was the same in the great offices of state where the king's uncle, Bishop Beaufort, replaced Archbishop Arundel as chancellor and the Earl of Arundel became treasurer. The lists of those attesting royal charters, and the scanty record of those attending the continual council in the first years of the reign, both reveal how restricted was the circle of those in the king's confidence. Beyond the royal dukes only the names of the Earls of Warwick and Arundel, and later Dorset and Salisbury, occur with any frequency, followed by an equally restricted number of bishops and household knights.[11]

But if the suspect nobility had no place in Henry's councils, they were certainly called on to serve alongside him in the field. Three dukes and eight earls contracted to serve on the Agincourt campaign, though death and dysentery at Harfleur so reduced their number that only York, Gloucester, Suffolk, Oxford, and Huntingdon fought at Agincourt. Nor did they escape unscathed; for York, Arundel, and both de la Pole brothers perished in 1415, and at Baugé in 1421 Clarence was slain and Huntingdon and Somerset made prisoner. Among the lesser nobility the wars brought a steady stream of fatalities. Most of the nobility were absent from

[11] I am indebted to Dr J. I. Catto for allowing me to see his lists of the witnesses on the Charter Rolls (PRO, C 53/180-5) for the first years of the reign. See his discussion, below, pp. 88-9.

England—cut off from their estates, families, and leadership of local political society—during the almost continuous fighting from 1417 to 1422. No more than four earls or dukes and thirteen lords attended the parliaments in these years held in the king's absence. The presence of virtually all the able-bodied nobility around the king for long periods, committed to his military ambitions and facing the hazards and demands of war, bred a sense of brotherhood and corporate responsibility which survived the king's death. They formed a kind of general staff around the king, to be detached as the occasion demanded for particular operations in the field or at a siege—as for instance in 1418 when Gloucester was sent to reduce Cherbourg and the Cotentin, or Exeter dispatched in 1419 to subdue the fortresses in north-east Normandy and to invest Château Gaillard. Nor must we forget the naval victories off Harfleur won by Bedford in 1416 and Huntingdon the year after. Those who had been on trial in the early years of the reign were now given commands of the highest responsibility in Normandy and the *pays de conquête*. The Earl of March became king's lieutenant in Normandy in 1418, and when Henry returned to England in 1421 he left Clarence as his lieutenant-general in France, with Salisbury covering the region of the upper Seine, and Exeter in charge of Paris, while Mowbray remained as marshal of the army.

As was to be expected, the rewards for such services came from the spoils of France. About the pecuniary profits from booty and ransoms it is difficult to get much evidence, but Henry distributed lands and dignities to some, though not all, of his principal captains. In 1418 Clarence received the vicomtés of Auge, Orbec, and Pont Audemer, and Exeter the comté of Harcourt. In 1419 Salisbury became Count of Perche, Warwick Count of Aumale, and the young Edward Holland briefly Count of Mortain. Two of Henry's former retainers as Prince of Wales, Sir John Grey and Sir William Bourchier, received the comtés of Tancarville and Eu.[12] All the nobility held the captaincies of important towns and fortresses, most notably Thomas Beaufort, Duke of Exeter,

---

[12] *Complete Peerage*, v, 177: Allmand, *Lancastrian Normandy*, pp. 70-1.

to whom Henry entrusted his three most important acquisitions, Harfleur, Rouen, and Paris. Such dignities, fiefs, and offices were not perquisites to be exploited, but carried military and territorial responsibilities for the defence and rule of the conquered lands. The wars in France turned the higher nobility into professional soldiers, committed them to the maintenance of the conquest, and gave them the will to act in unity and with decisiveness when faced with Henry's unlooked-for death. Just as he had prevented any renewal of the feuds of his father's reign by offering a measured restoration to favour, so his leadership of the nobility created new bonds of loyalty and personal devotion, an exhilaration in his service such as was expressed in Salisbury's letter to the king after he had redeemed the defeat at Baugé, and a pride in their contribution to his and England's achievements, manifested in such divers works as the *Vita Henrici Quinti*, commissioned by Humphrey, Duke of Gloucester, and the *Boke of Noblesse* commissioned by Sir John Fastolf.

But as well as leading his nobility a king had also at times to *rule* them: to show his own mastery and to assert the pre-eminent dignity and prerogatives of the crown. This is the most difficult aspect of his relations with the nobility to describe or analyse, for in so small and intimate a group the king's own personality was of major importance. We may feel broadly certain of his personal magnetism, the confidence he inspired, and the fear of his anger, but these vital aspects defy measurement or description. We know that he was insistent on marks of respect to his person and estate. The incident reported by Monstrelet in which Henry reprimanded the Burgundian lord and Marshal of France, Lisle Adam, for looking him full in the face when addressing him, to receive the reply that among Frenchmen it was the mark of an honest man to speak thus to another, betrays a certain touchiness which may have been absent from his relations with the English nobility.[13] But presumption of any kind Henry would not tolerate, and undoubtedly he knew how to unnerve by a display of displeasure. We have only to recall how Henry dealt with his uncle and mentor, Henry Beaufort,

---

[13] Monstrelet, *Chronique*, iv, 9–10.

Bishop of Winchester, when he secured nomination to the cardinalate from Pope Martin V. As the king remarked to his brother Gloucester, 'he had as lief set his crown beside him as to see him [Beaufort]wear a cardinal's hat', and the letter which Beaufort wrote to Henry in March 1420, excusing himself from attending the king's marriage, reveals the self-confident prelate reduced to agonies of indecision and apprehension under the royal threat of depriving him of his wealth.[14] We know, too, of the fear which the young Earl of March expressed to his confessor in 1415 that the king intended 'to undo' him. The huge marriage fine of 10,000 marks imposed upon him by Henry is the only occasion of his use of heavy fiscal penalties to ensure political subservience and good behaviour in the mode of King John and Henry VII. It was, moreover, exacted almost to the full. Although in 1413 the king took recognisances totalling 80,000 marks from three earls and seven lords, this was part of the determined campaign to stamp out lawlessness and exact respect for royal authority discussed in another chapter.[15] The exemplary action taken against Lord Ferrers of Chartley in Staffordshire and against the retainers of the Earl of Arundel and Lord Talbot in Shropshire in 1414 showed that Henry would not brook the use of armed retainers by the nobility to pursue their vendettas or pervert justice.

The converse of this firmness against self-help was the king's readiness to arbitrate and compose the disputes between his magnates. This was a looked-for and essential function of the crown, but its effectiveness depended on the king's own reputation for impartiality as well as the acceptance of his judgements. In the latter part of the reign, and notably on Henry's final visit to England in 1421, a number of magnate disputes over land were submitted to his arbitration. Perhaps the most famous is that over the castle and lordship of Berkeley which arose on the death of Thomas, Lord Berkeley in 1417, when the inheritance was disputed between his daughter, the Countess of Warwick, and his nephew James, the heir male. The Earl of Warwick, who was serving

[14] McFarlane, 'Henry V, Beaufort and the Red Hat'.
[15] *Forty-Third Report of the Deputy Keeper of the Public Records*, p. 585; *CCR, 1413-19*, pp. 97-9, 240; *Rot. Parl.* iv, 465 and PRO, SC 8/26/1289.

with Henry in France, secured a grant of the custody of the castle which the king had taken into his hands, and when the inquisition taken by the local escheator awarded the estates to James, he refused to surrender them. Warwick's influence was so great that James sought support from the Duke of Gloucester, then Guardian of England, promising him a thousand marks if he would get him possession of Berkeley castle. But it was only on Henry V's return in 1421 that Warwick bowed to pressure and surrendered the castle and James was summoned to parliament as Lord Berkeley. Even so, after Henry V's death Warwick renewed his bid, and, by an arbitration in 1424, in fact secured most of the estates, leaving James with only Berkeley castle itself. A similar dispute arose between claimants to the Arundel inheritance on the death of Earl Thomas in 1415 without direct male heir. Here the death of Arundel's cousin in April 1421 conveniently opened the way to the acceptance of the king's arbitration by the three coheiresses. In numerous lesser disputes involving the propertied classes the land in contention was taken into the king's hand to facilitate agreement.[16]

It is often said that in the late middle ages the English nobility were engaged in a perpetual scramble for royal patronage to supplement their own incomes, and that the crown was forced to buy support and loyalty by largesse on a substantial scale. Some kings chose to do this—though even they directed their liberality to favourites—but Henry V showed no sign of purchasing the support of the nobility at the expense of the crown. Royal grants were few, carefully measured, and aligned to service and responsibilities. Henry's endowment of his brothers was minimal. Clarence was given 2,000 marks a year at the exchequer (if he could collect it) and was essentially supported by his wife's and

---

[16] For the Berkeley dispute, see J. Smyth, *Lives of the Berkeleys*, ed. J. Maclean, 2 vols. (Gloucester, 1883), i, 42–8, 100 and W. Dugdale, *The Baronage of England*, 2 vols. (1675–6), i, 362–4, also *Proc. PC*, ii, 289, 293, *CFR, 1413–22*, pp. 207, 212–14. For the Arundel lands: *CPR, 1416–22*, pp. 238–9; *Proc. PC*, ii, 297–8, 335. For other disputes: *CPR, 1416–22*, pp. 78, 135, 139, 253, 295, 317, 414, 417 and *Cal. Signet Letters*, no. 906. There were also disputes over the Despenser inheritance involving Joan, Lady Bergevenny and Edward, Duke of York: *CCR, 1413–19*, pp. 110, 133–4, 165, 174–5.

stepson's inheritance. Gloucester initially received only 1,000 marks in annuities but later acquired the lordships of Pembroke and the Isle of Wight. Bedford was even required to surrender the estates of Henry Percy, given him by Henry IV as warden of the East March, when Percy was restored in 1416; he received 3,000 marks p.a. from royal revenues in recompense but these were difficult to collect and he retained many of the Percy lands until his death. Similarly with Henry's half-brother Thomas Beaufort, Duke of Exeter; on his elevation in 1416 he was granted £1,000 p.a. at the exchequer, but when the Lords were asked to give approval for this many said it was too small a reward for his outstanding service in the defence of Harfleur.[17] In no case did Henry V alienate crown lands even to his own family, and most of the estates which came to the crown's hands through forfeiture or escheat were retained or leased at realistic farms. The king's brothers and some others high in royal favour received occasional grants of wardships or valuable farms, but some of these were deducted from their annuities and gratuitous rewards were few or none.[18]

At a time when so many magnate estates were in the king's hand through untimely death in war or forfeiture for treason, Henry V showed himself particularly conscious of his obligations as feudal overlord. Ordering an inquiry into allegations that the estates of his ward, Fulk Fitzwarin, had been plundered, Henry affirmed that 'the king is bound to render the lands of minors in his keeping to them when they come to full age in the same state as they came to his hands'.[19] To the widows and brothers of those who had served him best he frequently committed the lands and marriage of the infant heir. But if defrauded of his own feudal rights he could be merciless. In 1421 the widowed Countess of Oxford married

[17] For Clarence, CPR, 1413–16, pp. 94, 306–7; for Gloucester, ibid., pp. 146, 170, 395, 397; for Bedford, ibid., pp. 259–60, 370 and Bean, loc. cit. (n. 7 above); for Exeter, CPR, 1416–22, p. 50, St Albans Chronicle, pp. 102–3.

[18] For leases of lands in the crown's custody, CPR, 1413–16, p. 344, CFR, 1413–22, p. 132 (Arundel); CFR, 1413–22, p. 135 (York); ibid., pp. 137, 393 (Stafford); ibid., p. 321 (Devon); ibid., p. 406 (Welles); ibid., p. 409 (Clarence). For grants of wardships and farms: CPR, 1413–16, pp. 328 (Sir William Phelip), 360, 372–3 (Lord Fitzhugh), 394 (Earl of Huntingdon); CPR, 1416–22, pp. 9, 37, 117 (Lord Fitzhugh), 32 (Duke of Clarence), 110 (Duke of Exeter).

[19] CPR, 1416–22, p. 207.

The King and his Magnates 49

her esquire Nicholas Thorley without the king's licence,
thereby depriving the king of a profitable marriage. All her
lands were seized into the king's hands until she made fine
for her transgression, while the wretched Nicholas was
clapped into irons in the Tower to await the king's pleasure.[20]
It must be said that there are some other instances where
Henry V's determination to serve royal interests led him—as
it did Edward I and Henry VII—to drive a hard bargain and
deal rough justice to those who were vulnerable to royal
pressure. In 1418 he persuaded Joan de Bohun, Countess
of Hereford, shortly before she died, to sell Chirk and Chirk-
lands to the crown for the bargain price of 4,000 marks,
taking advantage of the fact that the Earl of Arundel to
whom it should have descended had died without direct male
issue in 1415 leaving a disputed succession. And when the
death of the countess next year released her dower lands,
Henry initiated litigation for a redivision of the Bohun
estate between himself and Anne, Countess of Stafford
as coheirs. The original division in 1380 had left the house
of Lancaster with the slightly smaller share and with considerable lands in Brecon and Radnorshire from which
revenue had fallen drastically since the Welsh revolt. The
case was conveniently heard in the exchequer on precisely
the day that Henry opened parliament on his last visit to
England in 1421. Not unexpectedly, judgement was given
in the king's favour and he selected blocks of manors in
Essex, Oxford, and Dorset which could easily be annexed to
the duchy of Lancaster, leaving the countess with the prob-
lematic Welsh border estates.[21] Perhaps even more suspect
are his motives in instigating the imprisonment of his step-
mother Queen Joan on charges of necromancy in 1419. For
the dowager queen—whose Breton connections certainly

[20] For commitments of wardships to the Countess of Suffolk, see *CPR, 1413-16*, p. 383, *CPR, 1416-22*, pp. 256-7; to the widow of Gilbert Talbot, *CPR, 1416-22*, p. 258; to Lady Clifford, *CFR, 1413-22*, p. 433; to the Duchess of Clarence, *Proc. PC*, ii, 334. For Nicholas Thorley see *Proc. PC*, ii, 303, *CFR, 1413-22*, p. 433. For other fines for concealments etc., see *CPR, 1416-22*, pp. 296, 298, 411, *CCR, 1413-19*, p. 15, *CCR, 1419-22*, pp. 117, 128.
[21] *CPR, 1416-22*, pp. 172, 381; *CFR, 1413-22*, p. 389; *Proc. PC*, ii, 294-5; C. Rawcliffe, *The Staffords, Earls of Stafford and Dukes of Buckingham, 1394-1521* (Cambridge, 1978), pp. 14-17.

made her unpopular in England and a pawn in Henry's
diplomacy—enjoyed estates worth 10,000 marks p.a. On
her imprisonment these were taken into the king's hands
and used for the expenses of war and the royal household.
In fact they were restored to her in 1423-4, apparently in
accordance with Henry's last wishes; and the dying king
is similarly said to have repented of his retention of some
of the entailed lands of Lord Scrope and instructed that
they be restored. But these injustices were trifling by comparison with the systematic intimidation and spoliation of
the landed classes practised in the last years of Henry VII's
reign. Henry V sought neither to pander to his magnates
nor to cow them. That they perceived and valued this, and
took his rule as their model, we may see from the rhyming
chronicle of Robert Hardyng, the servant of Henry's devoted
north-country knight, Sir Gilbert Umfraville. Hardyng
praises his own master's rule because, as with the king, 'the
common profit without oppression was his labour and
diligence'.[22]

This chapter has been confined to Henry's relations with
the small group of upper nobility who had a very distinctive
place and role within the English State. The great magnate
families had political and dynastic traditions of their own
which, if flouted or endangered by royal policy, could lead
them into opposition to the crown. Ultimately they alone in
the realm had the power to withstand and destroy the king,
and on his handling of them depended the realization of all
his other plans and policies. These are obvious truths, though
to give substance to any analysis of this relationship means
too often searching for straws in the wind. In particular
one half of this relationship—how the magnates viewed the
king and what influence they exerted upon him—is almost
totally lost to view. At Henry V's accession his magnates
were, in the main, young and inexperienced, the heirs to
faction and suspicion, uncertain of their future roles and

[22] A. R. Myers, 'The Captivity of a Royal Witch; the household accounts of
Queen Joan of Navarre, 1419-21', *BJRL*, xxiv (1940), 262-84, xxvi (1941),
82-100; *CFR, 1413-22*, pp. 321, 344, 373, 422; *Rot. Parl.* iv, 213, 242. C. L.
Kingsford (ed.), 'The First Version of Hardyng's Chronicle', *EHR*, xxvii (1912),
p. 747.

prospects. By the mid point of his short reign he had won their respect and devotion, and they had identified themselves with his purpose and vision. In large measure this marked their recognition of his military genius. In the prowess, fortitude, inspiration, coolness, and discipline which he displayed, Henry V perfectly exemplified the chivalric ideal, and men counted it to their honour and repute to serve under him. But this comradeship of arms was part of a general confidence in his kingship, and in those matters where royal power touched baronial interests Henry had already won this when he sailed to France in 1415. His emphasis on his own royal title and dignity, and the prerogatives of the crown, was matched by his recognition of the concern of his magnates for their rights and inheritances. While claiming their loyalty and service, he offered them amnesty and restoration, thereby making confidence in his kingship the test of their confidence in their own future. Moreover, in rewarding loyalty, he eschewed partiality and self-indulgent generosity, and his dealings with the nobility remained largely free of arbitrariness and caprice. He thus created no new factions, and the old ones withered away. Against those who threatened disobedience his threats were not idle, and were seriously heeded, for his justice was quickly seen to be impartial and inexorable. He handled his magnates with assurance, shrewdly playing upon their ambitions and weaknesses; but he was readier to trust than to intimidate and did not give the impression of secretly harbouring resentment or suspicion. In short, he commanded his magnates' loyalty by inspiring confidence, and did not need to buy it by favour or constrain it by fear. His achievement was to consign the factions and feuds of Richard II's reign to the dustbin of history and to enable his own generation to find their proper role in service to the king and the realm. In so doing he not merely restored their own fortunes and honour but restored, too, the strength and dignity of the crown. A king who ruled his magnates as Henry V did had nothing to fear from them or anyone else.

III

The Restoration of Law and Order

EDWARD POWELL

For contemporary writers, as for historians ever since, the history of Henry V's reign amounted to a catalogue of his triumphs in France. The domestic affairs of England intruded only briefly as the chroniclers hurried on to recount the king's exploits overseas. Such an emphasis was of course inevitable given the time and energy he devoted to his French campaigns. Henry spent less than half his reign in England, and much of that in active preparation for war. On the other hand the king's prolonged absences abroad raise an important, and as yet unanswered, question concerning his domestic policies. An essential preliminary to reopening the war with France was the establishment of peace and order at home. Henry did not need reminding of the dangers of leaving a discontented realm to seek foreign conquests. As a boy he had accompanied Richard II on his expedition to Ireland in 1399, which allowed Henry of Lancaster time to slip back into England and acquire support sufficient to usurp the throne. The Earl of Cambridge's plot and renewed Lollard activity on the eve of the Agincourt campaign provoked anxiety at the king's departure, and according to the *Gesta Henrici Quinti* some of his advisers tried to persuade him to abandon the expedition.[1] Henry was not to be deterred, however, and his confidence proved to be justified. During his long campaigns in France there was remarkably little serious disorder in England. Professor Bellamy reflects the general consensus of opinion when he identifies Henry V's reign as one of the few periods of comparatively good order among the disorderly centuries of the late middle ages.[2] My

[1] *Gesta*, p. 21.
[2] J. G. Bellamy, *Crime and Public Order in England in the Later Middle Ages* (London, 1972), pp. 5-12.

principal aim in this chapter is to investigate this state of affairs, and to ask how Henry was able to ensure public order at home during his absences abroad. In particular, what measures had the king taken to settle the country before his departure?

Such questions are all the more pertinent in view of the striking contrast between the measured calm of Henry V's reign and the insecurity and turmoil of his predecessor's. Henry IV never entirely escaped the shadow of his usurpation of the throne, and the early years of the reign were times of acute instability for the new king. His dubious title to the crown precipitated a series of magnate revolts, and the manifest uncertainty and weakness of his position encouraged the outbreak of rebellion in Wales, led by Owain Glyndwr, war with Scotland, and threats to the crown's overseas possessions of Calais and Guienne from the kingdom of France. In short, Henry IV was assailed on every front, and until 1407-8 when the worst dangers of rebellion had been overcome, the regime was at full stretch, financially and militarily. In order to appreciate Henry V's achievement in restoring public order, therefore, we must briefly examine the problems which faced his father.[3]

Disorder was most serious and prolonged in the counties bordering the Welsh marches: the Glyndwr rebellion broke out in the northern marches in 1400, and spread across the principality, reaching its height in 1405; the last rebel stronghold was not captured until 1409, and the effects of the revolt were still being felt in the border counties at the beginning of Henry V's reign. Complaints about the depredations of the Welsh and the inhabitants of the marcher lordships were constantly reiterated throughout Henry IV's reign. Legislation was enacted to allow redress to the English victims of border raids, but it appears to have been totally ineffective. Until 1405, indeed, Henry was too preoccupied with the military challenges to his throne to spare much thought for the administration of justice. Only in the second half of his reign, when the threat of rebellion and invasion had begun to recede, did parliament draw his attention to

[3] For general accounts of Henry IV's reign, see McFarlane, *Lancastrian Kings*, pp. 5-113; Jacob, *Fifteenth Century*, pp. 1-121.

the poor state of public order prevailing over much of the country. In ·1410 the Commons complained of riots and disorders throughout the north and midlands, and requested the issue of general oyer and terminer commissions as a remedy. Petitions were received at the same parliament alleging a series of attacks on Lancastrian retainers and tenants in Staffordshire. The commons of Northumberland complained in 1411 of the prevalence of robbers and thieves in the county and nearby liberties, and deplored the rarity of judicial visitations. During this period also, concern was shown over the unofficial war raging in the Channel between English privateers and their continental counterparts, which disrupted maritime commerce and impaired foreign relations, notably with Flanders and Brittany.

No serious attempt was made to deal with these disturbances. Henry's reluctance to intervene in local disorders may have stemmed from a desire to avoid investigating the unlawful activities of his supporters. Some of these, concerning the Earl of Arundel's lieutenants in Shropshire and Thomas Barnby, the king's chamberlain in North Wales, were later revealed under Henry V. Where Lancastrian interests were threatened, however, Henry IV was quick to take action: special measures in the court of king's bench were ordered for the apprehension of those who had attacked Lancastrians in Staffordshire. By· contrast the king responded to the complaints of widespread disorder in 1410 and the demand for oyer and terminer commissions by reserving his right to issue such commissions as he saw fit, and only one, to Devonshire, appears to have been sent out as requested. Admittedly, several statutory measures enacted during Henry IV's reign aimed at the sterner and more efficient implementation of justice: for example the introduction of the death penalty for heresy, the consolidation of the Ricardian statutes of livery and forcible entry, and the statute of 1411, which provided justices of the peace with summary powers for dealing with riots. But these were not followed up by the energetic programme of law enforcement necessary after the usurpation and the years of rebellion and uncertainty which ensued. It was left to Henry IV's successor to carry out such a programme.

The question of public order was, therefore, one of the most pressing problems which faced Henry V on his accession. It would perhaps be too much to speak of a 'crisis of order' in 1413, but certainly the new king was expected to take decisive action to prevent matters deteriorating further. In the first parliament of the new reign in May 1413, the Commons complained at Henry IV's failure to implement his repeated promises to restore law and order, and petitioned his son to suppress disorder throughout his dominions.[4] Henry V's response to these demands was characteristically prompt and forceful, and the first two years of his reign saw a vigorous campaign of law enforcement. Important legislative measures, enacted chiefly at the Leicester parliament of 1414, were reinforced by a flurry of special judicial commissions and proceedings in many parts of the country. The court of king's bench, which had remained stationary at Westminster for the whole of Henry IV's reign, accompanied parliament to Leicester in 1414 and held sessions in Leicestershire, Staffordshire, and Shropshire, investigating all manner of criminal offences. Special commissions were also sent to Yorkshire, Devon, Nottinghamshire and Derbyshire, and North and South Wales, while of course the Lollard revolt provoked a spate of judicial activity throughout the south and midlands.

The main purpose of this chapter, therefore, is to present a detailed consideration of Henry V's programme to restore order, and to suggest how it fitted into his wider schemes of military conquest. Before doing so, however, it is necessary briefly to review the judicial machinery which the crown had at its disposal in the early fifteenth century, and to assess its strengths and weaknesses as a tool of law enforcement in the hands of a capable and energetic monarch.

Fifteenth-century England possessed the most sophisticated and well-organized legal system in Europe. At its heart were the great central courts of the crown, king's bench, common pleas, chancery, and exchequer, sitting at Westminster. In the counties, the two officials traditionally associated with judicial administration, the sheriff and the coroner, retained

---

[4] All references to the activities of parliament in Henry V's reign will be found in *Rot. Parl.* iv.

important functions, but during the fourteenth century ordinary criminal jurisdiction had been transferred to the justices of the peace. The link between central government and the localities was provided by the commissions of assize and gaol delivery, which were staffed by central court judges and pleaders. Assize judges went out on circuit twice a year, hearing a wide range of civil cases and trying serious criminal offences which were beyond the competence of the couny justices of the peace. Well before Henry V's accession, then, a system of royal justice had evolved, based on the quarter sessions and assizes, which was to endure in its essentials until the twentieth century.

In view of such institutional precocity it is paradoxical that the late medieval legal system should long have been notorious for its corruptness and inefficiency, and that the period in general should be regarded by many historians as one of unparalleled lawlessness. Yet the evidence is unequivocal: the practice of bribery, maintenance, and intimidation is extensively documented; while in the two centuries after 1300 the country was periodically subject to widespread outbreaks of violent crime which the crown could do little to restrain. To put these points in perspective, we should add that our knowledge of the inadequacies of the law, and of the disorder it failed to contain, derives principally from the records themselves. Before 1300 such records are much sparser, and it may be that our picture of the late middle ages as a time of declining standards of public order compared to previous centuries is simply the product of a growth in judicial activity and better record-keeping. As K. B. McFarlane remarked, 'it is odd that it is the very richness of their sources which has given the later middle ages a bad name'.[5] Nevertheless, even if we accept this argument, the problem remains of how to reconcile the undoubted sophistication of the judicial machinery with its apparent inability to enforce the law.

The impasse stems partly from modern preconceptions as to how an efficient legal system should function. Because late medieval institutions of justice bear a striking resemblance

[5] McFarlane, *Nobility*, p. 114.

to our own in certain respects, we assume that we can judge them by modern criteria, according to the number of crimes solved and criminals apprehended, convicted, and punished. Such an assumption is only valid, however, if it can be shown that the coercive powers of medieval courts were roughly comparable with those of their modern counterparts. This of course is manifestly not the case: one of the most fundamental differences between the medieval and the modern State is the comparative lack of coercive power which medieval governments had at their disposal. They simply did not have the financial resources to maintain the standing army and permanent police force which would have been necessary to implement a primarily punitive system of justice. As a result, in its efforts to enforce the law and maintain public order, the crown was bound to rely heavily on the support and co-operation of the local community. Principally this meant the landowning classes, the aristocracy and gentry who ran the counties and who filled the commissions of the peace and the local administrative offices of the crown. But it also included the lesser ranks of society, the yeomen and substantial villagers who served on juries which presented offenders before the justices of the peace and coroners and determined the guilt or innocence of accused felons. Inevitably this degree of local influence rendered the system vulnerable to perversion. Medieval communities were intensely suspicious of unjustified external intervention and sought wherever possible to maintain control over their own affairs: where a whole community closed its ranks against the central government and refused to co-operate in the investigation of crime, even a king as forceful as Henry V was virtually powerless, as we shall see in the case of Devonshire in 1414.[6] Similarly the strict course of justice might be diverted by sectional interests. Justices of the peace often used their powers as a tool of faction or class interest, while trial juries were extremely reluctant to convict a fellow-villager of homicide, even if his guilt was apparent.

The effect of local influence in the administration of justice was not, however, purely negative: the surest way for

---

[6] See below, pp. 62–3.

a locality to avoid external interference was to police itself effectively. Unlike visiting royal justices, the local community had to live with the settlement imposed after violent conflict and disorder. Its primary concern therefore was less to punish offenders than to reconcile hostile parties and re-establish peace and concord. In consequence the coercive aspect of justice often took second place to the conciliatory and restitutive aspects, especially when disorder arose from disputes among the gentry classes. The leading regional magnate or a group of county gentry would act as arbitrators between the disputants and attempt to settle the issues in contention in a form acceptable to both sides. Arbitration of this kind flourished vigorously in England throughout the late middle ages. The practice had its own well-defined procedures which functioned separately from the law courts though often in conjunction with them.[7] For the local communities where it thrived it was the ideal mechanism for the internal resolution of conflict.

The maintenance of law and order thus depended upon a partnership between the crown and political society in the provinces. The machinery of royal justice would have broken down without the active co-operation of the king's subjects. On the other hand the king was the ultimate guarantor of the system, explicitly bound to uphold the laws and do justice by the terms of his coronation oath. It was his task to foster the conditions in which the network of local courts could work smoothly and the peaceful resolution of disputes could be achieved with the minimum of central interference. This was a matter more of political management than of legal administration, since although the courts were generally able to cope with the crimes and offences of the lower orders of society, they were not adequate to contain disorders provoked by disputes among the magnates and gentry, which posed the most serious threat to public order throughout the late middle ages. Powerful commissions of oyer and terminer were useful in dealing with such disturbances, both as a formal expression of royal authority and to catch the small fry. But in bringing unruly magnates and gentry into line, the

---

[7] E. Powell, 'Arbitration and the Law in England in the Late Middle Ages', *TRHS*, 5th series xxxiii (1983), pp. 49–67.

king had to resort to less formal methods, using a judicious combination of threats and persuasion to put an end to private feuding. The process is well illustrated in a story told of Henry V in the *Brut* chronicles.[8] In the first year of his reign two knights, one of Lancashire and one of Yorkshire, prosecuted a fierce quarrel in which many of their supporters were killed. On hearing of this the king summoned them to his presence at Windsor. They appeared before him as he was about to sit down to a dish of oysters. Henry upbraided them roundly for their conduct and asked by what authority they raised up his liege men to fight and slay each other. The two knights begged for mercy and the king replied: 'be the feith that he owte to God and to Seint George, but yf they agreyd and accordyd be that tyme that he had etyn his owystrys, they shulde be hangyd bothe two or evyr he sopyt'. The knights withdrew and when summoned before the king a few minutes later, had come to terms to settle their quarrel. In the last resort, therefore, despite the elaborate machinery of justice, public order might depend quite simply on the strength, or otherwise, of the king's own personality.

Having completed this cursory examination of the late medieval legal system, it is time to return to the early months of Henry V's reign. As we have seen, the first parliament summoned by the new king in May 1413 submitted urgent petitions for the restoration of order throughout the realm. Henry responded almost immediately with administrative measures designed to help the law to function more smoothly. The Statute of Additions, enacted at the May parliament, stipulated that persons cited in a writ or indictment should be described according to their place and county of residence and their profession. This eased the sheriff's task of locating and identifying defendants and reduced the likelihood of mistaken identity. At the same time, on the advice of the central court judges, the king's council established stricter regulation of the return of writs to the court of king's bench. It appears that under Henry IV sheriffs had often failed altogether to return writs which they had been instructed to serve on behalf of king's bench.

[8] *The Brut*, ii, 595.

The first part of the country to which Henry turned his attention was Wales and the Welsh march. Although the Glyndwr rebellion had been effectively suppressed as an organized revolt in the second half of Henry IV's reign, the settlement of the region—the restoration of public order and the re-establishment of civil administration—had yet to be achieved. During the early summer of 1413 powerful commissions of oyer and terminer were appointed for North and South Wales, led by the Earl of Arundel and the justices of king's bench and common pleas. In addition the king ordered a commission of justices in eyre to hold sessions in the duchy of Lancaster lordships in the march of South Wales. During the summer and autumn, and again in the spring of 1414, these groups of justices sat throughout Wales. They received rebels who submitted to the king's grace, sold confiscated lands, reconciled to the crown communities which had risen in revolt (usually on payment of a corporate fine) and heard complaints against corrupt officials.[9]

Outside Wales the new king had, however, done little to reduce the level of disorder by the end of 1413. In January 1414 his attention was forcibly drawn to the problem by the rising of the Lollards led by Sir John Oldcastle.[10] Accusations of Lollardy had been brought against Oldcastle which led to his conviction for heresy before Archbishop Arundel in September 1413. Sentenced to death, Oldcastle was allowed forty days respite by the king during which, on 19 October, he escaped from the Tower with the aid of Lollard sympathizers. As the acknowledged leader of the Lollard sect, Oldcastle quickly hatched a plot to overthrow the government, and instructed his followers in various parts of the country to gather armed support and to meet him just outside London. The plan was to kidnap the king and his brothers at Eltham on Twelfth Night, seize the capital, and, apparently, to depose the existing hierarchy of king,

[9] *CPR, 1413–16*, pp. 112–13, 114, 179. PRO, JUST 1 (Eyre Rolls, Assize Rolls, etc)/1152-3, KB 9 (Court of King's Bench, Ancient Indictments)/204/3 mm. 18–27.
[10] See K. B. McFarlane, *John Wycliffe and the Beginnings of English Non-Conformity* (London, 1952), ch. 6.

magnates, and prelates.

The rising, of course, failed miserably. Henry had caught
wind of the conspiracy and was waiting for the rebels when
they gathered outside London on the evening of 9 January.
Some were killed, many captured, and the following day an
oyer and terminer commission was appointed to deal with
the rebels in London and Middlesex. In two days sixty-nine
had been condemned to death, thirty-eight of whom were
executed on 13 January. Commissions of inquiry were set up
in twenty-one counties to investigate the activities of Lollards
and rebels, arrest offenders, and to return their findings to
the court of king's bench. The surviving returns show that
the response to Oldcastle's call to arms was pitifully small—
less than three hundred in all—and after his initial ruthlessness
the king was disposed to be lenient. In March 1414 a general
pardon was issued to participants in the rising if they submitted to the crown, with a few named exceptions headed by
Oldcastle himself, who was not finally recaptured until 1417.

With hindsight we can see that the Oldcastle revolt presented no great threat to Henry V's throne, and certainly it
was suppressed so effectively that Lollardy was forced
underground for ever and ceased to function as a coherent
movement. Contemporary observers could not take such a
detached view, however, and the rising provoked considerable
anxiety amongst the lay and ecclesiastical establishment,
recalling as it did memories of the Peasants' Revolt thirty
years before. The horror generated by the threat of popular
revolt is reflected in the hyperbolic account of the rising in
the St Albans chronicle. The chronicler, Thomas Walsingham,
grossly exaggerated the numbers involved, and depicted
hordes of deluded rustics thronging the highways of England
en route to join Oldcastle's forces in London.[11]

Clearly, the ruling classes of the realm expected the king to
take rapid and decisive action to prevent further unrest. The
need for strong measures was brought home also by an
incident in Devonshire a few weeks after the Oldcastle
revolt. In late February 1414 an oyer and terminer commission was dispatched to the county to investigate allegations

---

[11] *St Albans Chronicle*, 78.

of piracy and counterfeiting of coin. The justices found themselves obstructed at every turn by the local community: of the thirty or so presenting juries summoned, all but a handful refused to make returns of any kind. Baffled, the justices returned to Westminster, their commission unfulfilled. The reasons for this extraordinary act of defiance are uncertain, but we may suspect that the community was reluctant to lose the benefits brought to it by the pirates who operated so profitably from the south Devonshire ports.[12]

These events appear to have determined Henry to give the highest priority to the restoration of law and order, as his first parliament had requested. The king's thoughts were already turning towards France, but it was evident that he could not leave the country in such a disturbed state. Before undertaking any expeditions abroad, a campaign against disorder at home was essential.

The campaign opened at the second parliament of the reign. Originally summoned to meet at the end of January, this parliament was postponed because of the Oldcastle revolt and finally assembled at Leicester on 30 April 1414. Its purpose, as set out in the chancellor's opening speech, was threefold: to root out Lollardy; to enforce maritime truces made between the crown and foreign princes; and to restore public order—in the chancellor's words 'for the chastisement and punishment of the rioters, murderers, and other malefactors who more than ever abound in many parts of the kingdom'.[13] Legislation was brought forward to deal with each of these matters. All judicial officials of the crown, from the central court justices downwards, were instructed to give active support to the ecclesiastical authorities in the location and extirpation of Lollardy: justices of the peace were given particular responsibility in this regard. An elaborate Statute of Truces was enacted in an effort to curb the activities of English pirates in the Channel, who had preyed with impunity upon foreign merchant shipping in breach of royal truces and to the detriment of diplomatic relations with potential allies such as the Dukes of Brittany and Burgundy. This statute, which established conservators

---

[12] *CPR, 1413-16*, pp. 148, 263-4. PRO, KB 9/205/2-3.
[13] *Rot. Parl.* iv, 15.

of truces in all major ports to enforce its provisions, rapidly proved unworkable, however, and it was soon watered down in subsequent legislation. To counter domestic disorder, measures were introduced to enforce observance of the Statutes of Riots of Richard II and Henry IV, and to involve the court of king's bench more directly in the prosecution of rioters.

Much of the legislation of this parliament was framed in response to petitions and complaints from the Commons, and from references in the parliament rolls it is clear that an animated debate over law and order took place at Leicester. One statute, for example, referred to 'diverses et hidouses compleintz . . . faitz en cest present Parlement'. In particular, petitions had been presented which reflected the breakdown of order in Shropshire and Staffordshire. Edmund Ferrers, lord of Chartley in Staffordshire, complained of the attacks of Hugh Erdswick of Sandon, to which Hugh made counter-charges of his own; while Thomas Marshall, John Bruyn, and others, collectors of the 1413 parliamentary subsidy in Shropshire, petitioned against Robert Corbet and Richard Lacon, knights of the shire for the county in 1413, who had appointed them and then allegedly done everything possible to hinder their activities.

A powerful remedy was needed to check this rising chorus of complaint. The king sought one by reviving the use of king's bench as a travelling court of trailbaston for the suppression of local disorders. This aspect of the court's jurisdiction, known as a 'superior eyre' to distinguish it from the old general eyre, had been frequently invoked during the fourteenth century. Henry IV, perhaps fearing the opposition such visitations might provoke, had never used the device, and king's bench remained stationary at Westminster throughout his reign. The superior eyre was, however, well suited to Henry V's purposes: king's bench, as the name suggests, was closely identified with the person and interests of the king and its proceedings were invested with peculiar authority. Already as a mark of his concern over law enforcement Henry had ordered king's bench to accompany parliament to Leicester, where it held sessions for a month from mid-April. As a result of discussions in parliament it was decided that king's bench should hold further sessions in Staffordshire and Shropshire to hear and determine indictments arising from the disturbances there. The court spent over three weeks at Lichfield in Staffordshire from mid-May until early June 1414, and a fortnight at Shrewsbury in Shropshire in the second half of June.[14] King's bench made a comprehensive review of the criminal administration of each county where it sat, calling in the coroners' rolls and all undetermined indictments taken before the justices of the peace. The court also summoned juries from all hundreds and liberties to make presentments concerning the recent disorders. In the two counties, Shropshire and Staffordshire, king's bench received a total of nearly 1,800 indictments, and issued process against some 1,600 persons. The sheer speed and volume of proceedings in king's bench during the summer of 1414 is impressive in itself: a number of cases were determined on the spot and many more concluded at Westminster in the two terms following the superior eyre.

The perambulation of king's bench through the north-west midlands was the first of a series of extraordinary judicial sessions ordered by Henry V in the wake of the Leicester parliament. Early in June 1414 a comprehensive commission of inquiry led by Lord Fitzhugh was despatched to investigate disorders in Nottinghamshire and Derbyshire. At the end of July a group of justices was sent to Devonshire with two commissions: the first to inquire into all treasons, felonies, and trespasses committed in the county; the second to discover who was responsible for obstructing the oyer and terminer commission which, as we have seen, met such a frosty reception in Devon the preceding February. Finally, in early August, a general commission of inquiry was held in Yorkshire under Robert Tyrwhitt, a justice of king's bench.[15]

A significant feature of this spate of judicial activity is that it was carefully co-ordinated from the centre. Except for the superior eyre all the proceedings just outlined, and the Lollard commissions of January 1414 as well, were commissions of of inquiry rather than of oyer and terminer. This meant that

---

[14] For the proceedings of king's bench during the superior eyre, see PRO, KB 27 (Court of King's Bench, Plea Rolls)/612–13.
[15] PRO, KB 9/204–5.

the commissioners were empowered only to receive indictments and order arrests, whereas justices of oyer and terminer
could also try and convict offenders. The findings of these
inquiries were returned to chancery and forwarded to the
court of king's bench for determination. By restricting the
commissioners' powers the government lost a degree of speed
and flexibility in dealing with local disorder. On the other
hand, by using king's bench as a general clearing-house for
the commissions, it was able to exercise closer supervision
and to gauge more accurately the extent and severity of
disorder throughout the country in order to formulate an
effective response.[16]

This policy of centralizing law enforcement bears the
mark of the king's own personality. Henry maintained close
contact with king's bench throughout its sessions as a superior
eyre. After the dissolution of the Leicester parliament he
followed the court to Staffordshire and resided at Burton
abbey while it sat in nearby Lichfield, exchanging frequent
correspondence with the justices. Several of the king's
signet letters survive in the king's bench files for this term.
When the court moved on to Shropshire the king appointed
Edward, Duke of York to preside over the Shrewsbury
sessions. There is at least one case, involving William and
John Mynors of Staffordshire, in which Henry is known to
have intervened personally in the court's business: the two
brothers were summoned before the king himself to account
for their offences. Later, on the king's instructions, they
received a pardon in king's bench. There are several other
examples where the king's influence is clearly visible, and
some of these will be discussed below.

As a result of the extraordinary judicial proceedings set
in motion during 1414, enormous pressure of business built
up in king's bench in the second half of the year. As we have
seen, process was issued upon 1,800 indictments during the
superior eyre alone, and each commission of inquiry returned
to king's bench brought in hundreds more. By Michaelmas
term 1414 the court was struggling to cope with a flood of

[16] PRO, KB 27/614–20.

cases far beyond its normal capacity. A remedy was needed to ease the congestion and to offer large numbers of defendants a quick and readily available method of resolving the suit brought against them by the crown. This was provided, at the third parliament of the reign in December 1414, by the proclamation of a general pardon, conceded by the king in return for a generous tax subsidy. Such pardons had been issued at periodic intervals since the middle of the fourteenth century. They could be obtained by individuals and corporations on application to chancery at a cost of 16s.4d., and entitled the beneficiary to exemption from a variety of financial liabilities and to immunity from prosecution at the king's suit on a comprehensive range of criminal offences. The terms of the 1414 pardon included even treason, murder, and rape among offences pardonable in this manner, disregarding the 1390 Statute of Pardons which expressly excluded them from general pardons.[17] Not surprisingly, the pardon was at once in great demand, and nearly 5,000 copies were granted in the three years following the proclamation. From Hilary term 1415 virtually every case brought in king's bench arising from the special inquiries of 1414 was determined by the presentation of a general pardon.

The proclamation of the general pardon of December 1414 poses the critical question of the effectiveness of Henry V's campaign to re-establish public order. On the face of it the offer of a full pardon to all comers, including traitors, murderers, and rapists, looks very much like an admission of defeat. The statistical evidence would appear to confirm this impression. The vast majority of those who appeared in court to answer charges either presented a pardon or made a fine. Convictions were very rare indeed: in the course of the superior eyre in Shropshire and Staffordshire, for example, only one person was convicted out of over 500 who came to court. On the basis of the statistics, therefore, it is impossible to refute the conclusion drawn by Elizabeth Kimball from her study of the Shropshire peace roll: 'unless the majority

---

[17] For the terms of the 1414 pardon, see PRO, C 67 (Patent Rolls, Supplementary)/37, m. 60.

of these indictments were not valid, serious crime was not being punished in Shropshire, or for that matter anywhere in England'.[18] If Henry V was seeking primarily to punish crime in 1414, his plans undoubtedly failed. Indeed this failure was so complete and so uncharacteristic of the king, who had executed swift and ruthless justice upon the Lollard rebels in January 1414, as to suggest that it was not his primary intention to punish crime, and that he sought to settle the disturbances by other means.

What then were these means? To answer this question we must look beyond the bare record of the court's performance, the rates of appearance and conviction, and consider more closely the nature of the disorder which was revealed by the inquiries of 1414. The records disclose that many of the worst offenders fell into two broad, and to some extent overlapping groups upon which the crown relied heavily for the administration of the realm: the county gentry, who helped run local government, and the professional administrators and servants of the house of Lancaster. The disorders in the midlands, for example, which provoked complaints at the Leicester parliament, were chiefly the result of gentry disputes escalating into open confrontation; while in North Wales the effects of the Glyndwr rebellion had been greatly exacerbated by the corrupt administration of Thomas Barnby, chamberlain of the principality from 1406 until he was removed from office by the king's justices in 1414. Although the king's chief administrative officer in Wales, Barnby was accused of consorting with the rebels, appropriating confiscated lands to his own profit, and all manner of lesser offences.[19] The situation was complicated further by the fact that in many areas disorder was a legacy of the divisions of Henry IV's reign and the abuse of power by his supporters.

The delicacy of the problems Henry V faced in this regard can be illustrated by the example of Shropshire, which according to Chief Justice Hankford, 'more than any other

---

[18] *The Shropshire Peace Roll, 1400–1414*, ed. E. G. Kimball (Shrewsbury, 1959), p. 45.
[19] Barnby's career is examined by R. A. Griffiths, 'The Glyn Dŵr Rebellion in North Wales through the Eyes of an Englishman', *Bulletin of the Board of Celtic Studies*, xxii (1967), 151–68.

county in England abounds in murder and rapine'.[20] Throughout Henry IV's reign the most powerful magnate in the
county was Thomas, Earl of Arundel, lord of Clun and
Oswestry in the Shropshire march, and one of the most
trusted supporters of the Lancastrian usurpation. Henry IV
entrusted Arundel with the responsibility of defending
Shropshire against the Welsh rebels, and the earl's supporters
were allowed a free hand in running the county. Arundel's
chief lieutenants were Richard Lacon and John Wele, con-
stables of Clun and Oswestry respectively, and his following
included a number of leading Shropshire gentry, notably Sir
John Winsbury, Robert and Roger Corbet of Moreton Corbet
and John Burley of Broncroft. Under Henry IV this group
dominated county administration, regularly filling the offices
of sheriff, justice of the peace, and shire-knight. With the
earl's acquiescence the Arundel retinue in Shropshire freely
abused this monopoly of power to line their own pockets and
advance their private interests. It is clear, for example, that
Lacon and Wele were very much a law unto themselves on
the marches, while Roger Corbet was indicted in 1414 on
several counts of extortion and for leading an armed band
which destroyed the house of John Wytheford, his opponent
in a property dispute. In reaction to such excesses opposition
to the Arundel affinity gradually took shape, and by the
end of Henry IV's reign had found its leader in the young
John Talbot, Lord Furnival, whose family had recently
acquired lands in Shropshire. In 1413 hostility between the
two sides found expression in a dispute over lands leased from
Wenlock priory. During the spring and summer of 1413
armed bands from each faction roamed the county, terrorizing
supporters of their opponents and leaving a trail of destruction in their wake. Arundel's affinity also used their administrative control to discomfit their enemies. Richard Lacon and
Robert Corbet, shire-knights for Shropshire at the 1413
parliament, nominated five Talbot men for the unpopular
post of subsidy collector for the tax granted by that assembly.
When the latter tried to collect the tax in November 1413,

[20] PRO, KB 27/613, Rex, m. 36. For what follows, see E. Powell, 'Public
Order and Law Enforcement in Shropshire and Staffordshire in the Early Fifteenth
Century' (Oxford Univ. D.Phil. thesis, 1979), pp. 300–17.

they were constantly harassed by Arundel's supporters and
their servants. Finally at the peace sessions of March 1414,
Arundel himself presided over the indictment of Talbot's
leading supporter, John Bruyn of Bridgnorth, for a wide
variety of offences. The record of the superior eyre of king's
bench at Shrewsbury in 1414 provides graphic evidence of
the fear inspired in Shropshire by the power of Arundel's
followers. The county grand jury laid charges against them
only on condition that every one they accused should give
security not to take reprisals against them. In subsequent
proceedings on the Shropshire indictments, the court took
care to see that this condition was fully observed.

How, we may ask, did the king attempt to deal with
such disorders? It would have been inappropriate, and
politically impossible, for the government to have hanged or
imprisoned this type of offender. Inasmuch as the Earl of
Arundel was one of the Lancastrians' most valued servants,
the mere indictment of his retinue in king's bench represented an important exercise of political authority by Henry
V. The king's main aim was not so much to punish the
warring factions as to separate them, resolve their quarrels,
and restore observance of his peace. Because of the crown's
dependence on the magnates and gentry for the administration of local government, Henry had to tread warily in
dealing with the criminal activity of these classes. The failure
of judicial inquiries in Devon illustrates how the local
community might withdraw its co-operation if it felt its
interests threatened. On the other hand, when disorder got
out of hand, as it did in the midlands before 1414, the king
was forced to intervene.

Reconciliation, then, was the keynote of Henry's policy
of law enforcement. In this regard the king's methods accorded with his broader policy of disowning the legacy of
faction and distrust inherited from his father's reign and
reconciling the country to the Lancastrian regime. His
approach demanded a skilful combination of firmness and
generosity. As in the episode narrated by the *Brut* chronicler,
some offenders were summoned before the king in person for
a stern lecture. Many leading protagonists of the disorders
were also bound in recognizances for large sums to maintain

the peace henceforward. In the case of Shropshire several of Arundel's leading adherents, including Lacon, Wele, and the Corbet brothers, appeared in court together and made bonds for £200 each to keep the peace. In addition Arundel was made to take out bonds totalling £3,000 to guarantee their good behaviour. Prior to this the king had already taken bonds for huge sums from Arundel, John Talbot, and his brother Gilbert, Lord Talbot. As a mark of disfavour Talbot had also been appointed royal lieutenant in Ireland for six years. For the most part, however, a fine or pardon was sufficient to buy off the king's suit and gain readmittance to his peace.

Military service was the means whereby many offenders were allowed to work their way back into royal favour. Henry V did not regard participation in the disorders of his father's reign as a disqualification against serving in the French wars. Indeed the reverse seems to have been the case, and we may suspect that the courtrooms of 1414 had an aura of the recruiting-office about them. This policy, of course, had the advantage of calming local feuds by physically removing the protagonists from the scene for an extended period. William Mynors of Staffordshire, whom we saw summoned before the king at Burton abbey during the superior eyre, took part in the Agincourt campaign of 1415 and subsequently in the conquest of Normandy. After the death of Henry V he remained in France to become a mainstay of the Lancastrian occupation, and one of John Talbot's most trusted lieutenants. Talbot himself, although exiled to Ireland during the Agincourt campaign, was summoned to Normandy by the king in 1419, and spent the rest of his long career defending Henry's French conquests. Besides good soldiers, the king also needed experienced administrators in France, and an immediate choice was Thomas Barnby, the former chamberlain of North Wales dismissed for corruption by royal justices in 1414. Although corrupt, Barnby was clearly efficient and he did not remain in disgrace for long. Just over a year later he was appointed treasurer of Harfleur, the port captured by Henry V after a bitter siege during August and September 1415. Perhaps the best example of the link between the disorders and subsequent service in France is provided by the muster roll of the Earl of Arundel's retinue at the siege of Harfleur.[21] The roll reads like a list of those indicted in king's bench for their misdeeds in Shropshire. Arundel's esquires included Richard Lacon, John Winsbury, John Burley, and Roger and Robert Corbet. The only important name missing is John Wele, the constable of Oswestry, but we know from other sources that the king had entrusted him with the defence of the Shropshire march during the Agincourt campaign. Still more revealing is that these followers of Arundel were accompanied in the earl's retinue by their own servants. Among the archers named in the muster roll are Hugh Purce, Roger Onslow, and Thomas Pendale, all servants of Richard Lacon, and Richard Leach and Richard Oswestry, who served the Corbet brothers. Each of these men had played his part in the Shropshire disturbances and was prominent in the indictments submitted to king's bench.

By these methods Henry V was able to defuse the explosive hostilities which had built up during his father's reign. After the king's brief but decisive intervention the process of reconciliation could be pursued within the local community itself. For example Talbot's supporter John Bruyn, who accompanied his master to Ireland in 1414, returned from exile in 1417 and was able to make peace with his enemies in Shropshire. Through the mediation of mutual friends a panel of arbitrators was set up, led by the abbot of Shrewsbury and the prior of Wenlock, which considered the grievances of all parties and devised a settlement in which both sides received financial compensation for the injuries they had sustained.[22] In addition the arbitrators instructed the parties henceforth to keep the peace with one another, and since no evidence has been found of subsequent disorders, it appears that they did so.

The success of Henry V's programme of law enforcement is demonstrated by the lack of serious disorder in England during his long absences abroad between 1415 and 1422. The king never found it necessary to interrupt his French campaigns in order to deal with outbreaks of violence and lawlessness at home. It would be quite wrong, however, to assume that public order was perfectly maintained. As is evident from petitions to parliament there were regions of the country, notably the northern and Welsh marches, where the king's peace was still freely broken. In 1414, for example, the commons of Northumberland complained against the depredations of men from the liberties of Tyndale, Redesdale, and Hexhamshire, and requested that the lords and officials of those liberties be instructed to co-operate in the arrest and punishment of such malefactors. A statute was passed to that effect, but it clearly remained a dead letter, for a complaint in very similar terms was presented to parliament in 1421. In 1417, shortly after the king's departure for Normandy, the Commons submitted a petition in general terms against armed bands composed, it was alleged, of Lollards, traitors, and rebels, who assembled to break into private forests and parks. Attempts were made to arrest the leader of one of these gangs, nicknamed Friar Tuck, who had been active in Surrey and Sussex, but he remained at large and was still active as late as 1429.[23] Nor was the government able to check an epidemic of counterfeiting coin which swept the country from 1415 onwards, the product it appears of a European bullion shortage exacerbated by the weight and frequency of Henry V's demands for money to finance his wars. Despite a statute granting new powers to justices of the peace and assize justices in cases of counterfeiting,[24] and the use of confessed coiners as 'approvers'—informers who accused their former associates—the problem worsened towards the end of the reign, and was only alleviated by the easing of financial pressure on the country after Henry V's death.[25] In some respects the French wars directly impeded the smooth running of the judicial system. When he embarked on the conquest of Normandy Henry ordered the suspension of all assize business for the duration of the expedition, in the interests of those who were accompanying him overseas: no assizes were taken until 1421 when the ordinance was

[23] J. C. Holt, *Robin Hood* (London, 1982), pp. 58–9.
[24] 4 Henry V st. 2 c. 8.
[25] KB 27/620–60; J. Day, 'The Great Bullion Famine of the Fifteenth Century', *Past and Present*, lxxix (1978), 3–54.

revoked at the Commons' insistence because of the delays it caused in bringing disputes into court. On balance, nevertheless, the significant fact is not that problems of law enforcement remained after 1415, but that public order ceased to be the serious political issue that it had been throughout Henry IV's reign and at Henry V's accession.

In the final assessment, the evidence of Henry V's reign seems to confirm the old cliché that medieval kings eased the problem of endemic disorder by undertaking foreign wars. On this argument England was quiet during the king's absences because he had taken all the trouble-makers with him. But this does not do full justice to Henry's achievement. The wars of Edward I and Edward III ultimately served only to aggravate the problem of domestic disorder. Moreover the degree and speed of the transformation between the turmoil of Henry IV's reign and the calm of Henry V's was remarkable and unprecedented. As we have seen, foreign and domestic policy were of course inextricably linked: but it took a king of extraordinary ability to combine the two so effectively, and, working within the limitations of his slender resources, to make each serve the interests of the other. It would perhaps be an exaggeration to say that the battle of Agincourt was won in the courtroom of king's bench, but there is no doubt that in order to explain Henry's successes in France, we must first look to his achievement in restoring order in England.

IV

The King's Servants

JEREMY CATTO

Who were the men who executed the complex of military, diplomatic, and financial means which served the political ends of Henry V? An achievement such as his conquest of Normandy could scarcely have been effected without an unusually able cadre of servants, bringing to new levels of professionalism and skill more than one of those arts of government which were beginning to be studied in the century before Machiavelli. As Tito Livio Frulovisi emphasized, relying on the impressions of Humphrey, Duke of Gloucester and his friends, the conquest was won by attention to detail: 'neither lacked they mines to undermine the ground, carpenters to make and raise engines, labourers to delve the ground and to lade ditches, masons to heave stone for shot, to make walls, to subvert strongholds, nor gunners to shoot the guns . . . there failed them no manner of skill or science'.[1] Henry's logistical preparation for war in 1413 and 1414, organized by Nicholas Merbury as master of the ordnance, the supply of arrows, of bows and bowstrings, cannon, siege-towers and scaling ladders, battering-rams and mining equipment, were graphically described by Wylie from the voluminous and detailed accounts rendered in the exchequer. Behind them were more delicate operations: the collection of ready cash, the pawning of the king's jewels, the recruitment of men by indenture and array, and the opening of a vigorous diplomatic campaign ranging from Portugal to the Teutonic Order. Such efforts could hardly have been begun, and certainly not carried through with success, without the intelligent co-operation and hard work of the king's servants in the widest sense, those commissioned

[1] *Titi Livii Vita*, p. 33; *First English Life*, p. 80.

to act temporarily or permanently in his name. Vigorous government does not of necessity involve institutional innovation. Finance and diplomacy were well-tried hand-maids of war, the main business of Henry V's ancestors. But fourteenth-century wars had certainly required a high degree of organizing ability on the part of the king's house-hold officials, as the campaigns of Edward I and Edward III had shown. The character of the men about Henry V's household, their recruitment and rewards, and their part in their master's triumphs is a subject which requires some attention.

Any attempt to distinguish in the early fifteenth century a professional civil service, exclusively devoted to the royal interest and will, must be a chimaera. Contemporaries made no sharp distinction between the king's service and that of other potentates, where the departments of state were matched in less elaborate form: an exchequer, with its own barons, had served the Dukes of Lancaster, while the Yorkist kings would adapt the practices of 'private' estate officials to the crown lands.[2] The king's knights and esquires normally served for a few months at a time, being drawn from the leading gentlemen of the counties who might serve other masters. The king's clerks in the lawcourts, exchequer, or chancery might seem to approximate more closely to the professional bureaucrat; but while they may have been professional, their skills were too particular, and their organization too sectional to constitute an administrative cadre. For the same reason, albeit the great departments of state had in Tout's phrase 'gone out of court', and were no longer a part of the king's household, they had no political independence nor even, so far as can be judged, a spirit of passive administrative resistance to the political will of their masters. The independence they had was sociological, not political: they had developed as separate series of profes-sions or mysteries, reflected topographically in the common households of the several types of clerk. The custom of the lawcourts, chancery, and privy seal was to live together in

[2] On the relation of royal service to others, see R. A. Griffiths, 'Public and Private Bureaucracies in England and Wales in the Fifteenth Century', *TRHS*, 5th series xxx (1980), 109–30.

Inns or hostels kept by a senior clerk, and situated in the neighbourhood of Chancery Lane where the Inns of Chancery used to be and the Inns of Court still are. In the Inns, as in the academic halls of Oxford and Cambridge, the juniors were apprenticed in their professions. The royal courts of law, which sat in different parts of Westminster Hall, demonstrate most clearly their combination of political subordination and professional independence: Henry V on his accession dismissed Chief Justice Gascoigne, but his appointment of Sir William Hankford as the new Chief Justice and all his other judicial appointments were made exclusively from the tight circle of Westminster lawyers and King's Serjeants-at-law who had been trained in the Inns of Court.[3]

Much the same development had been taking place in the chancery. The king's original writing office was now the sole channel of his official will expressed in solemn charters, patents, and writs, and it was also beginning to function, from the dais in Westminster Hall, as a court of equitable jurisdiction. The chancery clerks were another closed corporation, headed by the master of the rolls and eleven other clerks of the first or second benches, and including beneath them a larger body of junior clerks or cursitors and apprentices assigned as personal clerks to their seniors. There is not the slightest evidence that the procedures of the chancery, its mysteries of wax or ribbon and formulaic Latinity, were used to delay or frustrate the will of Henry V, whose two chancellors, Henry Beaufort and Thomas Langley, were among his closest confidants. Nevertheless, chancery was a world of its own. Its clerks were not yet civilians with a university training; even less were they common lawyers. They must have had some grounding in Roman procedures, and in judicial matters the chancellor and the master of the rolls were advised by doctors of civil law like Mr Ralph Greenhurst, the king's notary in chancery. The career of Simon Gaunstede, Henry V's master of the rolls, is typical of the usual practice of promotion from inside the office, though his occasional service as an envoy was a new departure

[3] G. O. Sayles, ed., *Select Cases in the Court of King's Bench, 1377–1422*, Selden Society, lxxxviii (London, 1971), p. xiv.

for a chancery clerk. Their almost wholly clerical and bachelor status in the early fifteenth century helped to preserve an exclusive way of life.[4] Standing orders issued by Henry V show that they lived together in hostels in Chancery Lane, of which the largest was that of the master of the rolls, and that they were forbidden to mix with the apprentices at law.[5] Here they carried on most of the business initiated by individuals, for which fees were charged, and kept the rolls and files of the department. Chancery, therefore, was not only a department of royal government but an esoteric profession. Its traditions could still be further elaborated, as the adoption of a standard 'chancery English' orthography and style would show in the following generation; though here the clerks would follow the forms personally used by Henry V.[6] Not yet legalized or laicized, its clerkships were not the sinecures they would become by the seventeenth century; but their narrow duties and specialized training cannot have fitted most of them for the larger tasks of diplomacy and government.

The king's exchequer was only superficially similar. Though physically divided into the receipt on the east side of Westminster Hall and the expanding audit department, the exchequer proper, on the west, its unity was preserved by its clerks' frequent promotion from one side to the other. The skills of the exchequer clerks, unlike those of chancery clerks, had many applications; they were those of the receiver and the accountant, the product of a widespread business training which was put to use with small variation on every landed property. Consequently, new blood flowed into it from the service of other lords. As hereditary chamberlain of the exchequer, the Earl of Warwick nominated a series of ministers from the Beauchamp estates to one of the chamberlainships in both the receipt and the account sections; and promotions from the royal household, like that of the cofferer William Kynwolmersh to be under-treasurer and

[4] T. F. Tout, 'The Household of the Chancery and its Disintegration' in *Essays in History presented to Reginald Lane Poole*, ed. H. W. C. Davis (Oxford, 1927), pp. 46–85.

[5] G. W. Sanders, *Orders of the High Court of Chancery* (London, 1845), i, 1–7.

[6] Malcolm Richardson, 'Henry V, the English Chancery, and Chancery English', *Speculum*, lv (1980), 726–50.

clerk of the receipt in 1417 were not uncommon. On the other hand, there were a number of exchequer families like the Everdons, kindred of John Everdon, Edward II's baron of the exchequer, from whom in Henry V's reign auditors were still being recruited. Laicization had proceeded further than in the chancery, and among the lay clerks were fore-runners of the future placemen: the Hertfordshire gentleman Henry Somer, for instance, chancellor of the exchequer from 1410 to 1439, was also under-treasurer during Archbishop Arundel's ascendancy in Henry IV's council, an early intrusion of faction into the exchequer. His career in the office com-bined lay status with pluralism, political patronage, and perhaps a sinecure tenure.[7] It is reasonable to suppose that the exchequer clerks were less self-sufficient and inward-looking than those of the chancery, and their contribution to government less ceremonious and more substantial. The physical expansion of the exchequer in the fourteenth century, to accommodate the vastly increased business of the auditors of foreign accounts in new offices to the west of the audit department, marks its control over the great volume of financial dealings arising from the French wars.[8] The numerous accounts of Henry V's captains, his local lieutenants and diplomatic agents, are the basis of our in-formation on his vigorous conduct of his wars. They also illustrate the exchequer's own vigour in holding the partici-pants in these vast and complex operations under some sort of financial control. This adaptability may reasonably be attributed to the open society of the exchequer, into which the skills of the auditor and the accountant could be imported as well as they could be inherited, and where no esoteric knowledge and no departmental Inns were required.

In the third of the great departments of state, the privy seal, we come closer to the heart of the king's business. Warrants under the privy seal were the authority required for the chancery to seal charters or letters, and for the exchequer to disburse its funds; though the privy seal records have for the most part disappeared, there is no doubt that in

[7] J. L. Kirby, 'The Rise of the Under-Treasurer of the Exchequer', *EHR*, lxxii (1957), 666–77.

[8] H. M. Colvin, *The History of the King's Works* (London, 1963–73), i, 542.

the reign of Henry V the normal instrument of business was a letter under the privy seal. At first glance a department neither so solemn as chancery, nor so domestic as the king's chamber seems redundant: a quango. It was, to be sure, a narrow world of its own, with its diminutive staff (about fourteen clerks in 1413) living together at Chester's Inn in the Strand, the 'Hostel of the Privy Seal', and generally serving for a lifetime. The human side of the privy seal can be observed in the poems of one of its clerks, Thomas Hoccleve. Hoccleve's world was a modest one in which worry about his annuity alternated with drinking sessions in the local taverns: it is worlds away from the chancery clerks round the corner with their fat purses and their furs.[9] It is not coincidence, however, that the privy seal and not the chancery had a poet, nor that Hoccleve's *Regement of Princes* and other verses were written to present the glory and righteousness of Henry V in recitable English; nor that Hoccleve compiled a formulary containing nearly nine hundred forms for letters under the privy seal. The formalization of the privy seal constituted the recognition in England of the art of diplomacy: letters to foreign princes or to English lords were the material of the privy seal clerk's art, and the same rhetorical techniques could be used for propaganda purposes in poems on current events such as Hoccleve's verses on the Oldcastle rising. Propaganda was a consistent feature of Henry V's government, of course, ranging from the newsletters which the king sent home from France to inspired versions of contemporary events like the *Gesta Henrici Quinti*. It is probable that some of the surviving internal council memoranda like the assessment in November 1418 of policy towards the Dauphin were drafted, in this case in English, by privy seal clerks. The office was therefore a kind of secretariat to the council, divided into a stationary and a travelling department during the French campaigns, and it could even be seen, on a longer perspective, as an ancestor of the foreign office.[10] The clerks perfected the arts

[9] A. L. Brown, 'The Privy Seal Clerks in the Early Fifteenth Century' in *The Study of Mediaeval Records, Essays in Honour of Kathleen Major*, ed. D. A. Bullough and R. L. Storey (Oxford, 1971), pp. 260–81; cf. pp. 270–2.

[10] A. L. Brown, 'The Privy Seal in the Early Fifteenth Century' (Oxford D.Phil. thesis 1954), pp. 92–109.

of diplomacy as they were understood in the second decade of the fifteenth century, exactly as Coluccio Salutati, the former chancellor of Florence one of whose letters was said to be worth a thousand troop of horse, had perfected *dictamen* and propaganda for political purposes.

The privy seal took its orders either directly from the king by word of mouth to the keeper, or from the council which had, by the early fifteenth century, crystallized into an institution. An inner core now met almost daily; it had its own premises, the Star Chamber built in 1348 next to the Receipt of the Exchequer, though it frequently met elsewhere; its own clerk, the second in command at the privy seal, Robert Frye; and (though rather haphazardly until 1421), its own records, files kept in the privy seal office. The council could indeed act as a complete government, as it had probably done for long intervals between 1409 and 1413 during Henry IV's illness, and was to do from 1422 until 1437. After 1417 during the king's absence a rump council directed much of the routine business of the crown. It was, therefore, what circumstances of the moment made it.[11] Membership, and even more attendance, was flexible, but the indispensable core in 1413–15 comprised the chancellor Beaufort, the treasurer the Earl of Arundel, and the keeper of the privy seal, John Prophet, together with two 'ministers without portfolio', the former chancellor Thomas Langley, Bishop of Durham and Dr Henry Chichele, Bishop of St David's and then Archbishop of Canterbury, who had held no formal office under the crown. At this time the central figure was probably Beaufort, who alone drew a regular salary as councillor; but they had all acted together before, during the ascendancy of the Prince of Wales in 1409–11, when Beaufort, Arundel, and Chichele had been councillors, with Prophet and Langley who had served all regimes and offended nobody. Not one of them had achieved eminence through service in the departments of state; Langley and Prophet had come to be confidential secretaries of Henry IV from the service, respectively, of Archbishop Courtenay and John of Gaunt; while Beaufort and Arundel

[11] On the fifteenth-century council see A. L. Brown, 'The King's Councillors in Fifteenth Century England' *TRHS*, 5th series xix (1969), 95–118.

were part of Prince Henry's intimate circle. Nevertheless, it is likely if not certain that the chancellor and the treasurer fulfilled their official duties in person: Beaufort's almost continuous residence at Westminster in these years suggests that he sat in the court of chancery, though he had no formal legal education. Arundel's position as the head of a family which had made extensive loans to the crown in the fourteenth century fitted him for a financial office, and he was active in the inquiry into the Calais garrison finances, visiting the town in 1414.[12] Chichele's experience, like Langley's, was diplomatic, with the additional qualifications of a civil lawyer. All five, therefore, reached their place on the council through having worked closely with Henry V as Prince of Wales. As councillors, they were able to act generally without the king's presence, but in accord with his wishes.

The council's business is perhaps best observed in the full minutes of its meetings on Friday, Saturday, and Sunday 25–7 May 1415, shortly before the Harfleur campaign when it was probably more active than usual.[13] On Friday, meeting at Blackfriars in the presence of the Earl of Dorset, the councillors considered and allowed a petition of the king's squire Robert Twyford to be permitted to accompany Henry V to France notwithstanding the king's desire that he remain in England. Next, they interviewed ten Italian merchants from whom they demanded £2,000 as a loan for the war treasury; when this was refused the merchants were committed to the Fleet prison. On Saturday they ordered the justiciar of Chester to hold no assizes during the king's voyage, and on Sunday, afforced by the Dukes of Bedford and Gloucester with the Earl of Warwick and Richard Courtenay (Bishop of Norwich and treasurer of the chamber), they delegated a number of tasks to individuals and committees. The list of duties is of some interest for the light it throws on specialization in the council:

1. To consider instructions for ambassadors to the Duke of Burgundy: Chichele; Sir Hugh Mortimer, chamberlain of the duchy of Cornwall; Dr Philip Morgan, an ecclesiastical lawyer and envoy of some experience (who would execute the

---

[12] Kirby, 'Financing of Calais', 165–77.
[13] *Proc. PC*, ii, 165–9.

present mission); John Honyngham, another tried diplomat; and, on his return, Henry, Lord Scrope.

2. To consider the recovery of pawned crown jewels: Duke of Bedford; Beaufort, a principal creditor; Richard Courtenay, as treasurer of the chamber the responsible officer.

3. To consider arrangements with the seneschal of Aquitaine, Sir John Tiptoft: Duke of Gloucester; Earl of Dorset, admiral; John Prophet.

4. To appoint commissions of array in each county: Beaufort.

5. To cause the prelates to take active measures against the Lollards: Beaufort again.

6. On the provision of supplies for the king's voyage: Arundel, treasurer; Sir Roger Leche, treasurer of the household; Sir John Rothenale, comptroller of the household.

7. On the payment of sailors: Arundel, treasurer; Dorset, admiral.

8. On provision for Calais and the marches: Arundel; Sir Roger Salvayn, treasurer of Calais.

This minute illustrates several points. First, it shows that the council was in the habit of calling on other experts to deliberate on particular questions. Secondly, there is a marked degree of specialization, particularly in the fields of diplomacy, loans, and military supplies. Court offices and garrison offices entrusted to courtiers, like the treasurership of Calais, cannot have been sinecures. It is noticeable that the court and household, including the king's brothers, took part in the council's deliberations as well as serving in the field. If at other times the council's work was likely to be more routine than at this time of military preparation, the failure of many temporal lords who had been sworn of the council to attend its ordinary meetings need not be taken as evidence of their remoteness from the king's government. Many of them were habitually in attendance in the household, and may therefore have been party to important business transacted in the king's presence.

It is futile to discuss the household of Henry V as if it were merely a new phase of a public institution, the royal household. There was no necessary continuity between successive kings' households, and in some respects closer comparisons could probably be drawn between Henry V's and those of contemporaries like his friend Richard, Earl of Warwick. Its organization, it is true, was traditional, little different from that of his great-grandfather Edward III, and was much the same as the household of Edward IV, described in the *Black Book* of 1478. It consisted of an outer circle, the household under the command of its steward, always a knight of renown, and its treasurer, once a clerk but by 1413 usually a layman of knightly rank; and an inner circle, the chamber or court proper, under the chamberlain who was always a nobleman, and the treasurer of the chamber.[14] This office seems to have been downgraded after the death of its first holder under Henry V, Richard Courtenay, Bishop of Norwich, in 1415. The total strength of the household was probably smaller than the 350 and more of Edward III's household in 1360, but must have been larger than the Earl of Warwick's in 1421, calculated at 'well below a hundred': perhaps two hundred, therefore. But its size is not really significant as at any particular time it might comprise a selection of the king's ministers, noblemen, or ecclesiastics, or ambassadors of foreign princes. The duties of its officers might vary from the purely domestic to major tasks of government: commissions of inquiry into disturbance, raising cash for war, armaments and military supplies, missions abroad, and probably organizing secret intelligence. The household seems to have moved with the king, except perhaps when he was on very short journeys, and Henry V's itinerary, when he was in England, was one of the ways in which he modified the domestic customs of his predecessors. The constant itineration of earlier English kings had already been reduced, by the later years of Edward III, to gentle progresses up and down the Thames valley between Windsor, Westminster, and the royal manor houses at Sheen and Eltham, south of the river: Henry V seems to have spent longer than any of his predecessors at Westminster. In his first year he conformed more to the habits of earlier English kings, with the summer months spent at Windsor Park and two journeys to Canterbury; on 29 June 1413, when he was

---

[14] See in general, Fagan, 'Household of Henry V'.

on his way to Canterbury for the second time, the council
had to ask him not to stray too far from London in a time of
tension. But from the middle of 1414 he was constantly at
Westminster; from September until May 1415 he hardly
seems to have stirred from the palace, and from his return
in November until June 1416 he was there again. His other
preferred residence was Kenilworth castle in Warwickshire,
a stronghold of the duchy of Lancaster, where he stayed
from January until March 1414 and again from December
1416 to January or February 1417. He planned a new
residence, in the centre of his religious foundations at Sheen
palace near Richmond which had been abandoned by Richard
II; his only embellishment to existing palaces, it seems, was
his pleasure garden at Kenilworth; and it is remarkable that
he evidently made no changes at Westminster where he
must have spent so many months.[15]

The Westminster months, we may therefore be sure, were
devoted to the work of government, and the household
officers must be considered as potential agents of royal
policy. There was of course nothing new in Henry V's reliance
on his household knights and officers. Their predecessors
had served in a variety of military and administrative roles,
it has recently been shown, in the twelfth century and
before. Nor is there any evidence that the Lancastrian kings
chose men of low rank as a counterpoise to the aristocracy.
In so far as the household officers of Henry V had a common
background, it was in the tradition of service to the house of
Lancaster before 1399, a service which included a striking
variety of men. Most of them had also served Henry IV,
including those who had been associated with the Prince of
Wales in his earlier campaigns; and in spite of the rivalries of
the late king's declining years, there seem to have been few
or none of the dismissals or appointments on grounds of
factional allegiance that were taking place in France in 1413.
In fact both stewards of Henry V's household were public
figures with versatile records of service. Sir Thomas Erpingham
was a knight of renown who had served John of Gaunt.
His successor Sir Walter Hungerford had been a knight of

[15] Colvin, *History of the King's Works*, ii, 998–1000, 685; i, 536.

Henry IV's household and had an equally strong Lancastrian background. He was a spectacular profiteer from Henry V's wars, though his service, culminating as treasurer of England, was more financial than military. His presence at the numerous negotiations with the Dauphin and the Duke of Burgundy in 1418-20 may imply a role as a personal messenger of the king, and at Henry V's deathbed he was charged, with Lord Fitzhugh, with the direct care of the infant prince. His career exemplifies the political significance of the household.[16]

There seems to be no recoverable criterion of selection for Henry V's household knights and officers at the beginning of his reign. Some were officials of the duchy of Lancaster; others, like Sir Hugh Mortimer, were promoted into or rewarded by office in the duchy; and still others, though by no means all, had been associated with him as Prince of Wales.[17] Loyalty to the prince during the rivalries of 1409-11 certainly mattered at first, to the disadvantage of Sir John Tiptoft, Sir John Pelham, or indeed Archbishop Arundel; but Tiptoft was to serve the new king well, while neutral figures in 1410 like Bishop Langley, and perhaps Sir Thomas Erpingham, would suffer no interruption at all in their service. The king's knights and squires, who attended him in rotation, were ideally chosen for political reasons: according to the *Black Book of the Household* of Edward IV, 'by the avyse of his counsayll to be chosen men of theyre possession, worship and wisdom, also to be of sundry shires, by whom hit may be knowe the disposicion of the cuntries'.[18] It is noticeable, conversely, that a high proportion of them would represent their county in parliament. Only a very few, however, could be considered intimates of Henry V; among the closest were probably his chamberlain, Henry Lord Fitzhugh, and his first treasurer of the chamber, Richard Courtenay whom he made Bishop of Norwich. Fitzhugh, who was about 55 in 1413, had long been associated with kings: a Yorkshire landowner and veteran of the border

[16] On Hungerford see J. S. Roskell, 'Three Wiltshire Speakers', *Wiltshire Archaeological and Natural History Magazine*, lvi (1956), 301-41; Roskell, *Speakers*, pp. 357-8.

[17] Somerville, *Duchy of Lancaster*, i, 176-98; Griffiths, 'Henry Prince of Wales', pp. 167-203.

[18] A. R. Myers, *The Household of Edward IV* (Manchester, 1959), p. 127.

wars, he had been a commander at the battle of Homildon Hill in 1402. He had twice benefited from the débâcles of his close cousins the family of Scrope, in 1405, when his relationship with Archbishop Scrope had lured that prelate to his captivity and death, and in 1415 when he was granted the lands of his kinsman Henry, Lord Scrope, the Cambridge conspirator, and prudently exchanged them for an annuity. Nevertheless he shared in Lord Scrope's elaborate piety and interest in the contemplative life, and it is clear that he was the driving force behind Henry V's foundation of the Brigittine house of nuns at Syon. For Fitzhugh, as for the king himself, there was nothing incongruous in this combination of interior prayer and a life of campaigning.

Richard Courtenay's association with Henry V was briefer, but its intimacy may have been closer still. Born in 1381 into the distinguished house of Courtenay, he had been a bachelor of civil law and chancellor of Oxford in his twenties. He had accompanied the Prince of Wales in the Welsh campaign of 1407, and his differences with Archbishop Arundel over the visitation of Oxford had reached a crisis in 1410 during the prince's ascendancy in the council. He took part in both of the embassies to Charles VI in 1414-15, perhaps because he knew the king's mind better than his colleagues. As treasurer of the chamber he played an important role in the financial preparations for the Agincourt campaign, receiving the ready cash lent in return for the king's jewels in pledge. A curious sidelight on his activities just before and during the expedition comes from the trial for treason in France of the astrologer Jean Fusoris. Courtenay had met Fusoris in the course of his missions in Paris, and had brought a number of books and an astrolabe from him. Subsequently, claiming that he had not been paid for these, Fusoris persuaded the Archbishop of Bourges to let him accompany the final French embassy which met Henry V at Winchester in June 1415. From Fusoris's account a series of vignettes of Courtenay emerge: eating almonds in the garden of the Celestines in Paris, while his graver colleague Bishop Langley, upstairs in the library, was comparing the Celestine and Benedictine Rules; back in England, consulting his almanac and his astrolabe on the fortune of the proposed marriage of Henry V with the Princess Catherine; saying mass for the king and presenting to him Fusoris, on the basis of a common interest in astrology. At Harfleur Courtenay seems to have acted as an intelligence officer, attempting perhaps successfully to use Fusoris as his agent in Paris: only the king 'who is very discreet as you know', Courtenay wrote, being privy to the transaction.[19] Here perhaps we have a glimpse of the careful groundwork, directed by household officers, which preceded Henry V's military and diplomatic victories.

The duties of household officers, then, could cover every aspect of government. The chamberlain and other household men inquired into the disturbance in the midlands in 1414; a knight of the chamber, Sir Roger Salvayn, was made treasurer of Calais, a post which, as his accounts show, involved residence at Calais for at least part of the year; most officers served in missions to foreign princes from time to time. The only specialization seems to have been the financial *cursus honorum* of chamber clerks leading through the coffererhip, the comptrollership and the treasurership of the household to the office of treasurer of England. In practice this exalted office was filled by household officers, either as acting treasurer or as treasurer in name, from 1415 until the end of the reign. In the Agincourt campaign the duty of paying the wages of war had fallen on an auditor of the exchequer, John Everdon, but after 1417 it became the responsibility of the treasurer of the household.[20] Henry V like Edward I found that the sinews of war were more readily flexed by his intimate companions than by the custom-bound officials of the exchequer.

In the court of Henry V the household officers were only one element, if a central element, among a transient population of dignitaries and potentates. Some information on the presence of magnates and prelates in his household may be derived from the uncalendared witness-lists to royal charters enrolled in the charter rolls, which exist from 1413 to 1417, though in gradually declining numbers.[21] These

---

[19] *Fusoris*, pp. 141, 149, 213, 220, 233, 267–8; see Wylie, *Henry the Fifth*, i, 230, 500, 504–5; ii, 28.

[20] Fagan, 'Household of Henry V', pp. 225–8.

[21] Charter Rolls of Henry V, 1413–1417, in PRO, C 53/180–6.

lists were to some degree formalized, and they apparently contain some fictitious signatures; they are therefore an unreliable guide in detail, but their general pattern shows consistent development. In the first stage, from May 1413 to the Leicester parliament in June 1414, a rather narrow inner circle seems to have been present on virtually all occasions: Archbishop Arundel until his death, Beaufort, Langley, Chichele and Nicholas Bubwith among bishops; of lay peers, the Earls of Arundel (the treasurer) and Warwick; and the officials Lord Fitzhugh, Sir Thomas Erpingham, and John Prophet the keeper of the privy seal. They were joined by the beginning of 1414 by the Dukes of Clarence and York. The second period lasted from June 1414 until the Agincourt expedition in August 1415: the circle had now widened to include the Dukes of Bedford and Gloucester, recently come of age, the Earl of March, and Bishop Courtenay of Norwich. Bubwith had departed for the Council of Constance, while Bowet the Archbishop of York seems to have been a fairly frequent visitor. The last phase for which the witness lists provide evidence extended from Agincourt to the invasion of Normandy: death had removed the Earl of Arundel and Bishop Courtenay, and retirement disposed of Erpingham and Prophet (though the former sometimes continued to subscribe charters); and the only frequent new witnesses were the Earls of Dorset and Salisbury. It is fair to conclude that after the spring of 1414 Henry V's household was ceasing to be a group of intimates most of whom had served him as Prince of Wales, and becoming a body more representative of the nobility in general.

For information on the lesser men who neither held any formal office under the crown nor enjoyed an exalted personal status, we can only proceed by example. Sir John Cornewaill may be taken as a model of primarily military service to the house of Lancaster. He was born about 1380 to an elder Sir John Cornewaill, a companion of Richard II who had also served John IV, Duke of Brittany and had married his niece. His family had therefore experience of military service in the courts of princes, and the younger John followed his father's example in marrying a royal lady, Elisabeth of Lancaster the sister of Henry IV, who had recently been widowed by the execution of John, Earl of Huntingdon. His part in Henry IV's service seems to have been limited to military or naval commands as castellan of Sheppey and constable of Queenborough, though he was active in securing by royal grants the lands of alien priories. He was closely connected in military service and business affairs with Sir William Porter, a squire of Henry IV's chamber, and in the succeeding reign they continued to campaign together. Cornewaill's part in Henry V's wars is characterized by a series of remarkable 'firsts': first ashore at Harfleur on 14 August 1415, in company with his step-son the Earl of Huntingdon, Sir William Porter, and Sir Gilbert Umfraville; first across the Somme at Voyennes, some weeks later, at the turning-point of Henry V's long march; first across the river at Pont-de-l'Arche in June 1418, securing the Seine for the investment of Rouen. Unlike his companion William Porter, he played no part in embassies or negotiations beyond the surrender of towns; nor had he any place in the administration of the conquest. He certainly enriched himself in the wars, however, since he built Ampthill castle from the proceeds, and possessed jewels which after his death were acquired by Henry VI. He was one of the few captains of the Lancastrian army to be elevated to the peerage as Lord Fanhope, though not until 1433. He therefore received no direct rewards from Henry V, though without the opportunities offered by sustained royal favour he would hardly have prospered.[22]

In contrast the career of Dr Philip Morgan may be taken as an example of Henry V's diplomatic service. A Welshman who had graduated in canon law at Oxford, he distinguished himself in the court of Canterbury, where Chichele before him had made his name. He probably came to the notice of Henry V through the good offices of Chichele, or perhaps through his part in the trial of Sir John Oldcastle, and was first employed in the king's service in June 1414, in a mission to Burgundy and Holland. Thereafter his frequent

[22] *Complete Peerage*, v, 253–4, s.n. Fanhope; Wylie and Waugh, *Henry the Fifth*, i, 348–9; ii, 17, 119; iii, 115; McFarlane, *Nobility*, pp. 94, 98.

service on informal missions, notably his semi-secret visit to
the Duke of Burgundy from August to December 1415,
and on the negotiation of truces, shows that his expertise
lay in mastery of detail and the preparation of agreements
in legal form. The most vivid glimpse of Morgan at work
comes from the record of Henry V's negotiations with the
Dauphin at Alençon in 1418, where he took the lead and
acted as spokeman: breaking the deadlock over who was to
speak first, eliciting the French terms without committing
his own side, analysing the Dauphin's offer and its implications, Morgan was very much the professional diplomat, with
the terms of the Treaty of Brétigny at his fingertips. His
rewards, though modest by the standards of Sir John Cornewaill's fortune, culminated in the see of Worcester, which the
king evidently obtained for him from Martin V in 1419. His
pastoral activity as bishop earned the praise of an exacting
critic, Dr Thomas Gascoigne, while he continued to serve
on the council during Henry VI's minority. Unlike many
ambitious churchmen of the day, he does not appear, anxious
for promotion, in the pages of William Swan's letter-book at
the Roman curia. In Morgan and Chichele Henry V had
obtained the services of men more modest and austere than
the princely Beaufort and Courtenay.[23]

A third career may be cited to illustrate aspects of financial
specialization in the service of Henry V: William Alington,
who was his treasurer-general in Normandy from 1419 to
1422. As a tried specialist in war finance and logistics,
Alington had much to offer the embattled government of
Lancastrian Normandy, but he only attained direct office
under the crown as a result of lengthy service to other
masters. A Cambridgeshire gentleman of modest means, he
first appears as receiver of revenue in Brest under the captaincy of John Holland, perhaps in 1388, certainly by 1397;
and when Holland, now Duke of Exeter, became captain of
Calais he followed as treasurer. With the usurpation of
Henry IV and the execution of Holland in 1401, Alington
passed into the service of Prince Thomas of Lancaster, the

[23] A. B. Emden, *Biographical Register of the University of Oxford to 1500*
(Oxford, 1957-9), ii, 1312-13; *Foedera*, ix, 632-45; Wylie and Waugh, *Henry
the Fifth*, iii, 152-6.

future Duke of Clarence, and when the young prince was made titular lieutenant of Ireland, he became treasurer of the Irish exchequer. Thereafter his fortunes depended on Clarence, profitably at first, less profitably in the early part of Henry V's reign when he lost his post. With Clarence's return to prominence in Normandy he re-emerged, joined his patron at Caen, and within a year was treasurer-general of Normandy. His abilities ensured that he remained in office after Clarence's death in 1421 for the remaining year of the reign, but early in the minority he evidently sold his Norman assets and returned to England. He continued to play some part in public affairs, in the council and as speaker of the 1429 parliament, until his death about 1438. Alington's accounts as treasurer-general demonstrate his expertise in raising, husbanding, and expending money prudently; he managed to put the Norman finances in order and to contribute funds to Henry V's continuing wars. But his skills were of a kind which many gentlemen shared, and his career in the king's service was only possible through the friendship of other patrons, the Dukes of Exeter and Clarence. Because their expertise was widely diffused, financial officers were perhaps more dependent than other royal servants on patrons, and their periods of service accordingly precarious and short. Nevertheless they were able to reap rewards on a modest scale, like the grants to Alington of houses in Caen and the lordship of Varaville.[24]

Henry V's responsible servants, those who could be entrusted with commissions or provide him with advice, formed therefore no narrow or homogeneous coterie, and it is not easy to discern features common to them all. It is sometimes assumed that in this period the clerical civil servant was giving way to his lay successor. The evidence of Henry V's court does not bear this out. Since the Norman period at least, lay or knightly administrators had been prominent in the king's government; Sir Walter Hungerford, Sir Roger Leche, and William Alington esquire followed a long line of lay servants of the crown. In fact Henry V made, if anything, greater use

[24] On Alington see Roskell, 'William Allington of Horseheath, Speaker of the Parliament of 1429–30', *Proceedings of the Cambridge Antiquarian Society*, lii (1959), 30–42; Roskell, *Speakers*, pp. 197–9.

than his predecessors of the small body of ecclesiastical lawyers who served as his almost-professional diplomats. Officers of the exchequer had usually been laymen since the later years of Edward III; those of the chancery were mostly clerics until the second half of the century. Henry V's only change was in the other direction: to appoint a churchman, William Kynwolmersh, to the traditionally lay office of treasurer of England.

Whatever its cloth, Henry V's service was recruited from many sources. His father had largely relied upon the body of men who had administered the duchy of Lancaster, and the list of duchy officials in Henry V's service is almost equally long: Sir Thomas Erpingham, steward of the household; Sir Walter Hungerford, the next steward; Sir Roger Leche, treasurer of the household, Sir Hugh Mortimer, briefly treasurer of England. But the vast Lancastrian lands had occupied an army of officials, who doubled as receivers of other noblemen or officers in the exchequer, and Henry V's accession shook up the Lancastrian officialdom as it did office-holders under the crown. By that time the duchy officials were no longer a coherent group. It was perhaps more important that many of them had been associated with him as Prince of Wales, like Leche, for instance, Sir John Cornewaill, or Thomas, Earl of Arundel; but they too had combined his service with other associations. The patronage of powerful ministers advanced, if it did not originate the careers of some royal servants: a connection with Lord Fitzhugh in the royal household secured William Kynwolmersh the deputy treasurership when Fitzhugh became treasurer in 1416, and a servant of the Earl of Warwick, John Throgmorton, was made chamberlain of the exchequer on the earl's nomination in 1419. But the significance of party rivalries among office-holders which can be detected in 1410–12 seems to have diminished in the course of the reign. Though Sir John Tiptoft and Sir John Pelham were out of favour at Henry V's accession, they both found their way back to his service by 1417. We can only conclude that Henry V had no group of talented or thrusting young men to draw upon: he merely had better service from the same men, or the same sort of men, as had served his father.

Nor can it be argued that, albeit of differing origins, the king's servants were an upwardly mobile social group, the ancestors of a future nobility. On the whole, their rewards were modest. The parliamentary peerage remained almost totally impervious to newcomers during his reign; its effective numbers were actually reduced from 41 in 1414 to about 27 in 1421, through extinctions and the succession of minors. Of four new English creations, three (Bedford, Gloucester, and Cambridge) were members of the royal family, and the fourth, the earldom of Worcester, was awarded to a cadet of the Beauchamp family whose father had been a peer. Even the promotion of the Earl of Dorset to the dukedom of Exeter was for life only. Norman counties were marginally more available, but only two, Eu and Tancarville, were awarded to knights not already peers or royal kinsmen, to Sir William Bourchier and Sir John Grey respectively.[25] It is remarkable that no Lancastrian captain received recognition in this way until, at the earliest, the 1430s. Clerks had a somewhat better prospect of a bishopric: Archbishop Chichele and Bishops Courtenay, Catterick, Wakering, Lacy, Ware, and Morgan probably owed their sees directly to the personal will of Henry V. All the same, they may have had to request their promotion; John Prophet, according to a sad letter of his nephew, grandly declined to ask for a bishopric, and consequently was not offered one, although previous keepers of the privy seal had been so rewarded.[26] Royal service offered hard work, not a sure path to riches or prestige. Very few, if any offices could at this time be regarded simply as sinecures, and performance of duty by deputy seems to have been possible only for absentees who were serving with the king in the field, like the deputy of treasurer Fitzhugh. What Henry V did offer was the opportunity of enrichment at the expense of others, as is obvious from the fortunes made in France by Cornewaill or Hungerford. Richard II, Henry IV, and Henry VI were each weakened by the pressure of grants and annuities on their revenues and by the criticism this

[25] See writs of summons in *Reports of the Lords' Committees touching the Dignity of a Peer* (London, 1820–9), iii, 816–54; on Norman earldoms, *Complete Peerage*, v, 177, note f.
[26] Brown, 'Privy Seal Clerks', p. 280.

evoked; Henry V seems to have avoided to a large extent the need to reward his servants so directly.

The king's ministers, then (to use the term 'minister' in its widest sense), cannot be defined as a group by a common origin or apprenticeship, nor by a common destiny amid the fruits of Henry V's enterprise, but by the way men who had served, or would serve, other masters responded to his personality and will. As might be expected of a king who spent so much of his time in England in the palace of Westminster, it is clear that he personally attended to much of the detail of government. This can be shown simply by comparing the ordinary business of the regency council in England after 1417, as recorded in the patent and close rolls, with English business enrolled in France in the 'Norman' rolls under the duplicate great seal which travelled with him. It is confirmed by the evidence of letters under the signet, which were probably composed by the king personally. The few which survive deal with a host of minor matters which may have originated in petitions. The only two letters which may be in his own hand, to Robert Waterton on the safeguarding of French prisoners and to Sir John Tiptoft with diplomatic instructions, were highly confidential and are characterized by a peremptory tone and clear directions.[27] In this personal dominance, perhaps, lies the force which kept the kind of austere and pastoral bishops he liked, who would much rather be attending to their dioceses like Langley or Morgan, for years at probably unwelcome secular duties which they performed with professionalism and skill.

[27] *Cal. Signet Letters*, p. 180, no. 881; *Foedera*, ix, 427–30.

V

Religious Change under Henry V

JEREMY CATTO

While it could hardly be asserted that Henry V's achievements
in the ecclesiastical sphere can compare with his military or
political triumphs, there is a case for locating a major turning-
point in the history of the English church in the events of his
reign: whether by design or by some less eluctable process is
a matter for delicate judgement. From the Leicester parliament of 1414 until the triumph of toleration in the eighteenth
century, religion was established and enforced by public
authority, and dissentient voices subjected to the rigours of
statutory felony. By contrast, before 1400 religion was
outside the competence of the secular power, and after 1800
would become a matter of indifference to the cabinets of
Europe. But between these dates, in England as in other
countries, it would be a matter of the utmost importance
to government, and a source of the bitterest conflict, what
the allegiance of its subjects was, what they believed, and
how they expressed it in public worship. The period of
European history which opened with the Council of Constance was marked by wars of religion, and there is some
ground for claiming that the first of these, a tiny war to be
sure, was the pathetic skirmish at Fickett's Field outside
Temple Bar on the evening of Tuesday 9 January 1414. If it
seems ludicrous to place this adventure of Sir John Oldcastle
and his Lollards beside the massacre of St Bartholomew's
Eve or the battle of the White Mountain, it is worth remem-
bering that Oldcastle had been in touch with Bohemian
captains who would unleash, before Henry V's short life was
over, a terrible religious war, in the course of which in
prosperous Bohemia the civil power would be extinguished
for a generation. Not the least reason for the contrasting
destinies of Lollard England—to stretch a point—and Hussite

Bohemia (originally, perhaps, an equal misnomer) was the vigorous action of Henry V on that night and in subsequent months, compared with the vacillations of King Wenzel the Drunkard in his dealings with the Bohemian nobility and clergy and the masters of the university of Prague. Only by hindsight can the inference be drawn that the danger never existed; contemporaries thought otherwise.

The nature and effects of this vigorous action, seen in the light of the religious changes of the previous forty years, is the theme of the following pages. It is necessary, first, to recall the doubts and confusions over many religious issues beginning with the Great Schism and encompassing the whole spectrum of public and private religious life which had beset Englishmen, especially the educated, since the 1370s. But in the reign of Henry V, the anxious and confused debates which had racked the previous generation were gradually stilled, and in their place we can see a confident, coherent religious leadership emerging, consistent in the forms of public cult it wished to impose, and systematic in its attempt to control opinion and establish a measure of orthodoxy. Beginning with Robert Hallum, the attractive and far-sighted Bishop of Salisbury, and carried into effect by his friends Henry Chichele, Archbishop of Canterbury, Thomas Brouns the archbishop's chancellor and William Lyndwood his official, the achievement of Henry V's leading churchmen has traditionally been seen as the successful suppression of the Lollards; this was indeed the focus of their activities, but it has to be seen in its context. The religious controversies of the fifteenth century, unlike those of the seventeenth, continue to be seen in terms of doctrine, but for contemporaries practice was much more central. It will be necessary, then, to consider the public worship of the early fifteenth century, the form of which was in part adumbrated in the decrees of Chichele.

John Wyclif and the Lollards had effectually inaugurated the long and rich tradition of religious controversy in England. They had challenged beyond recall the accepted authority of pope or bishops to govern the religious lives of laymen: 'Christian men' as one of them put it 'are not beholden for to believe that the Bishop of Rome that lives now in sinful life is a member of holy Church'.[1] More radically still, they cast doubt on the forms of popular religion: the cult of saints and the Virgin, pilgrimages and the indulgences that went with them, images, and above all the Eucharist, a cult object in the fourteenth century even outside the mass, in the Corpus Christi cult and in manifold outdoor processions. None of this would have mattered very much in an earlier age when, like the Cathars at the beginning of the fourteenth century, they might have been isolated and allowed to wither on the branch. In fact, however, the circle of radical preachers from Oxford was only one of what appear to have been many interrelated and overlapping circles of graduates, many in responsible positions, who were concerned with the purification of popular religion and the promotion of individual conscience among the laity. Others had included the household and circle of Archbishop Thoresby at York, the Cambridge friends of Walter Hilton, and by the early fifteenth century the group round Robert Hallum at Salisbury. Though differing in their theological ideas and attitudes to authority, these coteries were united in the task they set themselves: the propagation among the laity of the inner religious life so that 'temporal men', as Hilton put it 'with much possession of worldly goods' could also 'in party savour of ghostly occupation'.[2] Their means had included extended preaching tours, the translation of the Scriptures, and the composition of contemplative guides in the vernacular like Hilton's *Scale of Perfection*. In the period before Henry V's accession these activities had been, so far as we can see, unofficial or, in the case of the Lollard preachers, positively defiant of authority. Moreover, they either evoked or perhaps responded to a new phenomenon in English religious history: independent private religious initiative on the part of laymen. Evidence for initiative of this kind ranges from new forms of personal cult introduced into the prayer books of the nobility, like that of the Holy Name in Sir William Beauchamp's missal, or the contemplative prayers of Mary, Countess of Derby, through the devotions associated with the burgeoning religious

---

[1] *English Wycliffite Writings*, ed. Anne Hudson (Cambridge, 1978), p. 122.
[2] Walter Hilton, *Epistle on Mixed Life*, ed. G. G. Perry, *English Prose Treatises of Richard Rolle of Hampole* (EETS, 1866), p. 24.

fraternities of which Margery Kempe's 'crying and weeping' is a striking example, to the *Two Ways*, the devotional tract composed by the Lollard knight Sir John Clanvowe.[3] If some, like the *miles emulus veritatis* for whom Wyclif wrote a tract, were open to the persuasions of the Lollards, others such as Adam Horsley of the exchequer listened to Walter Hilton; differences in lay religious practice are as characteristic of the age as controversy among the clergy. The charge of Lollardy was levelled at Margery Kempe as well as Sir John Oldcastle. Seen in a long perspective, these manifestations of lay religion appear as a remarkable religious renaissance, but to contemporaries they were alarming evidence of the disunity of the age.

Probably we shall never know how far the upper classes and the court of the first Lancastrian king had been permeated by Lollard sympathies. That a distinct circle of courtiers had actively helped the Lollard preachers in their mission is now reasonably clear. Very probably they had given material help in the multiple copying of the Lollard translation of the Bible and the Wycliffite sermon cycle.[4] By 1411, however, most of them were dead, and with. one exception no sure cases of Lollard sympathies can be traced in the following generation. Sir John Oldcastle, however, was certainly not isolated socially from other members of Prince Henry's circle, and both he and associates of the Lollard knights like Sir William Beauchamp were related to the highest nobility. The brothersin-law Henry, Lord Scrope and Henry, Lord Fitzhugh shared a different kind of personal piety, which is revealed in the large collection of devotional literature in English which passed from one to the other, including the crucial Tanfield manuscript, now lost, of Richard Rolle's works. Scrope, if we are to place any credence on his confession, abhorred the Lollards, but he as much as Oldcastle was among those who, as the *Cloud of Unknowing* had put it, 'stand in activity by outward form of living, nevertheless yet, by inward, steering

---

[3] R. W. Pfaff, *New Liturgical Feasts in Later Mediaeval England* (Oxford, 1970), pp. 65–6; *The Book of Margery Kempe*, ed. S. B. Meech and H. E. Allen (EETS, 1940); *The Works of Sir John Clanvowe*, ed. V. J. Scattergood (Cambridge, 1975).

[4] Anne Hudson, 'A Lollard Sermon Cycle and its Implications', *Medium Aevum*, xl (1971), 147.

after the privy spirit of God'.[5] The problem for ecclesiastical
authorities, in these circumstances, was not merely the
discovery and elimination of Lollardy; it must include the
rallying of doubtful and troubled laymen with private con-
sciences and uncertain religious allegiances.

The potential heresy or independence of the great had
probably been Archbishop Arundel's first concern. But he
was naturally keenly aware of the success of Lollard preachers
in the country. Their handiwork can now only be glimpsed
directly in the letter of Richard Wych about his preaching
in Northumberland and Durham round about 1400; but
its conspiratorial atmosphere of flying visits and safe houses
removes all shadow of doubt about the reality of the Lollard
missionary effort.[6] Before 1414, we can be sure that there
was a network of Lollard households, linked by itinerant
preachers, and its vigour is confirmed by the recruiting
drive through the midlands of Oldcastle's agent Thomas Ile.
When these households were discovered, their members
were sometimes accused of holding schools and conventicles
to impart heretical doctrine, and many of the Lollard tracts,
with their catechetical format, were perhaps compiled for
their use. How cohesive the network really was is another
matter. The latest substantial Lollard tract seems to have
been *The Lantern of Light*, whose author evidently expected
his readers to be outward conformists in their parish churches;
they were merely advised to withhold judgement on the
efficacy of their priests. This is far from the strident propaganda of some earlier literature, and may represent the
development of some variety of attitudes among the Lollards.
Moreover in the midlands and the west, or in ports like Bristol
and Newcastle, they lived among laymen who were subject
to a range of pressures and ideas. The life of Margery Kempe
vividly evokes the Guild of Corpus Christi at St Margaret's,
King's Lynn, in which the influence of recluses such as Dame
Julian of Norwich might compete with the more traditional
practice of pilgrimage and with the corporate worship of the
fraternities. Urban and village communities might include

[5] H. E. Allen, *Writings ascribed to Richard Rolle* (London, 1927), p. 29; *The Cloud of Unknowing*, ed. Phyllis Hodgson (EETS, 1944), p. 3.
[6] F. D. Matthew, 'The Trial of Richard Wyche', *EHR*, v (1890), 530–44.

counterparts of Scrope as well as Oldcastle, and the sparse and ambivalent traces of Lollardy make a poor showing compared with the anti-Lollard fury of the Canterbury mob who confronted Mrs Kempe. The many forms of the lay conscience, united only in its inwardness, posed therefore a challenge, rather than a simple threat to ecclesiastical leadership.

Who were the leaders, then, of Henry V's church? The Grossetestian idea of bishops free of secular cares had given way, by the fourteenth century, to the dominion of prelates long experienced in public affairs: Simon Islip, John Thoresby, William of Wykeham, above all perhaps Archbishop Arundel, had been for long periods ministers of the crown and political figures in their own right. Increasingly, if not exclusively, the fifteenth-century bishops were graduates. If some of them, notably Richard Courtenay of Norwich and Arundel himself, were cadets of great aristocratic houses, they had also received a university education. A growing proportion of the highly promoted seem to have been graduates in civil or canon law and to have practised in the prerogative court of the Archbishop of Canterbury: Hallum, Chichele, Philip Morgan, Thomas Brouns, and William Lyndwood had passed through this classic *cursus honorum* to service in Henry V's diplomacy and so to the episcopal bench. It would be inaccurate, however, to see these professional men simply as passive servants of the crown who patiently awaited preferment according to a predetermined policy. Each episcopal vacancy, it has recently been shown, was a political event in which a variety of interests conflicted and compromised.[7] The slight evidence which survives in the letter books of Gilbert Stone or William Swan indicates the active calculation and scheming which accompanied any opportunity for promotion.[8] Bishops and the professional office-holders and lawyers from whom they were recruited were political men, and many of them had the virtues of public experience as well as the weaknesses.

[7] R. G. Davies, 'After the Execution of Archbishop Scrope: Henry IV, the Percies and the English Episcopate, 1405–8', *BJRL*, lix (1976–7), 40–74.

[8] On Stone see the forthcoming Oxford D.Phil. thesis of Mr Charles Everitt, 'Gilbert Stone and his Pre-Humanist Secretarial Contemporaries'. Swan's letters are described by E. F. Jacob, 'To and from the Court of Rome in the Early Fifteenth Century' in *Essays in Later Mediaeval History* (Manchester, 1968), pp. 58–78.

If they were not philosophers like many fourteenth-century bishops, their practical intelligence had been demonstrated in their diplomatic successes. As bishops they seem to have sought consistently the quiet regularity which Lyndwood's *Provinciale*, a systematic source-book of English practice in church government, was designed to facilitate. Office-holders formed only one group, though the controlling group, on the bench of bishops; but even they, as diocesans, seem to have resided in their sees as often as possible. Thomas Langley and Philip Morgan, two of the busiest servants of Henry V, were evidently as conscientious in their spiritual duties.[9] Further evidence, necessarily less precise, comes from the practice of visitation, which evolved at the hands of the early fifteenth-century bishops from mere assertion of episcopal privileges to careful enquiry into clerical morals, as recommended by Gerson. On the whole, Henry V's bishops were coolly professional, and avoided the spectacular churchmanship of some other periods.

It is possible to detect among the bishops a loose group of men both in the close confidence of Henry V and active in ecclesiastical affairs. Its centre was in the prerogative court of Canterbury, the focus of church business especially since the outbreak of the Schism and the penalties of Praemunire had diminished the importance in England of the papal curia. Officials of the court controlled the business of convocation, determined most of the cases arising from ecclesiastical privileges, and provided an equitable jurisdiction not unlike that beginning to be exercised in secular causes by chancery and the council. They were also called upon by Henry IV and Henry V for diplomatic work, pre-eminently, though not exclusively, at the councils of Pisa and Constance. Doyen among these professional lawyers to whom the leading role in ecclesiastical affairs was entrusted after the death of Archbishop Arundel was Robert Hallum, former registrar of Archbishop Courtenay, auditor of causes in the court of Canterbury, Bishop of Salisbury since 1407, and leading conciliarist in the English hierarchy. It is unfortunate, if

[9] R. L. Storey, *Thomas Langley and the Bishopric of Durham, 1406–1437* (London, 1961), pp. 223–5; R. G. Davies, 'Martin V and the English Episcopate' *EHR*, xcii (1977), 311.

characteristic, that Hallum's discretion has left only sparse
traces for the historian of the powerful attraction of his
personality: only a few sermons and occasional decrees in
his register which bear his personal stamp now bring back his
evocative imagery and sense of beauty.[10] This is the aspect
of him remembered by Ulrich von Richental at Constance:
in singing mass he was aware, like some later English churchmen, of the beauty of holiness.[11] Liturgy, indeed, and more
specifically the Sarum Use, seems to have been a common
interest of the circle which gathered round him both in the
court of Canterbury and at Salisbury. This included Nicholas
Bubwith, Bishop of Bath and Wells, another close councillor
of Henry V, ambassador at Constance, and co-sponsor with
Hallum of a Latin translation of Dante's *Comedy*; the theologian Richard Ullerston, who compiled the programme of
practical reforms to which Hallum and Chichele committed
the English church and indeed the new pope at Constance;
and Chichele himself, the supremely professional churchman.
It is even more difficult to form a personal impression of
Chichele than of Hallum. He too was a canon lawyer who,
as vicar-general to Bishop Medford of Salisbury, had experienced most sides of diocesan business, and as Henry IV's
envoy at Pisa had acquired besides an international acquain-
tance. Jacob detected in his years of responsibility at
Canterbury qualities of tenacity and endurance which must
have appealed to Henry V.[12] Notes in his copy of Innocent
IV's commentary on the Decretals reveal a virtuous if not
particularly individual scholar, and his breviary at Lambeth
is equally conventional. Yet Chichele and Hallum, together
with other lawyers like Philip Morgan and Lyndwood himself,
presided over a remarkable recovery of nerve among senior
churchmen, and developed a response to the challenge of the
Lollards which was primarily neither theoretical nor repressive,
but drew its strength from the positive aspects of the canon
law and the religious customs which canon law implied.

[10] Hallum is best described by E. F. Jacob, *Essays in the Conciliar Epoch* (Manchester, 1943), pp. 76–8.

[11] Richental's chronicle, tr. L. R. Loomis, *The Council of Constance* (New York, 1961), p. 115.

[12] Jacob, *Chichele*, p. 110.

For taken as a whole, the response of Henry V's bishops to the religious crisis of the previous generation was not a theory or an abstraction, not an intellectuals' answer but a fact; it was not an attempt to convince the doubtful by philosophical argument, but an appeal for common worship, a common expression of private prayer to 'the bestower of all grace, *who maketh the desert a standing water, and watersprings of a dry ground,* to moisten the deserts of our hearts . . . praying moreover, as our custom is, for the whole orthodox church'.[13] A theological answer to Lollard doctrine was in fact attempted, probably under Henry V's sponsorship and on a large scale, in the incomplete *Doctrinale Antiquitatum Fidei* of Thomas Netter, one of the king's Carmelite confessors who assisted as an expert theologian in a number of Lollard trials. Begun probably about 1415, the work had filled three large volumes by Netter's death in 1430. By then it was too late to be effective against Lollard arguments which had ceased to be put, at least in public, and it survives mainly in institutional copies.[14] The refutation of Lollardy was an important part of the agenda of contemporary theologians. Richard Fleming, Bishop of Lincoln founded Lincoln College, Oxford in 1427 as a seminary for anti-Lollard preachers, and Reynold Pecock, the master of a similar foundation, Whittington College in London, wrote his vernacular *Repressor* to defend the clergy against Lollard critics. But these theologians did not follow their scholastic predecessors into philosophical controversy. They preached sermons, mostly unrecorded, and sometimes took part in Lollard trials; their theology was a branch of practical not speculative knowledge. Even Netter's *Doctrinale* was only an unusually long *catena* of patristic authorities. It was brought to life by his sense of the church's living tradition, palpable and visible in ecclesiastical worship and in the religious practices, the *sacramenta* and *sacramentalia*, which it was his life's work to explain and defend.

---

[13] Ullerston's sermon on St Osmund is in A. R. Malden, *The Canonisation of St Osmund* (Wiltshire Record Society, Salisbury, 1901), p. 238; see Jacob, *Essays in the Conciliar Epoch*, p. 80.

[14] Netter, *Doctrinale Antiquitatum Fidei*, ed. B. Blanciotti (Venice, 1757-9). See D. Dubois, 'Thomas Netter' (Oxford B. Litt. thesis, 1978).

It is not really surprising, then, that among the documents which survive there is none which hints at a conscious policy or plan in ecclesiastical affairs, to complement so acute a statement of policy options as the memorandum drawn up for Henry V before the Alençon negotiation in 1418, printed among the privy council proceedings. Religious issues could not yet perhaps be conceived in such material terms. It is clear enough that the Lollard threat was discussed in council in 1414, as a prelude to the statute on Lollardy in the Leicester parliament, and that some similar discussion preceded the decree of convocation which regularized the ecclesiastical process in July 1416. However, neither the fragmentary minutes of the privy council nor the registers of Chichele or his suffragans throw any light on the formation of policy. On the other hand, the decrees of Chichele and convocation give the impression of concerted action against the Lollards and common initiatives in the wider field of ecclesiastical reform and liturgical innovation. In the light of the leading bishops' and officials' shared experience in lawcourts and diplomatic mission, this is not surprising. The body of common assumptions and guiding principles may have had much the same effect as a conscious policy.

No assumptions or principles, however, could have been applied effectively without the personal involvement of Henry V, the first king since Henry III to have shown more than conventional piety, as two strictly contemporary sources, the *Gesta Henrici Quinti* and the deposition of Fusoris, testify.[15] The habit of private prayer and the patronage of the most austere religious Rules was nothing out of the ordinary in a friend of Scrope or Fitzhugh: courtiers had founded all the new Carthusian houses, and Fitzhugh had already been in touch with the Swedish Brigittines before the king projected his double foundation of Sheen and Syon. More significant was his clear awareness that the service of religion was a matter for his government. Lollardy, after Oldcastle's rising, was perceived as a challenge to royal authority, a new departure destined to be permanent. The religious changes of the reign completed the integration of

---

[15] *Gesta*, pp. 2, 154; *Fusoris*, p. 243.

religious and secular authority which had moved forward
rapidly since Wyclif has been accused of fomenting the rising
of 1381.

The most obvious changes at the time must of course have
been liturgical. Ritual in its broadest sense, including public
ceremonies and processions, is a division of propaganda of
obvious importance in a partly literate society, and Henry V
was a master of the art. The city of London furnished him
with a joyous entry after Agincourt in which a heavenly
host of angels, prophets, and apostles cheered him in, a
consciously sober figure in purple, the colour of the Passion,
on his way to offer at the London shrines: a scene which
made a deep and long-remembered impression and which
was repeated in 1421 on the arrival of Queen Catherine.[16]
Henry V's emphasis on the forms of public worship is striking.
His own chapel was a focus of musical invention, as the Old
Hall manuscript, which preserves some of its music, and the
extant motet of his choirmaster John Pyamour prove, and his
musicians enjoyed a European reputation. Pyamour together
with John Dunstable and others belonged to the group of
English composers, artistically inventive and technically
advanced, who were to fill the western European courts with
song and, increasingly, the English cathedrals with a musical
expression of affective piety.[17] The king's victories progres-
sively expanded the ceremonies of his chapel with new
invocations of St George, St Edward the Confessor, and the
Virgin, on the feast of whose Assumption the battle of the
Seine was won in 1416.[18] If he traded on the reputation for
piety which the rumour of his private worship brought him,
his desire for the intercession of his patron saints was undoubtedly genuine.

One of the aims of Chichele's additions to the liturgy
observed in England was to propagate the image of the king
as *miles Christi* in the new feasts of national and military
saints: St George, patron of the Garter, promoted to a
double feast to be observed by the laity in November 1415,

---

[16] *Gesta*, pp. 100–12; *The Brut*, ii, 426.
[17] Nigel Wilkins, 'Music and Poetry at Court', in *English Court Culture*, pp.
186–7, 200.
[18] *Gesta*, pp. 150–4.

for his protection of the *gentis Angligenae armata militia*;
SS Chad, David, and Winifred, local saints of the Canterbury
province now 'nationalized' at the second attempt; above all,
perhaps, St John of Beverley, the saint especially adopted by
the house of Lancaster, for whom SS Crispin and Crispinian
had to make way on October 25, the anniversary of Agincourt.[19] Lyndwood, who must have known, comments that
the feasts of St George and St John of Beverley were promul-
gated at the special behest of Henry V, and emphasis was
placed on the universality and publicity of the feasts. The
same idea is possibly reflected in Hallum's epithet for King
Edward the Martyr, *athleta electus Dei*, though this, in an
indulgence announced in January 1413, antedates Henry V's
accession.[20] But the rites of the church, refined and elaborated, might also answer the inner religious needs repeatedly
manifested among laymen; and there are some indirect
indications that in the interests of standardization Chichele
may have encouraged the adoption through the province of
Canterbury of the Sarum Use, which gradually superseded
the other local uses in the century before the Reformation.
The Sarum Ordinal was treated as standard in his liturgical
decrees, and Lyndwood justified it by claiming that the
Bishop of Salisbury was precentor of the province and
therefore had the duty of ordering its rites.[21] The influential
Salisbury chapter, the chapter of St Paul's, and bishops
associated with Chichele such as William Heyworth of Lichfield who adopted it in his diocese shared their view. The
Sarum *Manuale*, the priest's handbook of sacraments and
ceremonies performed out of church, presented with explana-
tory rubrics from English canonists such as William of Pagula
and John de Burgo, must have been compiled in this period,
and its pastoral-canonical directions and rapid popularity
suggest that it had authoritative backing. The Sarum Use, a
subject of conscious pride to its bishop and chapter in the
early fifteenth century, provoked both criticism and debate;

[19] D. Wilkins, *Concilia Magnae Britanniae et Hiberniae* (London, 1757), iii,
375–6, 379–80.
[20] W. Lyndwood, *Provinciale seu Constitutiones Angliae* (Oxford, 1679),
pp. 103–4; Jacob, *Essays in the Conciliar Epoch*, p. 77.
[21] Lyndwood, *Provinciale*, p. 103.

denounced by Lollards as an obstacle to 'moche prechynge of the gospel', and refined at Syon, a developing centre of liturgical learning, by Clement Maydeston, it attests the vitality and importance of public communal worship in the church's response to Lollardy.[22]

The forms of worship practised in fifteenth-century churches can only be reconstructed indirectly, from liturgical and musical manuscripts and in the light of Chichele's and other bishops' ordinances. The general direction of the changes, however, is clear: more ceremonies, the introduction of new feasts and cults, more elaborate music and emphasis on public processions, such as the Corpus Christi day procession at Lincoln from Wykford to the Cathedral in which Bishop Repingdon insisted all local clergy should take part 'for increase of devotion'.[23] It is striking that the many new feasts with accompanying indulgences which found their way into the service books of fifteenth-century English churches offered frequent opportunities for corporate expression of the same personal contemplative prayer as Repingdon intended. In the new occasional offices of the Five Wounds, the Crown of Thorns (*Corona Domini*), or the Compassion of the Virgin, meditations on the Passion of Christ were given liturgical expression, drawing on the same fund of religious feeling and sometimes on the same language as the *Revelations* of Julian of Norwich. The passage from personal devotion to public worship can be followed in the cult of the Holy Name. This was a development from private prayer first visible in the Rhineland, where Henry Suso propagated it. It soon had devotees in England, including Richard Rolle, and a votive mass of the Holy Name of English origin appears in the missal of Sir William Beauchamp, an associate of the Lollard knights, as early as 1388. By the early fifteenth century the mass had found its way into numerous missals and a number of fictitious indulgences had been attached to it. Among these, however, is one

---

[22] *Manuale ad usum percelebris ecclesiae Sarisburiensis*, ed. A. Jefferies Collins (Henry Bradshaw Society, Chichester, 1960), pp. xviii–xix. See also *The Tracts of Clement Maydeston*, ed. C. Wordsworth (Henry Bradshaw Society, London, 1894).

[23] Wilkins, *Concilia*, iii, 396.

ascribed to Hallum and dated 1411 which, though not in his register, is apparently genuine. Taken together with his support for the cult of St Edward the Martyr, his encouragement of devotion to the Holy Name suggests a more positive attitude to independent lay religious practices than is usually conceded to bishops of his generation. In the course of the fifteenth century the mass of the Holy Name was generally adopted, incorporating some of the language of private meditation in the ordinary worship of the English church.[24]

The vital relation between public worship and private devotions is nowhere clearer than in the religious foundations of Henry V. There was nothing random about these foundations; they were planned as a group, and they were to be palace monasteries, almost an Escorial, encapsulating the restored palace at Sheen. In the event the third project, the Celestine house, was abandoned, and the palace itself was demoted in importance after -1422, leaving only the Charterhouse at Sheen and the house of Brigittine nuns with their accompanying community of priests over the river at Syon. In conception however it was by far the most ambitious monastic foundation attempted by an English king, and one designed to place the monarchy at the spiritual centre of English life. The elements which contributed to this remarkable conception had not been evolved overnight. Carthusian houses in which the arts of contemplation flourished and spiritual direction was available had been established and patronized by the lay nobility for nearly eighty years before the foundation of Sheen, and a de la Pole, a Mowbray, and a Holland had been among the founders; while at Sheen, even so worldly a prelate as Cardinal Beaufort would find his confessor. The idea of a Brigittine foundation came from Henry, Lord Fitzhugh, chamberlain of the household, who had visited the mother house at Vadstena in Sweden.[25] Syon would also be the heir, through Fitzhugh, of a stream of northern spirituality which flowed ultimately from Richard Rolle, and in the early fifteenth century it would be a centre

---

[24] Pfaff, *New Liturgical Feasts*, pp. 62–71.
[25] On Sheen see E. M. Thompson, *The Carthusian Order in England* (London, 1930), pp. 238–41, 340; on Syon, M. B. Tait, 'The Brigittine Monastery of Syon' (Oxford D.Phil. thesis, 1975).

of liturgical learning and experiment. Both from there and perhaps especially from the Sheen Charterhouse, foreign works of spirituality were diffused, including the *Imitation of Christ* in several recensions and the *Dialogo* of St Catherine of Siena, translated as the *Orchard of Syon*. In the light of their popularity as confessors and the bequests they attracted, it is difficult to regard the influence of the monks of Syon and Sheen as restricted to 'an exclusive and tightly-knit spiritual aristocracy' as has been claimed.[26] The inner circle of Henry V's bishops was closely involved in the foundations. Langley and Courtenay had opened the negotiations in Paris for a Celestine house, while a commission of theologians close to the king, including Stephen Patrington, another of his Carmelite confessors and Abbot Heyworth, later Bishop of Lichfield, had been appointed to soothe the growing pains of Syon. There is no reason to assume that Henry V had any intention, as founder, of expiating his father's execution of Archbishop Scrope; on the contrary, he seems to have seen them as a 'gigantic power-house of prayer' for the Lancastrian dynasty.[27] Sheen and Syon were committed by their Rules to spiritual exercises and austerity of life which would serve as exemplars in Henry V's programme, hardly begun at the end of his life, of monastic reform. As, potentially, a kind of spiritual household for the king, organized under the advice of leading churchmen, their establishment placed the seal of ecclesiastical approval upon independent lay spirituality. Its energies, still undiminished in the fifteenth century, were now to be conducted along safe, well-insulated lines.

The student of Lollard trials in the period after Oldcastle's rising in isolation from less judicial aspects of the bishop's office might easily over-emphasize the repressive activities of the hierarchy. To contemporary laymen and lower clergy, the episcopal attitude to heresy sometimes seemed scandalously lax. Arundel himself had only complained to Henry V about Sir John Oldcastle on the prompting of the Canterbury convocation, and delays in the process were greeted with

[26] Roger Lovatt, 'The *Imitation of Christ* in Late Mediaeval England', *TRHS*, 5th series xviii (1968), 100.

[27] Tait, 'Brigittine Monastery of Syon', p. 55.

112   Jeremy Catto

clerical protests. Catching the mood at the convocation of
1416, Chichele proposed to sweep away the *pulvis negli-
gentiae*, the dusty negligence of the prelates with his brisk
new measures for dealing with Lollards in the church courts.[28]
In fact the bishops' attitude to heresy was complicated by
their need to sift the religious practices of laymen, to encourage some and detach, if possible, their subjects from others
by gentler forms of pressure than the hammer of ecclesiastical
process. Arundel's examination of William Thorpe had been
an early exercise in argument and persuasion. The archbishop's
response and that of his colleagues to religious enthusiasm
between 1413 and 1417 can be observed in the experiences
of Margery Kempe, the redoubtable wife of Lynn whose
plentiful tears and blunt reproof of swearing and loose talk
could be taken in various ways. Gravely suspected by the
monks of Canterbury, she was threatened with burning by
the townsmen; but when she and her husband made their
vows of chastity before Bishop Repingdon at Lincoln in the
summer of 1413, he 'commendyd gretly hir felyngys and hir
contemplacyons, seyyng thei wer hy maters and ful deuowt
maters and enspired of the Holy Gost'.[29] A few weeks later
she went to seek permission to wear the usual mantle and
ring of chastity from Archbishop Arundel. Preoccupied
though he must have been at the time with the unforseeable
consequences of Oldcastle's heresy, the archbishop was
evidently prepared to listen and approve while Margery
explained her weeping and her revelations, extending the
interview 'tyl sterrys apperyd in the fyrmament'.[30] Four
years later at York, during the crisis of the Foul Raid in
which Lollards were believed to be implicated, Margery had
a less sympathetic hearing from Archbishop Bowet. He was
nevertheless willing to hear her out in person, and anxious
as he was to remove her from his jurisdiction he allowed
her to dally at York and Bridlington and failed to secure her
promise not to 'teach' the people.[31] Her difficulties came
from contacts with laymen: to the citizens of Canterbury,

[28] Wilkins, *Concilia*, iii, 352, 378.
[29] *Book of Margery Kempe*, p. 34.
[30] Ibid., p. 37.
[31] Ibid., pp. 124–8.

the mayor of Leicester, the lay servants of Bowet, and the agents of the Duke of Bedford she was plainly a 'fals deceyver of the pepul', a Lollard and heretic. Margery Kempe's experiences afford a glimpse of the informal contacts between bishops and the diverse and often troublesome enthusiasts of the age. They show that the need to root out heresy was only one aspect of episcopal duty: anxious to respect the authority of the confessor and the example of the recluse, aware perhaps that in an age of 'revelations' church authorities could claim no monopoly of access to God, the bishops had to tread delicately, to advise, encourage, and persuade. A heresy trial, inappropriate for the great majority of religious individualists, was a last resort.

Yet heresy, in a way unprecedented before 1370, was everywhere spoken of: by the lord mayor of London, shocked by *The Lantern of Light*; by the Cambridge conspirators, discussing potential allies; by the villagers of Norton Underhill in Worcestershire, who knew what to make of a sermon by Mr William Taylor, the Lollard master from Oxford; by the retainers of Archbishop Bowet and the Duke of Bedford. Charges of Lollardy, true or false, would be laid on ever smaller pretexts as the term degenerated into a meaningless epithet of abuse. To what extent any of the accused were Lollards in the conspiratorial sense of Sir John Oldcastle is less obvious. Undoubtedly, there was still a Lollard party in 1413: among knights, Sir Thomas Cheyne of Drayton Beauchamp and Oldcastle himself; among clerks, Cheyne's parson Thomas Drayton, Richard Wych, the correspondent of Hus, and two more recent Oxford scholars, Peter Payne and William Taylor, can be shown to have connections with one another, as well as sharing Lollard beliefs on the sacraments and other religious practices and on authority in the church. These links do not appear to have continued for long after the Lollard rising. Payne fled abroad in the autumn of 1413, eventually reaching Prague; Oldcastle was burnt in 1417 and William Taylor in 1423. The others were never free of suspicion, though Drayton and Cheyne were able to avoid charges; nothing more is heard of Drayton after 1425, nor of Sir John Cheyne after 1431. Wych's fate was more bizarre. After conforming apparently in 1419, he had held a number of livings in Kent and ultimately in Middlesex, during the next twenty years; but at the last charges of heresy were brought against him, and he was burnt at Tower Hill in June 1440. The offerings of silver and wax images made at the site by Londoners do not suggest that he had had any recognizably Lollard influence upon them, whether or no he retained any of his former beliefs.[32] Lollardy as a group of believers in direct succession to the circle of Wyclif cannot be shown to have survived 1428, when the last Oxford pupil of Peter Payne was brought to trial. It is besides quite likely that William White, the leader of a group of suspects accused of heresy in Kent and Norfolk in the same year, had learnt his ideas from one of the surviving Lollard masters or from some associate of theirs, since his notion of transubstantiation conformed quite closely with Wyclif's; but there is no direct evidence of it, either from his accusers or from Netter, who mentions his trial in the *Doctrinale*. He may simply have read works of Wyclif or his disciples. If he did plan another Lollard rising, as a correspondent at the 1428 convocation wrote to William Swan, it was the last time that a Lollard preacher can be shown to have contemplated sedition. After the trials of his Norfolk associates, he had no disciples.[33] The great publishing enterprises of the Lollard sermon cycle and the translation of the Bible had long been completed, and as none of the datable Lollard tracts were written after 1420, there was nothing to hold any remaining sectarians together in common belief, worship, or achievement. The history of Lollardy from then until the Reformation is, at best, the history of a felony with no more coherence than a history of murder.

Conspiratorial Lollardy remained, if not on the ground then in the minds of Henry V and his ministers. Under the terms of the statute of 1414, royal and municipal officers were bound to detect Lollards and hand them over to the church authorities, while by the decree of 1416 archdeacons

[32] J. A. F. Thomson, *The Later Lollards, 1414–1520* (Oxford, 1965), pp. 53–4, 60, 148–50, 173–5, 211.

[33] On White and his associates see Thomson, *Later Lollards*, pp. 122–32, 173–6; *Heresy Trials in the Diocese of Norwich, 1428–31*, ed. N. P. Tanner (Royal Historical Society, Camden 4th series xx, 1977); Margaret Aston, 'William White's Lollard Followers', *Catholic Historical Review*, lxviii (1982), 469–97.

were directed to conduct regular enquiries into the fai‍
their flocks. In 1428 a questionnaire seems to have been
produced, probably from a draft by Thomas Brouns, by
which Lollard beliefs could be elicited systematically.[34] In
this developing programme we can see the church authorities
at last taking the initiative in the control of religious opinions.
Whether they continued to believe, after the trials of Taylor
and White, in any widespread conspiracy to upset the social
as well as the religious order is not clear in the formal documents in which measures against Lollardy are laid out. But
prosecutions would recur sporadically, according to the
urgency perceived by particular prelates: Chedworth of
Lincoln, for instance, seems to have been especially active
about 1460, and successive bishops of London in the 1490's.
The sharpening definitions of faith and heresy, and the
consequent elaboration of Lollardy as a label which could
be pinned on any form of nonconformity of belief or practice
which happened to be detected, powerfully reinforced the
role of the church establishment, usually backed by the royal
power, in the life of the laity. Guidelines suitably modified
would continue to be used by Henry VIII, Elizabeth, and
Archbishop Laud in their progressive definitions of England's
public religion. The authority of the English church was an
aspect of the sense of community which Chichele had also
encouraged by the new forms of public worship; a liturgy
in which personal devotions could be incorporated and the
call of private conscience could be harmonized. This too
would be modified by the Reformation, but the idea of a
national common prayer, expressed in the sixteenth century
in successive Books of Common Prayer, can already be
perceived in the measures of Chichele and Henry V. In all
but name, more than a century before the title could be used,
Henry V had begun to act as the supreme governor of the
Church of England.

---

[34] Thomson, *Later Lollards*, pp. 224–5; Anne Hudson, 'The Examination of
Lollards', *BIHR*, xlvi (1973), 145–59.

VI

Henry V the Soldier, and the War in France

C. T. ALLMAND

The baby Henry VI, a near-contemporary chronicler thought, 'beyng in his Cradel, was moche doubted and dradd, bicause of the gret conquest of his fadre', and thus began his reign at a great advantage.[1] The writer was, I think, saying this: in 1422, the regard and respect due to monarchy, even when personified by a young child not yet one year old, was such that Henry VI began his reign with most, if not all, the aces and a good set of trumps, too. Monarchy had had its difficulties in the relatively recent past of English history. Look at Richard II, if no further: even the reign of the first Lancastrian, Henry IV, had not been without its problems. His son, the greatest king of that house (and, in the view of the late K. B. McFarlane, 'the greatest man that ever ruled England') was to change all that.[2] For the brief period of a decade, monarchy was to resume its traditional and undisputed place in society. It led, and it led from the front.

As a man, Henry V was a complex character, not always easy to understand. But one thing about him is clear. The king was a man of great mental and physical energy. His mind was always active, and he readily caused ideas and plans to be transformed into reality. His expeditions to France were carefully prepared and organized, down to the details.[3] He liked to be at the very centre of government and administration, for that is where the action was, where the decisions were being taken. Even when he was in France, he kept in close touch with those who were governing England on his behalf, receiving reports and giving instructions as to what should be done, and how. He took his duties as

---

[1] *The Brut*, ii, 497.
[2] McFarlane, *Lancastrian Kings*, p. 133.
[3] Waurin, *Croniques . . . 1399–1422*, p. 168.

the personification of justice particularly seriously.[4] What was right mattered a great deal to him. He was also a man of straightforward and fairly traditional religious ideas, a staunch defender of orthodoxy, of the church and of churchmen. The Lollards goaded him as the 'priests' king' (the 'princeps presbiterorum') and in France we are told that he defended, the rights of the clergy against those who would attack them.[5] In England he supported the church, especially under its 'unconquered' champion, Thomas Arundel, Archbishop of Canterbury, against heterodoxy. The social and political threat which Lollardy constituted, as we understand it today, makes us appreciate the more readily why it was that Henry, as King, should have stood for traditional, orthodox teaching and practice in matters of religion.

In this firm stand, as in other ways, Henry appears as a conventional enough king. Indeed, one of the main problems facing the historian of today looking back to the fifteenth century is to ask whether there is not the possibility that contemporary, or near-contemporary writers on Henry did not, to a certain extent, fit him into a mould of predetermined shape, by deliberately depicting him as a busy administrator, a seeker after justice, a defender of God's Church, and so on, rather than by letting his achievements and his method of accomplishing them speak for themselves. There is, I think, something of a problem here. But don't let it detain us today. Rather, let us turn this problem upon its head, regard it as a problem no longer, but rather as an indicator (or as a series of indicators) of what men of the late middle ages expected of their kings. The shape of the mould is, in itself, important; that Henry was made to fit it perfectly is even more important still. It tells us that, according to the lights of the day, he fulfilled much, if not all, of what was expected of him by the men of the nation whom he ruled and led.

By long tradition one of the positive characteristics expected of a king was that he should be a soldier. The ability to lead in battle and defeat the enemy was an essential

---

[4] His strong sense of justice earned him the nickname of 'Justicia'. within his own lifetime (Bodleian Library, Oxford, MS Ashmole 845, fo. 224[r], kindly drawn to my attention by Christopher Phillpotts).

[5] *St Albans Chronicle*, p. 88.

element of medieval monarchy. This is so well known as to be a truism. Some of the great kings of the past had been outstanding soldiers, notably, I suppose, the first and third Edwards. There can be no doubting that Henry V's military ability, and the successes which it produced, was highly regarded by his contemporaries. His military achievement did more than anything else to raise both him, and monarchy, high in the esteem of his people. The war with France was the single most important theme of the reign; it was the dominant one, and that in itself is indicative of the importance attached by Englishmen of the time—and later—to the successful pursuit of conquest at the expense of the old enemy, the French.

There are two factors which need to be emphasized at the outset. Both need some explanation. Both are stressed in contemporary writings of different kinds, those of chroniclers and preachers alike. The first is this. England is seen as fighting two wars, not simply one; as a result Henry, as a soldier, has two roles to play. In the first he is seen as a kind of celestial knight, 'God's own soldier', defending the church and orthodoxy against the spiritual and social enemy, Lollardy.[6] Look at the *Gesta Henrici Quinti*, or *Deeds of Henry the Fifth*, written by a royal chaplain in the middle years of the reign, and notice how the reader is pitched right away into the battle against Sir John Oldcastle and the heretics who, by threatening both the spiritual and the social order, are guilty of a double form of treason. In the clerical writer's view, God is heaping trials upon the king from which he emerges, although scourged, perfected.[7] Through the experiences of these difficulties, told in almost epic form, Henry, the hero king, wins divine approval. This is also the central theme of a sermon preached, perhaps before parliament, in the early summer of 1421, probably before Henry's third and final crossing to France that year. In this, the preacher, like many before him (and one notable example of this which comes to mind is St Thomas Aquinas,

[6] R. M. Haines, 'Church, Society and Politics in the Early Fifteenth Century, as viewed from an English Pulpit', in *Church, Society and Politics*, ed. Derek Baker (Studies in Church History, 12, Oxford, 1975), p. 150, n. 54.

[7] *Gesta*, p. 11.

in his *De Regno*), likens the State to a ship, and its ruler to a pilot, the 'maistur, oure worthi prince'.[8] In this sermon, the preacher refers to the spiritual battles into which Henry has led his people only to emerge triumphant, together with the rewards, in terms of the world, which God has allowed him to reap as his recompense for his virtue in founding religious houses, encouraging devotion, and defending orthodoxy. God is seen as responding positively and favourably to such acts. He responds, too, to prayer, which the preacher compares to the oars which propel the ship forward. Put it another way, God is an Englishman. Put it yet another way, this tradition is reminiscent of the motto found on a drinking tankard discovered in the wreck of Henry VIII's *Mary Rose*: 'Sit nobis Deus, quid contra nos', which reads, in a free translation, 'If God is with us, what can stand against us?'

I have deliberately taken a little while to emphasize that, by first defending spiritual values and orthodox religious practice in England, Henry was seen by his contemporaries as having merited divine support in his war against the French, support which rendered him, one might say, unstoppable. Yet if the king appeared supremely confident—one may almost say smug—in his dealings with the French, it was not merely because he felt that God was with him. More than once Henry was to say that his war in France was not the result of ambition (he was no Alexander, or Napoleon, or Hitler, hell-bent on conquest for its own sake); no, in pursuit of his aims in France he could adopt the high moral tone of one who used force only as a last resort, after diplomacy had failed, because the French refused to do him justice, since they continued to retain lands which properly and justly belonged to him as King of England. In the English view it was the persistent denial of justice by the French which brought an English army into France; equally, it was their persistent resistance which led them to defeat at the hands of the English who, in this matter, were acting as the instruments of God. As wrote the author of the *Gesta*, ever anxious to point out a moral which redounded with credit

---

[8] Haines, 'Contemporary Preacher's View', 85–96; St Thomas Aquinas, *On Kingship to the King of Cyprus*, trans. and ed. G. B. Phelan and I. T. Eschmann (Toronto, 1949), pp. 3, 11, 58.

upon the English, war was but the last resort when a dispute between those having no superior on earth (two sovereign kings, in a word) could not be resolved by diplomacy or other peaceful means. In such circumstances appeal to 'a Heavenly arbitrament carried out by the sword' was the only way forward. In such a view wars, and better still battles, became acts of divine judgement. Both the chaplain and Thomas Walsingham were at pains to stress how, through a series of victories won since the reign of Edward III, England had received clear signs of divine approbation in her long struggle for justice against the French. It was they who had ignored these signs at their peril. Since England's cause was manifestly a just one, the war fought by Henry V was a just war, and his victories, too, were victories won in justice.[9]

Henry deliberately chose to make the most of his war against the French by sharing the undertaking with his people. The king was an excellent public relations officer, aware that without wide support he could do little, but that with it much was possible. That support was intended to show itself in different ways. Research has shown that for much of his reign Henry had the practical support of the majority of the highest nobility of the land who, in 1415 at least, on the first of the king's expeditions to France and the one which led to Agincourt, turned out in numbers to accompany Henry across the sea. That support was not merely the symbolic one of society's traditional military leaders going to war with their king and thereby registering their approval of his actions. Their presence also made it easier for Henry to raise the men whom he needed, since it was through the nobility and the leading country gentry that a king raised his army. There can be little doubt that the acceptance by the leaders of society that the war was worth fighting led to a wider acceptance of that view throughout the country. Only later in the reign did the number of high nobility serving decline, and this may have discouraged the shire gentry from continuing in the royal service at the end of the reign. Yet the evidence which has recently emerged from part of Yorkshire for 1421 suggests that any decline in

[9] *Gesta*, pp. 123–5; *St Albans Chronicle*, p. 121.

the willingness to serve was due more to a markedly worsening economic situation than to any real disinclination to pursue the king's war aims in France.[10]

The more general involvement of Englishmen in war was furthered in a number of other ways, some of which had been developed by Henry's predecessors. At each meeting of parliament, a speech was made by the chancellor setting out the problems and difficulties faced by the king and his people at the time. At each such meeting held in time of war, reference was made to the successes won by the king; to the need to finance the enterprise; to the need to give the king both moral and practical support in the struggle. It may have been before either parliament or convocation which met before Henry's final departure for France in June 1421 that the sermon depicting the king as the country's 'maistur mariner' was preached. Here was a full-blooded appeal to the concept of the king and the kingdom at war together against a common enemy. England and her king were safe in the knowledge that the venture had divine approbation to support it. I mention the possibility that the sermon could have been preached before convocation with good reason. For there is no doubt that in this reign, with a king who was a staunch supporter of the clergy and the orthodox faith, there was an outstanding response from the clerical body to calls for substantial financial backing for the war. That suggests, to say the least, that the clergy was willing to accept Henry's main thesis that he was fighting a just war.

While on the subject of the clergy, we may also refer to the significance of prayer in time of war. It was commonplace in this age for the pulpit to be used as a place from which to exhort the faithful to intercession in a political cause. Bishops were accustomed to receiving orders to instruct their clergy to seek God's intervention for a favourable outcome in war. Whether they were always successful in persuading the faithful of the urgent need for such prayer

---

[10] M. R. Powicke, 'Lancastrian Captains', in *Essays in Medieval History presented to Bertie Wilkinson*, ed. T. A. Sandquist and M. R. Powicke (Toronto, 1969), pp. 376, 378; Allmand, *Lancastrian Normandy*, pp. 242-4; A. E. Goodman, 'Responses to Requests in Yorkshire for Military Service under Henry V', *Northern History*, xvii (1981), 240-52.

is another matter; in June 1417 Henry Chichele, Archbishop of Canterbury, had to admit that he had detected signs of a certain slackening off of enthusiasm in the offering of prayers for the success of English arms abroad.[11] Yet our preacher of 1421 saw prayer as the force behind the oars which drove the ship of state forward. He, at any rate, had no doubts about its efficacy. How could he, with a king who had done so much for the church deserving so well at the hands of God? Prayer was also important in another way, as a form of communal worship which bound the country together in unity behind the king. The author of the *Gesta* wrote of the 'prayers and supplications being made in England' while Henry and his army were fighting in France.[12] There is here a further attempt to underline how, in worship, the country was united in spirit with the king and his men.

Finally, while discussing the significance of popular support, we cannot fail to refer to the relationship which Henry tried to establish with the city of London. There are indications, some of them very clear, that the king and the people of the capital understood one another well. In March 1415 Archbishop Chichele was at the head of a royal delegation which went to the Guildhall to negotiate a loan for the planned attack upon France. In July 1418, the city's common council decided to order the despatch to the king of 500 archers for a period of six weeks (together with a gift of £1,500).[13] Henry was at that moment about to begin what was to be for him and for his army the most difficult military operation to date, the siege of the Norman capital, Rouen, an undertaking which was not to be successfully completed for six months. In order to achieve this, the king needed all the help he could muster. Early in August 1418 he wrote a letter (in English, as was now his custom) to the mayor and alderman of London requesting supplies

[11] See, for example, W. R. Jones, 'The English Church and Royal Propaganda during the Hundred Years War', *The Journal of British Studies*, xix (1979), 18-30; A. K. McHardy, 'Liturgy and Propaganda in the Diocese of Lincoln during the Hundred Years War', in *Religion and National Identity*, ed. S. Mews (Studies in Church History, 18, Oxford, 1982), pp. 215-227; *Reg. Chichele*, iv, 176.

[12] *Gesta*, p. 89.

[13] C. M. Barron, 'The Government of London and its Relations with the Crown, 1410-1450', (London Ph.D. thesis, 1970), pp. 423-4, 618.

and provisions for the besieging army and, in another letter, he sought the help of soldiers who would come 'to be soulded or waged with the Kyng' at the siege.[14]

But the best-known evidence of the city's support for the king must undoubtedly be the account of the famous reception given to Henry and his army in November 1415 after the battle of Agincourt had been won. The occasion, described in the fifteenth chapter of the *Gesta*, reads like the account of a Roman triumph. And, in spite of the king's apparent reluctance to take any personal credit for the victory won against the odds, the theme is undoubtedly triumphalist. The last paragraph of the previous chapter sets the mood of the occasion:

> Nor do our older men remember any prince ever having commanded his people on the march with more effort, bravery, or consideration, or having, with his own hand, performed greater feats of strength in the field. Nor, indeed, is evidence to be found in the chronicles or annals of kings of which our long history makes mention, that any king of England ever achieved so much in so short a time and returned home with so great and so glorious a triumph. To God alone be the honour and the glory, for ever and ever. Amen.[15]

There then follows the account of the reception. One can visualize the event unfolding itself: the people in a state of considerable exitement at the thought of seeing their king, who had vanished with his army, nobody knew exactly where, only for them to reappear having won a great victory; the mayor, members of the guilds and corporation going out to meet him; the floats with their symbols and figures; the arms of the king and those of his favourite St George, the warrior-saint, juxtaposed; the chorus line of beautiful young girls; the inscribed legends, including one with the words 'Welcome Henry ye fifte, Kynge of England and of Fraunce'. There can be little doubt that this stage-managed occasion reflects the popularity of the king as a soldier. Henry made the most of his success to publicize his achievement. Others have, since that time, followed his example.

At this stage we should take a brief look at Henry's

[14] *Memorials of London and London Life in the XIIIth, XIVth, and XVth Centuries*, ed. H. T. Riley (London, 1868), p. 665.

[15] *Gesta*, p. 101.

campaigns to try to understand what was his achievement on the ground. As king, Henry led armies to France on three separate occasions, in 1415, in 1417, and again in 1421. On the first of these, having exhausted the possibilities presented to him by diplomacy, and with the French placed firmly in the wrong by their refusal to make any significant legal or territorial concession, Henry sought to show that he was not a man to be trifled with. It is important that we see this expedition in relation to the diplomatic exchanges of 1414 and early 1415; it was because he could not obtain what he wanted by negotiation that Henry resorted to force. Late in July he sailed from Southampton with a fleet of some 1,500 vessels and landed near Harfleur at the mouth of the river Seine, close to where the port at Le Havre was later to arise. Harfleur was heavily defended; the siege which the king pressed led to much destruction and lasted some six weeks. But Henry was determined; and he had with him the weaponry necessary to complete what he had come out to do. When it was clear that no rescue was likely to come, Harfleur surrendered, in a ceremony aimed at underlining the legality of the exercise of majesty by the King of England upon French soil. Now that Harfleur, 'the key of all Normandy' and a place of great strategic importance, was in English hands, the problem was what to do next. With part of his army either dead or incapacitated by serious illness, Henry's immediate subordinates counselled caution and an early return to England. But, as the author of the *Gesta* (who was there) pointed out, the king rather typically rejected this advice. He would make his own decisions. Calais, English since 1347, was to be the destination, and some flag-waving would be done on the way. Moreover, such a march could be constituted a challenge to the effectiveness of the French king's authority, and Henry may have wanted to throw down that challenge. Thus it was that what was left of the army set out for Calais. As we all know, it was a hard journey, and Henry's powers of leadership were taxed to the full. But in spite of everything, order and discipline were maintained. It was on this occasion that the soldier who broke ranks to steal a pyx, which was a sacred vessel as well as a valuable one, from a church, was condemned and immediately hanged before the assembled army.[16] Against all the difficulties, Henry was getting his force in the direction of Calais when his road was blocked by the French army, rather as had happened to the Black Prince at Poitiers in 1356. On 25 October 1415 Henry and his men fought and defeated the numerically superior French at Agincourt, a triumph for discipline as the word was understood at the time. A few days later, on 29 October, the news reached London and, as we have seen, the return of the king and his army was soon celebrated in the capital. The success was the first stage in the creation of Henry's enviable reputation as a military leader. On 25 October 1416, a year to the day later, the victory won at Agincourt was commemorated by the singing of a solemn *Te Deum* in the royal chapel before mass, by order of the king himself.[17] It was an anniversary to remember: before long it was to become part of English historical tradition.

The year 1417 was to witness Henry's second invasion of Normandy. His chances of success had been considerably improved by developments in 1416. On 15 August, an English fleet under the command of the king's brother, John, Duke of Bedford, had defeated a combined Franco-Genoese fleet in the estuary of the River Seine, within sight of Harfleur whose garrison was being hard pressed by the French at that moment. The relief of Harfleur was important. But even more so for our purpose was the fact that this naval victory was no fluke, but in good measure the result of the conscious building-up of a fleet of royal ships during the past few years, a fleet whose numbers were to be swelled by the addition of eight carracks (the best fighting ships of the time) captured from the Genoese on this and later occasions. We now know how, in Henry IV's time and above all in the reign of his son, the size of the navy was deliberately increased by procuring some three dozen fighting ships, some specially commissioned, others purchased, others still, as we have seen, captured in battle.[18]

[16] Ibid., pp. 59, 61, 69.

[17] Ibid., p. 179.

[18] *The Navy of the Lancastrian Kings. Accounts and Inventories of William Soper, Keeper of the King's Ships, 1422–1427*, ed. Susan Rose (Navy Records Society, London, 1982), pp. 28–56, 248.

May I insist on one point here? It is my firm belief that Henry V appreciated the value of naval strength, and that this appreciation is another facet of his remarkable capacity as a commander and leader in war.

The naval victory of August 1416 had helped to clear, if not yet to rid, the Channel of enemy shipping. So it was that when Henry landed in Normandy almost a year later there was no opposition at sea. Opposition on land there certainly was, but the king was ready and equipped to deal with it. Instead of using Harfleur as a safe means of entering France, and then advancing directly up the River Seine to Rouen, the capital of Normandy, and thence to Paris, the capital of France, Henry chose to land on the southern side of the wide estuary (something made possible by his control of the sea) and to aim for the more western part of Normandy. Here, his sense of strategy became apparent. His first objective was Caen, visited by Edward III in 1346 and since that time well fortified. There was a delay of some three weeks while the place was captured, whereupon Henry moved southwards, thus at a stroke cutting Normandy into two and isolating those parts to the west from help from Paris, so that they could be, and were, picked off at will, although the Duke of Gloucester, Henry's youngest brother, was to face a stiff test at Cherbourg. Much of the winter 1417-18 was spent before the castle of Falaise (even today the place would not be easy to capture), this being the first of Henry's winter sieges. In the spring of 1418 the English army moved eastwards and then northwards. The River Seine was crossed and cut above Rouen, and it was in these circumstances that Henry was able to begin the siege of the Norman capital with the reasonable assurance that relief would not come from the direction of Paris. Yet, in spite of horrific conditions described for us by a contemporary witness, the city held out for some six months.[19] That the citizens managed to keep the English king and army in their tents for this second consecutive autumn and winter (the siege lasted from July 1418 to January 1419) was largely due to the state of the

[19] *The Brut,* ii, 397-422; *The Historical Collections of a Citizen of London in the Fifteenth Century,* ed. J. Gairdner (Camden Society, London, 1876), pp. 1-46.

defences. Henry's strategy of making sure that the French could not send help to the stricken city was ultimately entirely successful.

The fall of Rouen early in 1419 led inexorably to the rapid completion of the conquest of the remainder of Normandy. Once the duchy was his, Henry could aspire to greater ambition. By the end of the year he was in a position to dictate the future; the terms of the Treaty of Troyes, which some argue to have been the culmination of Henry's achievement in France, were already being drafted. In May 1420 the treaty was sealed. Now heir to the French kingdom, Henry married the French king's daughter, Catherine. On the very next day he set out again to begin another round of sieges, this time in the country to the south-east of, and up-river from, Paris. By the end of 1420 it was time to leave for England, where he had not been for almost three and a half years. He had to present his bride to the English kingdom; he had to have her crowned; and he needed more money. The coronation was quickly done; it was while he was touring England trying to raise money and men for the war that Henry heard that his brother, Thomas, Duke of Clarence, had been killed on the eve of Easter 1421 in a clash with the French and their Scots allies at Baugé in Anjou. For a while, English successes were under threat. But in the early summer Henry departed once again for France. Pausing only to obtain the latest information regarding the enemy's positions, he set off for the southern frontier of English influence. At the height of the summer he was at Chartres, moving southwards; before long he was close to Orléans (where eight years later the English met their Waterloo), but finding that he could not make contact with the enemy, wisely keeping out of the way, Henry turned eastwards and then northwards, hoping to brush up pockets of resistance which still existed in the region south and east of Paris. In October 1421 he began to besiege the town and fortress of Meaux, some thirty miles east of the capital, up the River Marne. The siege, which lasted until May 1422, a period of some seven months, has been termed 'Henry's masterpiece'.[20] Certainly his ability as a soldier was

[20] Wylie and Waugh, *Henry the Fifth*, iii, 339.

stretched to the full on this occasion. Perhaps the effort of yet another long winter siege was too much for him. It is likely that it was at Meaux that Henry contracted the illness which was to lead to his death. He was thirty-five years old when he died at the royal castle of Vincennes, now a suburb of Paris, on 31 August 1422.

I think that we may say, without too much controversy, that Henry V was above and before all else a soldier, and that the reputation which he enjoyed among his contemporaries was founded upon this fact. We may ask, then, what qualities did he show to justify this reputation? There was, first and foremost, his total commitment to the war, to the securing of what he regarded as justice. He was in France for more than half his reign, pursuing his claim and the war in what were sometimes very difficult conditions. The figure of the king in camp is the most typical which we can conjure up of the man. There is a feeling, difficult to avoid, that we are dealing with a man with an obsession. Obsessions are dangerous, if the ability to fulfil them does not exist. In Henry's case that ability did exist, expressing itself in the way most appropriate for a king, in a sense of leadership. Henry was also a man with a reputation for bravery in battle, a reputation which he shared with all his brothers, although in the case of Thomas, Duke of Clarence, foolhardiness may be more appropriate.[21] At Agincourt Henry showed his courage, both moral and physical; he did so again on many occasions when besieging fortresses and towns, and when fighting in the mines at Meaux. The anonymous preacher referred to the many dangers to which 'our peerless prince had exposed himself for the right of the realm and for the safety of the ship [of state]'.[22] Another of his attributes, very widely recognized, was his sense of discipline and order, without which there could be no victory. Discipline meant causing as little devastation as possible to land and property; it meant respecting the rights and persons of civilians; and it involved issuing special ordinances of war to control the behaviour and conduct of soldiers. All this greatly impressed

[21] This is certainly suggested by *The Brut*, ii, 447–8, 492.
[22] Haines, 'Contemporary Preacher's View', 92.

the men of his time. Waurin was not alone when, in what one may term his 'obituary' of the king, he referred to his discipline with evident admiration.[23] The reason for this admiration is easily found. Too many commanders of the period of the Hundred Years War were incapable of imposing order; the men who did so would, understandably, become the object of respect. One other of Henry's military qualities must suffice. I have already suggested that, in consciously implementing the creation of a fleet of royal ships, Henry was showing his awareness of a new facet of war whose importance had yet to be fully recognized. He did this in other ways, too. I have emphasized that in three separate winters, 1417-18, 1418-19, and 1421-2, the king undertook important sieges at a season of the year when war was normally called off. Furthermore as a number of chronicles (and notably *The Brut*) tell us, Henry had with him in France large quantities of weapons suitable for siege warfare, notably cannon, a weapon whose potential had been developed only over the past half century or so, and was still, therefore, relatively new.[24] In a word, we may say that Henry's approach to war was sufficiently flexible and adaptable for him to see what his needs were, and how they might best be met. Compared with the expeditions carried out, for example, by the Black Prince, half a century and more earlier, Henry's aim was something different. He was intent not merely upon raiding; because the French were withholding his right, his aim was to regain actual possession of that right. This he could only do by conquest, and it is as conqueror that he was regarded, and admired, by his contemporaries. We miss the point if we fail to notice how often words such as

[23] *The Black Book of the Admiralty*, ed. T. Twiss, 4 vols. (Rolls Ser., 1871-6), i, 459-72; Waurin, *Croniques ... 1399-1422*, p. 429. As another Frenchman put it, 'il estoit moult chevalereux et tant obey de ses gens, granz, moienz et petiz que homme de quelque estat qu'il peut estre; il estoit tres fort justicier' (*Chroniques de Perceval de Cagny*, ed. H. Moranvillé (SHF, Paris, 1902), p. 126.

[24] *The Brut*, ii, 382; *Les Chroniques du Roi Charles VII, par Gilles le Bouvier, dit le Héraut Berry*, ed. H. Courteault, L. Celier, and M.-H. Jullien de Pommerol (SHF, Paris, 1979), p. 65; *Perceval de Cagny*, p. 94. The importance of artillery to the English in the coming years is underlined by C. T. Allmand, 'L'Artillerie de l'armée anglaise et son organisation à l'époque de Jeanne d'Arc', *Jeanne d'Arc. Une époque, un rayonnement* (Centre National de la Recherche Scientifique, Paris, 1982), pp. 73-83.

'conqueror', 'conquest', and 'conquered' appear in the chronicles when describing the feats of war of Henry V. It was in this light that the world saw him.[25]

I have referred to what I termed Waurin's 'obituary' of the king. It was quite usual for chroniclers to sum up, in a short passage, the achievements of kings at the point where their deaths were recorded. Such a practice has, for us at any rate, the advantage of conveying how a person was regarded by his contemporaries, and how he might be remembered. Perhaps he was a tyrant, or a law-maker. In the case of Henry V, it was the king as a soldier who had so impressed contemporaries, both friend and foe alike, and so it was the soldier whom the chroniclers recalled. Already, during his own lifetime, Henry was in the process of becoming a legend —or almost so. Clerical writers such as the author of the *Gesta*, the preacher of the sermon in Bodley MS 649, and Thomas Walsingham, monk of St Albans, all emphasized how his activities, whether directed against heretics or against Frenchmen, had won the seal of divine approval. Henry had achieved victories with God's help because he merited reward for his support of virtue and religion. It was, therefore, Henry the conqueror whose feats came to be recorded in the chronicles. Not only, as Waurin pointed out, was the extent of his conquest greater than that achieved by any of his predecessors; equally impressive, to the author of the *Gesta* and to our preacher, was the speed at which his conquest had been carried out, a fact which struck two French writers, Pierre de Fenin and Perceval de Cagny, as well.[26] Likewise, the chronicle which we know as *Gregory's Chronicle*, whose assessment of Henry's reign was compiled almost a generation later, having referred to the king as 'the good and nobylle Kyng', the 'floure of chevalrye of Crystyn men', then went on to list the places (towns, castles, abbeys, and so on) 'that oure fulle excellent lorde the Kyng Harry the

[25] See, for example, *The Brut*, ii, 495, 497; Waurin, *Croniques . . . 1399–1422*, p. 429; *First English Life*, p. 185; *Mémoires de Pierre de Fenin*, ed. Mlle. Dupont (SHF, Paris, 1837), p. 196; *Chronique de Jean le Févre, Seigneur de Saint-Remy*, 2 vols. (SHF, Paris, 1876–81), ii, 67; *The Boke of Noblesse*, ed. J. G. Nichols (Roxburghe Club, London, 1860), pp. 16–17, 41.
[26] Waurin, *Croniques . . . 1399–1422*, p. 429; *Gesta*, p. 101; Haines, 'Contemporary Preacher's View', 93; *Fenin*, pp. 99–100; *Perceval de Cagny*, p. 112.

V wanne and conqueryde in Normandy and in Fraunce, to hym and to hys ayrys'. With such achievements behind him, it is scarcely surprising that Waurin should have reported that the funeral ceremony organized for the dead king in London should have been the finest accorded to a king of England for two hundred years.[27]

Henry, by one of those ironies of history, was followed to the grave after only a very few weeks by his father-in-law, Charles VI of France. A comparison—or perhaps one should say a contrast—between the verdicts pronounced on these two very different men who died within so short a time of each other can be instructive. We have seen how Henry was respected and admired for his military achievements and that the chief virtues which he exhibited were closely connected with war: his sense of justice demanded that he should fight to regain his right; while his sense of order and discipline and, one suspects, the fear of God which he instilled into people, made him a supreme master of men. Such characteristics caused Henry to be respected; his reputation as a soldier was nothing less than formidable, his achievements greater than those of any of his predecessors. Charles VI, by contrast, a man who had reigned for forty-two years, during thirty of which he had suffered from long bouts of mental illness, was loved rather than respected. Pierre de Fenin recalls that he was known as Charles-le-bien-Aimé; Perceval de Cagny tells us that no man was ever better loved by his people than he; while the anonymous and sometimes rather bitter 'Bourgeois de Paris' made it clear in his narrative of Charles's funeral that he had been held in great personal affection by his subjects.[28] There could be no greater contrast in human verdicts. Charles was loved and, one suspects, pitied because of his illness. Henry on the other hand, was never to arouse that same affection in men: instead, he was admired for his qualities and for what he managed to do. It is upon admiration, not affection, that his historical reputation has always been based.

I think that this point, that the impression made by the

[27] *Collections of a Citizen of London*, pp. 148–9; Waurin, *Croniques . . . 1399–1422*, p. 428.
[28] *Fenin*, p. 191; *Perceval de Cagny*, p. 127; *Bourgeois*, pp. 178–80.

man owed more to his achievement than to his qualities as a human being, is underlined if one looks at the use made of his reputation in later years. To the author of the *Libelle of Englyshe Polycye*, a tract on the use of sea power written *c.* 1437, what mattered was that Henry, the 'prince of honoure', should have stood up to the kingdom's enemies, and should have used a fleet to do so.[29] When, a year or two later, Humphrey of Gloucester commissioned the Italian humanist, Tito Livio Frulovisi, to write a life of his late brother, the growing xenophobic sentiment found in England in the 1430s demanded that the emphasis should be upon the conquests and 'feates' of the 'most victorious Kinge', for it was through strong measures and victories that peace between England and France was to be won.[30] If we advance another generation, we meet William Worcestre, in his *Boke of Noblesse*, trying to whip up support for military activity in France by asking the reader to look over his shoulder at the good old days of the past when England had been victorious by force of arms. Naturally, the method had to be selective, but many of the successes, both great and small, achieved by English arms, above all during the period which we know of as the Hundred Years War, are recorded. Inevitably, in such a context, the 'more effectuelle laboures and dedis of armes . . . done by that victorioux prince Henry the .v^th, he being parsonelly bothe at many sieges, leyng at assautes, at batailes, and journeis frome the second yere of his reigne into the day of his trespassement the space of vij yere', are the subject of favourable comment.[31] Let me quote a further passage from Worcestre, for it sums up what at least one Englishman of the next generation, but one who had been very close to those who had personally experienced the Lancastrian wars in France, thought of Henry V's achievement:

the seyd prince Herry V^the, albeit that it consumed gretlie his peple, and also by batailes yeveng, conquerid the towne of Harflete, and wanne bothe the saide Duchie of Normandie first and after the Roiaume of Fraunce, conquerid and broughte in subjeccion and wanne be his gret manhode, withe the noble power of his lordis and helpe of his

[29] *The Libelle of Englyshe Polycye*, ed. G. Warner (Oxford, 1926), p. 2.
[30] *First English Life*, p. 7; *Titi Livii Vita*, p. 2.
[31] *Boke of Noblesse*, pp. 40–1.

comonys, and so overleid the myghtie roialle power of Fraunce be the seide sieges lieng, first in his first viage at Harflete, and in the second viage he made manly besegid Cane, the cite of Rone, Falleise, Argenten, Maunt, Vernonsurseyne, Melun, Meulx, Enbrie, and at many other castellis, forteressis, citeis, and townes to long to rehers. Also had gret batailes on the see ayenst many grete carekkis and gret shippes that beseiged Harefleu after it was Englisshe. And had a great discomfiture at the bataile of Agincourt in the yere of Crist M^l iiij^{c}xv [= 1415], at his first viage, where many dukes, erlis, lordis, and knightis were slaine and take prisoneris the bene in remembraunce at this day of men yet livyng. And after allied hym to the Frenshe king Charlis .vj^{te} is doughter, because of which alliaunce gret part of the roiaume of Fraunce were yolden unto hym his obeisaunce. And now also in the said noble conquest hathe be kepte undre the obediaunce of [the] Englisshe nacion from the begynnyng of the said late conquest by xxxv yeris be continued and kept by roialle power, as first be the noble and famous prince Johan duke of Bedforde, regent and governoure of the roiaume of Fraunce by xiij yeris, with the eide and power of the noble lordis of this lande, bothe youre said royaume of Fraunce and duchie of Normandie was kept and the ennemies kept ferre of in gret subjeccion.[32]

And so one could go on. There is the so-called *First English Life* of 1513, written on the occasion of Henry VIII's invasion of France of that year as a kind of model of what might be achieved. Then there are the chroniclers and annalists of the later sixteenth century, Hall, Stowe, and Holinshed. And then, of course, there is Shakespeare, who places almost the entire emphasis upon an all-conquering king whose achievements are resurrected, so to speak, for the benefit of national sentiment in late Elizabethan England. Not that a sentiment of nationalism, even perhaps of jingoism (in the sense of our king always right and never wrong) is ever far away from some of the chronicles contemporary with Henry V. The king's dealings with the French are described in this way; the French seem unable or, even worse, unwilling, to understand that God is with the English. We have seen some of the reasons why Englishmen thought that this was so. It was, therefore, natural that the events of the reign should be narrated chiefly in terms of war and conquest,

[32] Ibid., pp. 16–17.

so that, as William Worcestre put it, they should be 'notorily knowen thoroughe alle Cristen nacyons, to the gret renomme and worship of this Reaume'. That is the way that Henry, 'imperii et tryumphalis memorie', and his achievements were seen by his contemporaries and near-contemporaries.[33] It was not for them to question too much. It would be left to future and far-distant generations to ask whether it had all been worth while.

[33] Ibid., p. 4; PRO, C 76/122, m. 14 (May 1440).

VII

The Management of Parliament

G. L. HARRISS

To the simple and fundamental question 'what was the function of the medieval parliament?' historians have given diverse and discordant answers. In the 'Whig' interpretation parliament was destined to limit the royal prerogative and safeguard the liberties of the subject, while the 'Tory' view identifies its true purpose as that of an instrument of royal government, sanctioning royal policies for the good of the realm. At particular stages of its development its function has been variously characterized as being the place where subjects could most readily present petitions, where judgement could be authoritatively rendered on the most important and contentious legal questions, where consent to taxation must be sought and received, and where the crown could proclaim its policies and deal publicly with complaints against its officials. All these functions parliament did indeed fulfil, but one further quality it had which must be emphasized. From the very beginning of its history parliament is seen as a public and solemn occasion, a meeting between the king and the realm at which the important concerns of each can be discussed and decided. As representatives from the local communities became an integral part of parliament in the early fourteenth century, it emerged as the only formal occasion at which the king could meet a broad spectrum of his subjects and they could speak to him, not as individuals but as the body of the realm. That parliament *did* represent the body of the realm in the late middle ages we need not doubt. We have the statement to that effect by Chief Justice Thorpe in 1365 when he declared that every subject was bound by its legislation, without the need for proclamation, since all were deemed to be present, and in Henry V's parliaments the Commons claim to represent 'the commune of

your land'.[1] Its representative character was likewise the
basis for its authority to impose taxation on all subjects.
Ever since the reign of Edward I the writs summoning representatives required them to come with full and sufficient
power from the shire community to do and consent to
whatever was ordained by common agreement. That reminds
us that parliament was there to do things, that it was not just
a talking-shop, and to do things that the king wanted done.
But because it represented the communities of the realm
these might also complain of what was being done to them,
by presenting grievances against royal government and royal
officials. Parliament thus directly reflected royal government,
and the varying character it displays, from reign to reign and
century to century, is to a large degree the mirror image of
the king's own purpose and rule. It is largely true to say that
a king got the kind of parliament he deserved. But that is *not*
to say that he could make parliament what he willed. It had
to be managed, and it could more easily be made to move
in the right direction by being led than by being driven.

During the late middle ages the scope and responsibilities
of royal government enlarged rapidly. In legislation and law
enforcement, in the organization of war and the system of
taxation and crown finance, institutions and procedures
were created which continued to function in the early
modern period. A representative parliament was an integral
part of this new web of government, for it incorporated those
principles of common consent and common profit on which
both royal administration and royal authority rested. Those
who rendered assent to laws and taxes in parliament were
those who enforced them in their localities; on them too the
crown relied to fight its wars and suppress rebellion. The
crown's lack of paid professional officials, outside the central
administration, as of any ultimate coercive authority of its
own, meant that a king could never impose government or
fashion policy by his will alone; both had to reflect and
serve the interests of his subjects. The representatives who
came to parliament, versed in an ancient tradition of 'self
government at the king's command', brought not only their

[1] Chrimes, *Eng. Const. Ideas*, p. 352; *Rot. Parl.* iv, 22.

expertise as local officials and their mandate to defend local interests, but a concern for good government and an attitude of co-operation on which the crown could build. A king thus had to rule by agreement or he would not rule at all. The agreement of parliament might, of course, be obtained by the awe of majesty or the threat of royal displeasure, though more often by appeal to the conventions that prescribed the subject's duties and obligations to the crown. Agreement was also bought by concessions to general grievances or particular interests. But it was most easily and fruitfully obtained when royal policy harmonized with the interests of subjects.

That gives the general picture; but how did the particular scene look when Henry V came to the throne? The answer depends on the overall view one takes of parliament's 'true' function. For over the preceeding forty years parliament could be either said to have displayed a precocious awareness of its power and destiny to limit the prerogative, or to have become the instrument for factious and obstructive opposition to the crown. The record, in short, is largely one of criticism and conflict. Parliament had invented and used the weapon of impeachment against the principal ministers of the crown in 1376 and 1386; it had participated in appeals of treason against members of the court and nobility in 1388 and 1397; it had even endorsed charges of misgovernment against King Richard, sanctioned his deposition, and approved his supplanter. Under both Richard II and Henry IV it had, at times, demanded that a wise and weighty council be formally appointed in parliament and charged to advise the king, had complained about the size and character of the king's household, and sought reform in the royal administration and restrictions on the king's right to give rewards. In granting taxes, it had removed these from the control of the royal exchequer and placed them in the hands of special treasurers to ensure that they were properly spent, even demanding in 1404 that these should account to parliament. In all these matters parliament had encroached on the prerogatives of the crown. It justified its demands as being for the good of the crown and realm, and it accompanied them by a barrage of criticism against the corruption of local and central government, the failure of the king to maintain order, to do justice, to manage his finances prudently, and to defend the realm and suppress rebellion—all summed up in the general charge of lack of 'bone governance'.[2]

Richard II and Henry IV had reacted to this in very different ways. Richard felt affronted by criticism and threatened by the attack on his friends and ministers—as indeed he was; failing to win the Commons' confidence, his response was to override complaint and exact obedience. Henry IV tried to cultivate the reverse image, turning a conciliatory ear to complaint and buying off criticism with fair promises. Neither was a real solution. Henry IV provided no ground for charges of tyranny, and his baronial opponents were never able to use parliament as the tool of faction; but by 1406 the instability of royal government and the chaos of its finances had provoked an irresistible demand in parliament for the establishment of a council to oversee royal government and control expenditure. Unlike the parliamentary commission of 1386 which deprived Richard II of authority to govern, the council which ruled from 1406 to 1411, with varying degrees of reference to Henry IV, was composed of the king's friends, not his enemies. Its nominal head was Prince Henry, now afforded the chance to redeem his father's broken promises by providing the 'bone governance' for which the Commons had reluctantly granted taxation. It is with the parliaments he met at Gloucester in October 1407 and at Westminster in January 1410 and November 1411 that our study of his relations with that body must begin.

The Commons' complaints against Henry IV's rule in 1406 were broadly of two kinds: on the one hand was the failure to meet external threats to Calais and Gascony, to protect English shipping, and to suppress the Welsh revolt; on the other the looming bankruptcy induced by runaway spending on the royal household and heedless generosity in granting away crown revenues. The articles of reform, which they demanded as the price of a further subsidy, gave the council full power over financial policy and prescribed the use of crown revenue for the household. Prince Henry

[2] A. L. Brown, 'Parliament *c.*1377–1422', in *English Parliament*, ed. Davies and Denton, pp. 109–140.

was to devote himself to mastering the Welsh rebellion while the council, and the new treasurer of the household, Sir John Tiptoft, implemented the financial reforms.[3] When parliament met a year later the external threats had largely receded and the Commons passed a vote of thanks to the prince and the Duke of York for their service in Wales, where the end of the rebellion was in sight. The council also faced the Commons with confidence, presenting a statement of how it had spent the subsidy, laying claim to their gratitude for its efforts, and seeking release from the oath given in 1406 to fulfil the articles of reform. The Commons still expresssed concern over purveyance, the security of shipping, and the cost of the Welsh rebellion, but they marked their approval with the grant of a modest half-subsidy for each of the coming three years.[4] By 1410, however, Henry IV aided by Archbishop Arundel had begun to reassert his control over expenditure while the prince, now returned from Wales, was bent on claiming the active leadership of the council and was pressing for a sustained programme of financial discipline. The Commons, perhaps with some prompting by the prince, revived their demands of 1406: Calais, the sea, and the Welsh and Scottish marches were to be securely and economically guarded; a new council was to be named; crown revenues were to be applied to household expenses and not granted away, and evasion and embezzlement of taxes was to be stopped; disturbers of the peace were to be punished. These discontents were exploited or encouraged by the prince —which is not clear—to secure the dismissal of Archbishop Arundel as chancellor and Tiptoft as treasurer and the appointment to the council of a younger generation of those who had fought with him in Wales—the Earls of Arundel and Warwick and Lord Burnell, together with his half-uncles Thomas and Henry Beaufort. The prince now stood committed to a programme of 'bone governance' for which he sought, in return, a regular lay subsidy for the remainder of the reign, without recourse to parliament, so that he could plan ahead with confidence. That was asking too much of the

[3] A. L. Brown, 'The Commons and the Council in the Reign of Henry IV', *EHR*, lxxix (1964), 13–30; *Rot. Parl.* iii, 573–4, 579, 585–9.
[4] *Rot. Parl.* iii, 609–12.

Commons; their confidence in him was still not complete, but they did, as in 1407, provide a half-subsidy for each of the three years ahead.[5]

The prince's government lasted just under two years. It ended in a quarrel with his father, probably over the dispatch of the Earl of Arundel's expedition to assist John, Duke of Burgundy against the Armagnacs. It was Henry IV who turned the tables on his son by forcing the resignation of the chancellor and treasurer, and the council of the prince's supporters, in the parliament of November 1411. For a moment the prince may have contemplated rebellion, but wiser counsels prevailed, and this time the Commons, having been brusquely told by the king that he would have no novelties in this parliament, bought royal favour by a humble apology and a tax which they placed at the king's free disposal. Nevertheless they insisted on recording their thanks to the prince and his council for having loyally done their duty according to their promise given at the last parliament. The prince, in reply, reproachfully declared that if they had granted him more money he could have performed even more for the honour, welfare, and profit of the king and all the realm.[6] But for the rest of his father's reign Prince Henry ceased to attend the council or to play any role in government.

Much in these parliaments is obscure and difficult to interpret, but it is clear that they form a sequence with the first three parliaments of the new reign, concerned with the problems of 'bone governance'. In the last few years of his father's reign Prince Henry had established a working relationship with the Commons and came to the throne pledged to a programme of good counsel, financial discipline, efficient and economical administration, and the maintenance of strong defences. Though alert and responsive to the complaints of parliament, it was his own conviction of a ruler's duty that informed his policy, and it was this that impelled him to resist any constraints on the executive and prerogative powers of the crown. In 1406 he had not wished the council to be bound to the articles of reform under oath and himself

[5] Ibid. iii, 623–33. This is my inference from Walsingham's statement in *Historia Anglicana*, ed. H. T. Riley (Rolls Ser., 1864), ii. 283.
[6] Ibid. iii, 647–9.

refused to take one; nor would he accept any obligation to account for the subsidy. Moreover he expected that the council's commitment to financial restraint should be matched by a guaranteed and significant revenue from taxation. A row had erupted over this in 1407 when the council tried to tell the Commons how much tax they were to grant, and in 1410 the prince threatened to withdraw unless they voted adequate supply. On each occasion the Commons stood their ground. Despite this the prince retained their confidence. That was due to at least three things. First, he publicly dissociated himself from the fair words and broken promises of his father's rule: he made his intentions clear and took pride in keeping them. The Commons knew where they stood. Secondly, his military achievements won repeated commendation from the Commons, who had berated his father's failure. Thirdly, his case was powerfully argued in parliament and he was kept closely in touch with opinion in the house. In this the Beauforts were of prime importance. John, as captain of Calais, and Thomas, as admiral, were key figures in protecting English trade with Flanders and both were commended by the Commons; when the prince himself succeeded John as captain in 1410 the defence of Calais was given high priority. Henry Beaufort, who opened the 1410 parliament, was an eloquent and impressive orator, while his cousin and retainer, Thomas Chaucer, was speaker in the parliaments of 1407, 1410, and 1411, and later that of November 1414.

Such was the background to the first parliament which Henry met as King in May 1413, two months after his accession. The tone was set by the new chancellor, Henry Beaufort, preaching on the text 'Ante omnem actum consilium stabile'.[7] He bade parliament make provision for (i) the sustenance of the king's estate, (ii) the establishment of 'bone governance' and the maintenance of the laws, (iii) assistance to foreign allies and resistance to enemies. All these looked directly back to Henry's policy as Prince; in particular the first two demanded regular taxation as the

[7] In the remainder of this chapter all statements relating to parliamentary proceedings are based on the text in *Rot. Parl.* iv, 3-165. Individual references will not be given.

price of 'bone governance'. On this occasion the Commons did 'for their great love and affection, for the good of the realm, and for good governance in future', grant the wool subsidy for four years and a whole lay subsidy, allocated to the defence of the realm and sea: a fitting welcome to the new king. But at the same time they underlined the principle that direct taxation was extraordinary and should be confined to open war, by disclaiming any obligation to grant further taxes for the maintenance of the permanent garrisons. With the coming of war this particular issue became submerged, though it surfaced again after 1420, as we shall see. Moreover the Commons were mindful of Henry's side of the bargain as well. Their speaker, Sir William Stourton, recalled to the king's face how often they had asked his father for 'bone governance' and had received promises of it, 'but how those promises were kept and performed the king himself well knows'. When the speaker then agreed to the king's request to put their special grievances in writing, the Commons disavowed his action, saying that they wished to make their complaints orally and under general headings. A week later Stourton was said to be ill and was replaced by Sir John Doreward, a follower of Archbishop Arundel. What lay behind this is not easy to say, but the fact that the Commons explicitly demonstrated that the speaker was the servant of the house and not of the king, may reflect their apprehensiveness as well as their hopes of the new reign.[8] The vigorous wielder of a new broom in government might only too easily sweep away their rights. The Commons' concern was again revealed in the second parliament, of May 1414, where they asked that when petitions were made into statutes the purport of them should not be changed by additions or diminutions. The king had, indeed, substantially amended six of the ten petitions enacted in 1413, mainly by mitigating the penalties demanded; but he adroitly side-stepped the protest, merely promising not to enact anything contrary to what was asked in a petition. While the Commons might claim to have always been 'assentors as well as petitioners', Henry was determined that legislation should ultimately reflect his purposes rather

[8] Roskell, *Speakers*, pp. 52, 155.

than theirs.[9] Thus, despite his record as Prince, Henry's relations with his early parliaments were far from trustful and relaxed. The Commons' old resentments against his father and wariness over his own forceful kingship meant that tact and consistency were called for in order to win their co-operation.

Let us now attempt a broader view of Henry's parliaments. What was their character; what did they do; how were they managed? Some elementary statistics can set the scene. Henry V summoned parliament more frequently than his father, holding eleven in a reign of nine and a half years compared to Henry IV's nine in thirteen years. But whereas Henry IV's parliaments sat for an average of nine weeks each, and those during Henry VI's minority for almost twelve weeks, under Henry V the average duration of a parliament was about four weeks. The pattern of short, frequent sessions was more characteristic of Edward III's parliaments. Yet we cannot wholly explain their frequency by the needs of war taxation, nor their shortness by the king's absence from five of them. Rather, they are a reflection of the tempo of Henry's government—brisk, business-like, effective. Henry V had no time for parliament as a talking-shop; he saw it as a tool of government, for furthering his own plans.

His overriding purpose was, of course, the assertion of his just claim to the French crown, and from the third parliament of the reign, in November 1414, the needs of war became dominant. That meant heavy taxation. Over the whole reign of nine and a half years Henry V received ten and one-third subsidies—almost exactly equivalent to what Henry IV had received in thirteen years. Of these, eight and one-third were granted in the five years of intensive war effort between November 1414 and November 1419, and all save one-third were collected in the five years February 1415 to February 1420. In both 1415 and 1417 two subsidies were collected in the space of a year and between June 1416 and November 1417 a subsidy was collected every six months. The nearest parallel to this unprecedented burden of taxation was the five years 1377–81 when the equivalent to five and two

[9] Gray, *Influence of the Commons*, pp. 261–77; Chrimes, *Eng. Const. Ideas*, pp. 159–64.

thirds lay subsidies were collected. It was the attempt to levy almost half this total within the year April 1380-1 which started the Peasants' Revolt. The effect on parliament had been traumatic and far-reaching. Unnerved and in dread of another upheaval, parliament became reluctant to grant further taxation for war and this contributed significantly to the shift of policy towards a long truce with France. The grudging compliance with Henry IV's demands, and the suspicion that the king misused what was granted, which led parliament to commit its grants to special treasurers or the council, and even at times to require account for them to be rendered in parliament, revealed that the Commons were still sensitive to the unpopularity of taxation. By contrast, both the liberality of the grants to Henry V and the absence of any such restrictions upon them showed that this era had passed. Parliament again had confidence in its power to tax, and confidence in the king's use of what it granted, such as it had not displayed since the years of Edward III's maturity. How was this change effected?

An answer must begin with Henry V's use of the traditional romano-canonical doctrine of necessity. War had long provided the classic case of necessity, for it endangered the existence of the realm and the safety of its inhabitants, and rulers could legitimately claim support from their subjects for defending them against such danger. The war had to be in a just cause and be waged in defence of the realm, and it is in the elaboration of these requirements that the distinctiveness of Henry's approach to parliament appears. It was hardly possible in 1414-15 to claim, as had Edward III, that England was threatened with invasion and the English tongue with destruction, and the more lurid propaganda of the earlier part of the Hundred Years War was little used. Instead, the French were solely and insistently accused of depriving Henry of his rightful inheritance in France, and his subjects were summoned to assist in the recovery of his royal estate. Emphasis had therefore to be laid not only on the justice of his claims but on the obstinacy of the French in refusing to restore his rights by peaceful negotiation.

This was the theme of Bishop Beaufort's address as chancellor to the parliament of November 1414 which furnished the first war taxation, and its force was both acknowledged and tested by the insistence of the Lords and knights that the king should try yet again for a negotiated settlement, even by compromising some of his demands.[10] War was not to be commenced lightheartedly and wise counsel could be a bridle to an impetuous king. Henry accepted it as such and a further embassy was dispatched. But a year later, when the astonishing news of Agincourt had just arrived, and Beaufort opened parliament with the text 'strive for justice and the Lord will fight with you', all hesitations were dispelled. In the glow of victory, and as gratitude for the king's homecoming, the Commons granted Henry the subsidy on wool for life and another whole lay subsidy. This was a striking tribute to their confidence in his kingship. The only previous life grant of the wool subsidy had been that made to Richard II under duress in the parliament of January 1398 which formed, as the Commons believed, a basis for tyrannical rule and set a precedent which they had consciously avoided under Henry IV. Nor did they now hedge their grants with conditions. They had granted Henry the lay subsidy of November 1414 'to dispose of according to your most wise discretion, for the defence of the realm', and that of 1415 followed suit. Indeed the words of their grant echoed the chancellor's own speech and endorsed Henry's vision of his purpose, voicing the gratitude of the realm to a king who had devoted his own wealth and courage to an enterprise which God had now blessed with victory, to the honour and exaltation of his crown, his fame, and the perpetual profit of the whole realm. A year later the same theme could still excite a warm response. Beaufort once more—this was to be his last parliament as chancellor—recalled the justice of Henry's claims and the continued obstinacy of his adversary in denying him his rights, even after God's verdict shown at Agincourt, and drew the inexorable conclusion that peace could only be secured by war. A lasting peace was the reward promised for the double subsidy now granted to launch the conquest of Normandy, and already in 1414 Beaufort had hinted that, when Henry had regained his patrimony in France, the

---

[10] *Proc. PC*, ii, 140.

burden on England could be lifted. But two further years of taxation, granted in the parliament of November 1417, were needed before the conquest of Normandy was achieved.

When parliament next met in November 1419 the murder of John the Fearless had put the French crown within Henry's grasp, and rumours of peace abounded. Meanwhile the war had still to be fought and paid for, and Bishop Langley, as chancellor, had a harder task than Beaufort. Significantly, although he rehearsed the familiar round of past victories and the hope of a just peace, it was to the stern doctrine of moral necessity that he reverted: 'necessitas causat bellum et non voluntas'. The necessity that impelled the king to fight required his subjects to pay. The war, he told the Commons, could not continue without notable reinforcements of men and money; but he now held out the hope that it would bring 'a peace without end between the two realms'. This time the Commons' response was nicely tailored to their perception of the situation in France: a whole subsidy was granted for February 1420, but then merely a third of a subsidy for the following Martinmas. It was a shrewd guess, for by May peace had been made at Troyes. Moreover they insisted on the subsidies being spent in England, while into an act permitting loans to be raised on the third part they inserted a telling proviso that they should not be charged or obliged to support the king's wars in France and Normandy. They had reached their limit, but in fact that ended Henry V's war taxation. Compared with that of Edward III and Richard II it had been short and sharp. It had confined itself to one plea—the recovery of the king's rights—and had sought to identify subjects with his cause. Edward III had used the same plea, but not so consistently or exclusively. In Henry's eyes the realm was not fighting for its own protection or survival, nor to conquer the land of its ancient enemy; it was fighting for the king's own title and inheritance. The king was the personification of the realm; his quarrel was its quarrel. Nor was this mere casuistry. The miracle of Agincourt and the prolonged campaigning in and 'colonization' of Normandy evoked a wider identification with the king's leadership and a deeper response of national pride than had the expeditions of the fourteenth century. The oratory of Henry's chancellors and the humble addresses of his Commons were more than mere hyperbole; they mirrored the sentiments of the realm.

This was evident in the changed circumstances created by the Treaty of Troyes which, by establishing peace between the two realms and recognizing Henry's title, eliminated the justification for further taxation on the accustomed plea. The parliament of December 1420 proved the most recalcitrant of the reign. There had been a contest for the speakership, Roger Hunt, probably the 'official' candidate, winning only after a close vote, and the Commons went on to press for immediate commercial benefits from the Treaty of Troyes, at the expense of Flanders, and to complain of the king's prolonged absence abroad. They expressed dissatisfaction about their petitions being diverted to the council or sent abroad to the king to be answered, but most striking was their demand for the confirmation of Edward III's undertaking in 1340 that Englishmen should never be subject to the king in virtue of his French title. That went to the heart of the new situation, and had immediate implications for the Commons' liability for taxation. For the Treaty of Troyes made the Dauphin and his supporters mere rebels against Charles VI and required Henry V, as 'Heir of France', to reduce them to obedience. The war was no longer between two nations, but between the King of France and his rebellious subjects, and Henry V's English subjects were in no way obliged to support this. Hence no taxation was sought in this parliament and 1421 was the first year of the reign in which none was collected.

It would appear, therefore, that Henry had kept his promise to lift the burden from the realm once peace was secured. Yet when Henry arrived in England in February 1421, after three and a half years' absence, it was already clear that the treaty had opened up the prospect of a prolonged war against Dauphinist France, and the king's intention was to return with a fresh army in the summer. How was this to be financed? Henry's first act was to summon a parliament to meet in May, to answer grievances and reform abuses arising from the king's absence, and to ratify the Treaty of Troyes. Nothing was said in the chancellor's speech, or in the parliament roll, about taxation; yet it is certain that this was prominent in the minds of Henry and the Commons, and very probably occasioned a struggle between them. As Adam of Usk makes clear, the victorious king found his subjects in no mood for further burdens.[11] Yet he had explicitly waived any demand for a tax from the recalcitrant parliament of 1420 so that its successor might be the more amenable, and, now returning in triumph 'like Julius Caesar', could expect parliament to mark its gratitude to him as it had in 1415.[12] Moreover, even while Henry was making pilgrimages to shrines and redressing grievances, his own brother was killed at Baugé, and in seeking to redeem that defeat the king would be exposing his body to the perils of war. Did not subjects have a duty to provide for the safety of their prince by sending him adequately equipped? A royal *viage* (expedition) was traditionally regarded as imposing a special obligation to aid the monarch. Henry, moreover, had employed his 'pilgrimage' in March and April in raising men and loans for the expedition, and a large sum, as much as £9,000, had been borrowed from a wide range of subjects. What security could be offered for its repayment? The obvious answer was a tax to be granted in the ensuing parliament. There is some indirect evidence that Henry did indeed seek a tax. A later source states that a tax was proposed, and John Strecche, a canon of Leicester, says that it was both asked for and received.[13] Then, too, the king had a statement of the financial situation prepared, dated 6 May, four days after parliament opened. It showed the existence of a permanent deficit—excluding the costs of war—which could only be eliminated by a permanent contribution from direct taxation.[14] But that, as we have noted, had long been anathema to the Commons. Was there, then, a confrontation between the king and the Commons over the principle of permanent or peacetime taxation in May 1421? Quite probably, although the parliament roll contains no mention of it. A compromise was worked out to save the

[11] Usk, *Chronicon*, p. 320.
[12] *St Albans Chronicle*, p. 126.
[13] *Henrici Quinti Angliae Regis Gesta*, ed. B. Williams (London, 1850), p. 152; Taylor, 'Chronicle of John Strecche', p. 52.
[14] *Proc. PC*, ii, 312-15.

faces of both sides. The king withdrew his demand and tapped ecclesiastical wealth instead. Convocation granted a tenth in the second week of May, thereby providing repayment for the loans, and on 13 May Bishop Beaufort purchased his restoration to Henry's grace with a huge loan of £17,666 13s. 4d.[15] That took the pressure off the Commons for the moment, but they must have made an unrecorded and deferred grant, for in December another parliament met, summoned to coincide with the birth of Henry's first son and heir, and on the very first day of that parliament—even before the election of a speaker—the Commons granted a whole subsidy. This would seem to be a unique departure from the well-established procedure that the subsidy bill came on the last day of the session. The grant was made in the accustomed terms: 'out of affection for the king and especially for the defence of the realm', and thus created no formal precedent; but the fact remained that the king had secured a tax for reinforcements though the realm was technically at peace. In the event this was the final tax granted to Henry V and the last for seven years during which the Commons consistently refused to support the war in France. Whether he would have been able to persuade them otherwise had he lived remains an open question.

Even when taxes were granted for war, on an indisputable plea of necessity, the Commons bargained for the redress of their grievances and concessions to their interests. Here again we can glimpse how the king handled parliament. The most direct concession by the crown was the grant of a general pardon, covering a wide range of criminal offences, trespasses, and evasion of royal dues. Such pardons had been purchased by grants of taxation under previous sovereigns; under Henry V they were accorded in 1413, for the first tax of the reign, and then in November 1414 and November 1416 when double subsidies were granted. That of 1414 was made more desirable by extending the range of offences covered.[16]

Next we may note the strong pressure applied by the mercantile lobby in parliament. In March 1414 Henry V introduced a Statute of Truces in an attempt to stamp out

[15] McFarlane, 'Henry V, Beaufort and the Red Hat', p. 110.
[16] See Dr Powell's discussion in chapter iii.

English piracy and eliminate friction with English allies, notably the Dukes of Burgundy and Brittany. Truce-breaking, and the disregard of safe conducts issued by the king, were made high treason and punishable by the death penalty. Conservators of the truces were appointed in each port to check on seizures and punish offenders, while English merchants who were themselves the victims of alien pirates were forbidden to take reprisals and referred to the king and council for satisfaction. Although measures to regulate piracy along these lines had been taken in the previous reign, by according them the permanency of statute and providing maximum penalties Henry showed that he was in earnest. Indeed the immediate and effective enforcement of the scheme soon provoked English merchants to complain that, while they themselves were disciplined and restrained from piracy, they could get no redress from foreign rulers for the offences committed against them by foreign pirates. In November 1416 Henry agreed to a partial relaxation by authorizing the merchants to take reprisals if they had failed to get recompense for their losses by lawful means. The merchants continued to complain against the statute, but it was not until 1435 that they got it repealed. The mercantile lobby waged an even more prolonged campaign to restrict the operation of alien merchants in England. Resentment against their privileged position was coupled with the suspicion that their profits were at English expense and resulted in a net export of bullion. Legislation restricting their trading activities, requiring them to purchase English goods with their profits, and putting them under the surveillance of English hosts, went back to Richard II's reign. But the crown habitually dispensed from it for the sake of good diplomatic relations, the flow of trade, and the loans with which the alien merchants purchased royal protection. In 1413 Henry showed himself accommodating, in accepting petitions for the enforcement of earlier legislation and hosting laws, but reserved his power to dispense in individual cases. In 1416 he accepted demands for the expulsion of Bretons and for the hosting laws to be enforced, but in 1420 renewed petitions on the hosting of aliens suggest that the king was still dragging his feet.

Henry's readiness to make concessions in these matters, particularly in the parliaments of November 1414 and 1416 when large subsidies were at stake, never amounted to the annulment of his legislation or the surrender of his prerogatives. Then in 1420–1 the merchants saw their chance to exploit the Duke of Burgundy's acceptance of the Treaty of Troyes for their own interests. In their eyes Flanders had now become an English satellite, and some long-resented barriers to English trade could be removed. In particular, the duke should be compelled either to lift the embargo on imports of English cloth into Flanders or to give English merchants the monopoly of imports of raw wool. Further, now that England commanded the Dover Straits, foreign shipping should pay a toll for passing through to Flanders. Both these the king refused; he had no intention of alienating his hard-won ally at this juncture. What Henry did agree to was a petition from the mayor and company of the staple at Calais that all wool sales at Calais should be in English coin, for the effect of this was to increase the business and profits of the Calais mint and make a contribution to the costs of the garrison. This went with his policy of restoring the currencies of England and France, to counteract the effects of debasement practised by Charles VI and Duke John the Fearless. A sound currency was vital to the restoration of the economy which the war had dislocated, and the parliament of 1421 legislated for a systematic recoinage in England and Calais.

This raises the question of how Henry V responded to the petitions of the Commons and to what extent his legislation was based upon these. In his study of late medieval legislation, H. L. Gray noted that far fewer 'common petitions' were presented in Henry V's parliaments than in those of his two predecessors: only 150 in his eleven parliaments as against the 500 in Richard II's twenty-four parliaments and 400 in Henry IV's nine parliaments. Further, the number of statutes enacted under Henry V was only half that in the reigns of each of his two predecessors. On the other hand a larger proportion of the 'common petitions' in his parliaments— over one-third—became statutes.[17] In other words, although

[17] Gray, *Influence of the Commons*, p. 260.

there were fewer petitions they were more productive of statutes. These 'common petitions' dealt with problems of common or public concern, to which the king was asked to provide solutions by legislation or administrative action. But they could easily become the vehicle for denunciations of misgovernment, detailing administrative abuses or the malfeasance of officials. A marathon petition in the Good Parliament (1376) contained sixty-one articles of complaint, ranging over the whole field of government, central and local; yet only one-tenth of it was translated into legislation. Nothing remotely like that was seen in Henry V's parliaments, mainly no doubt because the good and abundant government, for which the Commons had clamoured, was now being provided. Indeed the best answer to a petition was not another statute but the enforcement of the law and strict and economical administration. Henry V's work in these respects has been discussed in other chapters. But the smaller number of common petitions may also suggest closer royal surveillance, an unofficial vetting to eliminate those that were otiose or unacceptable. That would be in line with the brisk and streamlined handling of Henry's parliaments.

It is in this light that we need to reconsider the other phenomenon noted by Gray, that virtually all the statutes of the reign were based on 'common petitions', confirming a trend strongly visible from the accession of Henry IV. Gray saw this as marking 'the triumph of popular legislation' and giving the Commons 'control' over the making of laws. But such deductions have been shown to be mistaken.[18] In the first place—as the petition of 1414 acknowledged—Henry, like any other king, enacted only what he wanted, refusing some petitions and answering others by reference to existing statutes or by taking administrative action. Even when abroad he insisted on having petitions referred to himself to answer, and the Commons' protest against this in 1420 significantly coincided with the attempt by the mercantile lobby to press their intemperate demands on the king's inexperienced lieutenant, Humphrey, Duke of Gloucester. Henry also safeguarded his ultimate control over legislation

---

[18] Chrimes, *Eng. Const. Ideas*, pp. 236–49.

by requiring that statutes made in his absence should only remain operative until the next parliament after he returned. Secondly, legislation could be initiated in either the Commons or the Lords, the decision between them being largely determined by convenience and particular interests and not indicating a political or constitutional struggle. Much legislation dealt with minor or local reforms and arose directly from the Commons' own experience and interests; in identifying ills and remedies in the body politic, they were fulfilling their own essential and irreplaceable role, not usurping the king's. What is significant, however, is the initiation of royal legislation through the Commons. The fact that—as Gray noted—the important statutes of Truces, Lollards, and Riots in 1414 were all introduced into the Commons in the precise words of the acts, shows that they had already been drafted by royal clerks. Important fiscal measures like the recoinage bill of 1421 and the preference for the royal household in 1413, though clearly originating with the crown, were framed as common petitions.[19] Why major royal legislation of this kind should have been introduced in the lower house rather than the upper is not easy to answer. We may see a parallel in the increasing readiness of individuals, even such exalted ones as the Earl of Salisbury, the Duchess of Kent, and Bishop Beaufort, to use the Commons as sponsors or intermediaries for their private petitions. This may reflect the desire of the petitioners for public attestation of what they sought and were granted, although it probably also saved time to forward directly to the Lords private bills already furnished with the Commons' assent, along with the 'common petitions'. The formula for this was standardized in this reign and suggests that the Commons had evolved a regular procedure for scrutinizing bills. Moreover the normality of the Commons' assent to such bills, and to those originating with the king and Lords (such as that granting the manor of Isleworth to the nuns of Syon in 1421), was establishing that 'two-way traffic' in legislation between the houses which was formally recognized by the middle of the

[19] Gray, *Influence of the Commons*, pp. 278–80, 285.

century.[20] In 1420 the Commons protested against the endorsement of private bills as 'by the authority of parliament' which had not received the threefold assent of king, Lords, and Commons and though the king rejected this, like their earlier claim in 1414 to be assentors as well as petitioners, it already reflected more than mere aspiration. Obscure and technical though the evidence is, the reign of Henry V seems to mark the point when the Commons became fully integrated into all stages of the legislative process. But that in no way diminished royal control over legislation.

Of itself legislation is an inadequate measure of the importance of parliament, which had always been the place where matters of great concern to the king, the nobility, and the realm were dealt with. Henry V's parliaments fully realized this traditional function. In them the Treaties of Canterbury and of Troyes were ratified and the Emperor Sigismund's peace proposals submitted to the advice of the realm; the sentence on the conspirators of 1415 was affirmed, Sir John Oldcastle was adjudged a traitor, and confiscation pronounced on Queen Joan for witchcraft; dukedoms were conferred on the king's brothers, the heirs of the traitors to Henry IV were restored, and a new division of the Bohun estates between the king and his aunt was enacted. Parliament had this unique quality, that it embraced and served the interests of all estates of the realm, from the highest to the lowest, and this made it a peculiarly effective instrument of government for a king like Henry V. For Henry's policies and his view of kingship demanded an identity of interest between the king and the realm, and in parliament this could most appropriately and publicly be given expression. We have observed the fruits of this in the provision of good government, in taxation, petitions, and legislation, and in the speed and effectiveness of the parliamentary timetable. Only very dimly can we perceive the means by which this was achieved.

[20] The whole subject is discussed by A. R. Myers, 'Parliamentary Petitions in the Fifteenth Century', *EHR*, lii (1937), 385–404, 590–613, and in *English Parliament*, ed. Davies and Denton, pp. 169–71. See too J. G. Edwards, *The Second Century of the English Parliament* (Oxford, 1979), pp. 61–5, 86–7.

Two officials stand out as most influential in this; the speaker in the Commons and the chancellor in the Lords. Almost certainly the speaker led the house in debate as well as presiding over it, and very probably indicated the crown's wishes to the Commons. He was, as the Commons had demonstrated in 1413, their spokesman not the king's. But the speakers of Henry V's parliaments were all trusted royal officials or well known to the Duke of Bedford who acted as Guardian of England in 1415, 1417, 1419, and 1421. Four of them (Stourton, Hungerford, Beauchamp, Flore) were officers of the duchies of Lancaster or Cornwall; three (Hungerford, Beauchamp, Chaucer) held posts in the royal household. Two of them served more than once: Flore, in 1416, 1417, and 1419, Chaucer in the crucial parliaments of 1414 and 1421, having already held the office in the prince's parliaments of 1407-11. Both those who contested the speakership in 1420—Roger Hunt and John Russell— were old parliamentary hands and were officers of the crown, and Russell who was defeated went on to become speaker in 1423-4.[21] Of like calibre and service were others who sat as knights of the shire—Sir Humphrey Stafford, Sir John Tiptoft, Sir William Philip, John Willicotes, John Hotoft, and Henry Somer. Some members of the king's council sat in the lower house and many others there were men known to him and well informed of his wishes. The king did not lack his advocates in the Commons, though we know nothing of their advocacy.

Thomas Chaucer was cousin to Bishop Beaufort, and Beaufort was chancellor until 1417. When Beaufort presented the king's policy to the Commons at the outset of parliament, his speeches were carefully framed and fluently expounded; they were attuned to the mood of the Commons and laid the basis for that confidence in the royal purpose on which the speaker would need to build. For Beaufort, in particular, sought to convey a sense that Henry's government was directed towards a well-considered and achievable goal. In his final parliament as chancellor, that of November 1416, he reviewed the achievements of the reign to that date. In

[21] For the careers of these speakers, see Roskell, *Speakers*.

the first parliament the king had striven to establish peace and good governance in the realm, and such had endured; in the second, at Leicester, he had made good and necessary laws; in the third he had secured the assent of all estates for the expedition to establish his just rights; and in the following two parliaments he had sought peace from his adversary without avail. Thus in this, his sixth parliament, he had to prepare for war in order to achieve that full and final peace, following which—Beaufort concluded—he and they would have rest. For just as the Holy Ghost created the world in' six days and rested on the seventh, so Henry had laboured to accomplish the promises of his coronation oath in six parliaments so that with the seventh might come their rest and reward. It was not, of course, to be. Four more years and two more parliaments, held without the king, passed before the peace treaty was signed, and in that time much of the spirit of partnership in a noble and just venture which Beaufort had invoked seeped away. But though these later parliaments brought tensions with the crown and increasing reluctance to grant it money, there was no attempt to limit the crown's authority, no suspicions of the king's honesty or competence, and no challenge to his policy.

On any score Henry V's handling of parliament was out-standingly successful. In proportion to the length of his reign, he got more money with less trouble than any other king of England. He never encountered the fury of indignation that brought king and parliament to crisis in the reigns of each of his predecessors and in that of his son; nor did he come to shun the summoning of parliament as did Edward IV and Henry VII. His approach to parliament was perhaps more like that of Edward I before 1290; he called it frequently, and invited its co-operation in the full confidence that it would serve his purpose. Above all he led it. For it was not merely among his nobility and churchmen, nor even in the battles and sieges where his life was mostly spent, that Henry V proved a great leader. The parliaments over which he presided attested his political leadership of the realm.

VIII

Financial Policy

G. L. HARRISS

Let me make it clear at the outset that my subject is Henry V's financial policy and not the state of his finances. The sufficiency or otherwise of a king's finances indeed affected his exercise of authority; but it was the means by which he accumulated revenue and the purposes on which he spent it that better illuminate his kingship. For a king's rights over his own resources and to those of his subjects were conditioned by his obligation to use these for the common good of the kingdom. The practice of royal finance could therefore never be separated from political theory and constitutional rules, the more so as subjects were apt to judge royal government principally by the yardstick of its financial demands on their own purses and property. An examination of Henry's financial policy will thus take us close to the heart of his practice of kingship, to where his own interests and purposes impinged on those of his subjects.

The medieval view of the State as an association of ruler and ruled for the common good was embodied in certain fiscal conventions and institutions. The king—or rather, the crown—possessed an endowment, termed in Latin *fiscus* and in English 'livelihood', which was intended to support the king's household, his servants, and the normal charges of government, leaving subjects to contribute from their wealth to the exceptional or extraordinary needs of the realm. These were associated primarily with its defence in time of war, when subjects were consulted and gave their consent to taxation. In this sense there existed a symbiotic relationship between the crown and its subjects whereby the livelihood of each sustained the State which sheltered and nourished both. Consequently, in respect of their financial obligations at least, those who granted taxation saw themselves

as partners in government, free to—and indeed bound to—
criticize the king if his financial policies were to the detriment
of the crown and the commonwealth. During the forty
years preceding Henry V's accession such criticism had been
bitter and sustained. This may partly be attributed to persistent defeats in war, and a steadily widening gap between the
crown's own income and expenditure, both of which stimu-
lated opposition to its demands for taxation; but these
demands were made less acceptable by the incapacities or
extravagance of particular monarchs. A king who failed to
defend the realm or could not sustain the royal estate from
his own resources had little claim upon his subjects, for he
was not fulfilling his own obligations, and was unfairly
increasing theirs. This was the charge made against Richard
II at his deposition—that he had heedlessly squandered the
revenues of the crown on favourites and had then been
compelled to levy unwarranted taxes on his subjects. That
could be interpreted as tyranny. Conversely, if a king practised
'bone governance', spending taxes effectively and managing
his own 'livelihood' to the best advantage so that it could
sustain the royal estate, he would find his subjects more
ready to assist him in time of genuine need. The fact that
such a theoretical delimitation of the respective obligations
of ruler and ruled could hardly work in practice was beside
the point; for the granting of taxation was determined by
convention and persuasion, and on political rather than
purely budgetary grounds.

From this point of view Henry IV did little better. He
came to the throne with virtually no experience of central
government and with little appreciation of how finely balanced
royal finances were. Two things in particular soon precipitated
financial confusion. First, to stabilize his throne, Henry IV
freely distributed grants of land and annuities, confirming
virtually all those of Richard II and rewarding, as he was
bound to, his own Lancastrian supporters. He kept an open
household, the costs of which soon soared above even the
level of Richard II's. Secondly, for the first eight years of
the reign he had the additional expense of suppressing the
Welsh revolt; expeditions had to be sent to Wales and garrisons
maintained along the marches. Together these produced a

continuing and increasing deficit and critical shortages of cash to pay commanders in Wales, the wardens of the northern marches, and suppliers to the royal household. The crown's political and financial credit sank as the exchequer, to stave off demands from its creditors, gave them assignments on future revenues, rather than cash. The creditor received a wooden tally which authorized him to receive payment from a local revenue collector when this became available. The system was well established, but was open to abuse if the exchequer issued tallies in excess of the revenue available. Such 'dud cheques' then rebounded on the exchequer, creditors complaining that they had been given just sticks instead of money. They would try to persuade the exchequer to take their tallies back, cancel them, and issue fresh ones on revenue that was available. If this happened they were credited on the exchequer rolls with what historians have dubbed a 'fictitious loan', and these afford a rough guide to the extent to which a government was losing a grip on its finances, and issuing promissory instruments in excess of revenue. Although the level of fictitious loans does not accurately represent the extent to which the exchequer defaulted, and though we cannot equate paying creditors by tallies of assignment with unsound finance, yet a high level of cash payments and a low level of assignments is an indication of tight financial discipline.[1] Mr Steel has laboriously analysed these phenomena on the receipt rolls and his tables reveal some striking differences between the reigns of Richard II, Henry IV, and Henry V:

	% Cash	% Assignment	% Fictitious loans of assignments issued
Richard II	41	41	14.25 for 1386-99
Henry IV	29.6	51.1	24.3 for 1399-1413
Henry V	54.8	31.7	12.6 for 1413-22

This steep rise in the proportion of assignments and fictitious loans in Henry IV's reign reveals a significant decline in real revenue, for although Henry IV issued broadly the same

[1] The system of assignment is described in the introduction to Steel's *Exchequer*, and the following table has been compiled from his appendix of tables, C 1-4, with the exception of column iii which I have calculated on the basis of his tables B 1-4 and D 1-4, to give equivalent periods for each reign. See also my article on 'Fictitious Loans', *Ec. HR*, 2nd ser. vii (1955), 197-9.

quantity of assignments as Richard II, they were now chasing a smaller amount of money and the competition to cash them was becoming fiercer. Influential creditors put pressure on the crown to give them preferential treatment, to the point where the crown's own claims were impeded and the exchequer thrown into confusion.

Henry IV's financial difficulties also produced complaint in parliament which came to a head in 1406 when the king was forced to surrender much of the direction of royal finances, and even grants of royal favours, to the council of which the Prince of Wales now became the nominal head. The ending of the Welsh revolt helped to ease the financial strain, and made possible much more stringent control of finances. The council now prepared estimates for the principal charges over a year or half a year, allocated fixed sums to them, appropriated taxes to the principal military needs, and drew up a clear scale of preferences, to ensure provision for the royal household, Calais, and the northern marches. Estimates were likewise prepared of income, and attempts made to increase the efficiency of revenue collection and reduce the number of annuities. Available revenue was allocated to expenditure within the accounting year and this enabled the exchequer to pay more of its creditors in cash and ensure that its assignments would be met. By these measures royal credit began to recover and criticism and opposition in parliament gradually subsided, as the Commons extended a grudging recognition to the council for its efforts towards financial solvency and control.[2]

The experience of grappling with what had, in 1406, become a crisis of confidence in royal credit, and of applying principles of budgetary control to royal expenditure, deeply influenced Henry V's own financial policy as King. Unfortunately the council minutes and memoranda are far less full for his reign than for the period of his administration as Prince, but they make clear that the practice of budgeting was continued. In February 1415, as planning for the Agincourt

[2] Evidence for fiscal planning and control is contained in *Proc. PC*, i, ii and in the warrants for issues, PRO, E 404. See Mr Edmund Wright's forthcoming Oxford D.Phil. thesis on royal finance in the period 1406–13.

expedition got under way, the treasurer of England was charged

to declare the state of his office and what revenues can be collected in the near future, and the state of the household, chamber, and wardrobe and of all the countries and marches here and overseas of which the king has to bear the charge, and also the debts incurred since his coronation, and the annuities; so that before departing the king can make provision according to the burden of each charge; and thus the king's conscience will be clear and he can set forth as a well ordered christian prince ('come prince chrétien bien governé') and so better accomplish his voyage to the pleasure of God and comfort of his lieges.

The treasurer certainly did his homework, producing in due course an elaborate assessment of the hereditary crown revenues and the customs and subsidies for the year commencing at midsummer, and the charges to be met for all the standing garrisons. The rest of the statement relating to the costs of the domestic departments does not survive. The only other surviving statement for 1421 is in more summary form, and is fragmentary. This too provides estimates of the hereditary revenues and the customs and subsidies for a year, and for the cost of Calais and other garrisons, the salaries of the royal bureaucracy, and the total sum due in annuities.[3] These two chance and imperfect survivals show that Henry's policy was guided by overall planning, and that this was held to be the mark of a 'prince bien governé'.

Even without these documents I think we would be able to deduce from the receipt rolls that the king was keeping a very firm control over expenditure. As we have seen, a far higher proportion of the exchequer's dealings were now in cash than had been the case even under Richard II; and the contrast with Henry IV's reign is particularly decisive and dramatic, as though Henry V was signalling his break from old practices. In the first two years of the reign the exchequer received £210,234 in cash and made assignment on only £14,301—a proportion of less than 7 per cent. This reflected orders, issued to all revenue collectors in 1413, to bring their receipts to the exchequer and pay no annuities or assignments. Exemptions from this were then introduced in favour of

---

[3] *Proc. PC*, ii, 148, 172–80, 312–14.

special creditors, and assignments were carefully matched to revenue. The use of tallies as purely promissory instruments ceased; they became creditworthy again and those who received them could expect to collect revenue at the specified time. Of course the system never worked perfectly, and fictitious loans occurred, but these fell to 12.6 per cent for the whole reign, slightly below the level in Richard II's and half that for Henry IV's.[4]

The restoration of exchequer credit was the necessary prelude to mobilizing its resources for war. The scale of Henry V's ambitions, and achievements, surpassed even those of Edward III; yet unlike his predecessor Henry was not backed by the extended credit network and vast financial resources of the great Italian banking houses. His expenditure was virtually limited by the taxation he could raise, for this provided the only security on which he could borrow from his subjects. He therefore had to make his subjects partners in his enterprise, and a further difference between war in the age of the Edwards and in that of the Henrys underlines this point. Before the middle of the fourteenth century kings could in varying measure exploit their prerogative right of purveyance to take victuals and materials for war on a large scale from their subjects at nominal cost; they even tried to summon men-at-arms and to array foot soldiers and archers for overseas service, equipped and partly paid for by local communities. But the restrictions imposed on these rights late in Edward III's reign meant that by the fifteenth century virtually all victuals and equipment had to be bought —usually from London merchants—while the wages of war had to be paid, at fixed rates, for six months in advance before the expedition sailed. This meant, therefore, that the exchequer had to accumulate a large store of cash in preparation for each campaign. For his two major expeditions Henry V did this on an almost unprecedented scale. In the year 1414–15 the exchequer received £104,000 in cash revenue and £27,000 in loans giving £131,000 available in cash. In 1416–17 its cash revenue was even larger: £110,000 with £51,000 in loans making a total of £161,000. These

[4] Steel, *Exchequer*, table C 4 and pp. 149–51; E 404/29/5, 91, 111, 114, 118–19, 131 and many others.

totals were only exceeded by the first year of Richard II's reign, in which a double subsidy was levied. The effort in these two years was extraordinary, but throughout the reign the lay and clerical subsidies were always received in cash, the inflow each Michaelmas term reaching £50-60,000 and rising to over £80,000 when the two great expeditions were being assembled. How different this pattern was from the preceding decades is clear from a glance at Steel's tables which show that in no single term since 1380 had cash receipts reached even £50,000.[5] Thus by mobilizing his cash resources, refusing to anticipate future revenue, and giving top priority to his war needs, Henry V managed to dispatch all three of his expeditions across the Channel more or less on time. That he successfully launched his armies and maintained the momentum of his campaigns is the best verdict on his financial policy. However, the narrow limits within which he was working were revealed when, in May 1415, it was found that there was insufficient money to pay the wages of the assembled troops for the second quarter. Commanders had to be given crown jewels as pledges for later payment, though in the event many of these were still being redeemed years after Henry's death. The same problem recurred in 1417, and on this occasion the second quarter's wages were paid from a total of £31,600 raised in loans from Bishop Beaufort and others on the security of the jewels.

Let us look briefly at these loans. For the three expeditions of 1415, 1417, and 1421 Henry V borrowed on a larger scale than at any time since Richard II's Irish expedition of 1394-5. Loans might be raised either by sending commissioners with royal letters to the gentry, churchmen, and communities in the shires, or by direct approach to important individuals and wealthy corporations. A widespread loan was neither a very efficient nor a very popular way of raising money and Henry used it only twice on a large scale, when he was straining every nerve to provide for the expeditions of 1417 and 1421. In 1417 he raised some £5,000 in this way, and in 1421 £9,000—almost certainly the most any

[5] Steel, *Exchequer*, tables B 1-4 and pp. 151, 156; *Foedera*, ix, 241, 272.

medieval king secured by this method. This was the fruit of his own journey through England in the crowded months of his last visit, in the spring of 1421, doing justice, visiting shrines, seeking recruits, and inducing people to lend. Such loans were not 'forced' in the sense of being compulsory; in theory they were freely given, although subjects were held to have a duty to assist the king for the common safety of the realm. Moreover subjects received no interest on their loans, though they could require good security for repayment, usually from the tax they would pay. But many always refused to lend and on this occasion, in 1421, no taxes had been granted. To raise such large sums Henry must have employed a mixture of personal persuasion and threat. Adam of Usk speaks bitterly of him 'rending every man throughout the realm who had money, be he rich or poor' and complains of the 'grievous taxation', 'accompanied with murmurs and smothered curses' of the people.[6] There are other signs of reluctance to lend as the reign wore on. A general loan authorized by parliament in 1419 yielded practically nothing—Henry himself was in France—and in 1421 the city of London, which had lent 10,000 marks in 1415 and 1417, would advance only £2,000. Many of those who lent in 1421 had little option, like Henry's new queen, Catherine. Henry certainly knew how to twist the screw on those who had money in hand. In 1415 he threatened the alien merchants in London with imprisonment unless they lent; in 1417 he was more subtle, offering to waive the high duties on their exports which parliament had just imposed, in consideration of a loan. But it was his uncle and chancellor, Henry Beaufort, bishop of the rich see of Winchester, who felt his hand hardest. When sent to the Council of Constance in 1417 to procure the election of a pope favourable to English interests, Beaufort deposited with the king a loan of £14,000. If this was intended as security for his good behaviour, Beaufort's acceptance of a cardinal's hat against Henry's wishes proved a costly miscalculation; for the king stopped repayment of his loan and exacted a further £17,666 13s. 4d. from him in 1421 as the price of his

---

[6] G. L. Harriss, 'Aids, Loans and Benevolences', *Hist. Jnl.*, vi (1963), 1–19; Usk, *Chronicon*, pp. 133, 320; *CPR, 1416–22*, p. 385.

restoration to royal favour. Although Beaufort was allowed to claim repayment from the customs in Southampton, he was still owed more than £20,000 from both his loans at the time of Henry's death.[7]

This was far from being the sum of Henry V's debt and default. The arrears of the wages for the Calais garrison totalled £28,710 by 1421, and were to provoke a mutiny in 1423; many of the captains who served on the Agincourt expedition were still owed wages for their second quarter (for which they held jewels), as were some who had the guard of fortresses in France, while in England the Earl of Northumberland claimed almost 10,000 marks for the keeping of the east march. These are all evidence of the strain which Henry's plans placed on his finances, particularly during the last three years of the reign. Yet Henry did not run up debts light-heartedly. Set beside the £200,000 in which Edward I was indebted after ten years campaigning in Scotland or the £300,000 which Edward III owed overseas in 1340 they are insignificant. Among Henry V's first acts had been the provision for the payment of all his father's household debts and of his own debts as Prince—all who had claims were invited to bring them to the exchequer for settlement. But these good intentions were overtaken by the demands of war, and at the end of his own reign many of his father's debts remained unpaid, and a sum of 40,000 marks was provided to discharge both these and his own.[8]

Thus Henry V made severe demands on his subjects and incurred substantial debts, and by 1420 there were signs of strain. But his indebtedness never produced a collapse in royal credit which frustrated his plans, or impaired his standing as a 'prince bien governé', as happened to Edward III, Henry IV, and Henry VI, and he bequeathed no legacy of financial chaos, as had Edward I. His wars undoubtedly stretched royal resources to the limit, but by careful planning,

[7] *CPR, 1416–22*, pp. 47, 67; *CCR, 1413–19*, pp. 312, 323; *Proc. PC*, ii, 165–6, 282–3; *CPR, 1413–16*, p. 364; *CPR, 1416–22*, p. 107; *CCR, 1413–19*, pp. 425, 430, 434. McFarlane, 'Henry V, Beaufort and the Red Hat'; G. L. Harriss, 'Cardinal Beaufort, Patriot or Usurer? ', *TRHS*, 5th ser. 20 (1970), pp. 129–48.

[8] For Calais, *Rot. Parl.* iv, 159 and Kirby, 'Financing of Calais'; for wages of war, *Rot. Parl.* iv, 247, 320 and *Proc. PC*, iii, 44, iv, 42, 254; for royal debts, *CCR, 1413–19*, pp. 17, 180 and *Rot. Parl.* iv, 172–3.

which gave priority to war needs, he had effectively concen-
trated and mobilized his resources to launch his expeditions.
And as debts and arrears began to accumulate the reputation
for careful husbandry and good credit which he had cultivated
from the very beginning of the reign bore the strain of the
financial and political tensions. At his death there was no
sign of financial or political collapse.

Let us now turn to the other side of royal finance, the
management and employment of the king's hereditary
revenues. As we have seen, the canons of good kingship
required the king to preserve and use his livelihood to support
his estate and household, reward his servants, and contribute
to the government and defence of the realm. He was at fault
if he dissipated his 'own' by prodigality, but he was equally
at fault if he unjustly used royal power to deprive his subjects
of their 'own' and reduce them to poverty. How did Henry V
measure up to this?

It is best to start with the crown lands, and more particularly with Henry's patrimony as Prince. From the moment
when he assumed direct command in Wales in 1403, he
initiated a systematic exploitation of the duchy of Cornwall
and the earldom of Chester, to offset the loss of his Welsh
revenues. In both alienated lands were resumed and the
demesnes brought under the close supervision of the prince's
council, which also introduced uniformity into the accounts.
In the duchy rents were increased by ten per cent in the
seven-yearly reviews made in 1406 and 1413, and in Chester
two exceptional taxes, or *mises*, were levied and annuities
paid from local revenues were substantially cut back. This
intensive pressure on Chester was relaxed after Henry
became king and henceforth it became increasingly integrated
with royal administration and contributed special taxes to
the king's expeditions and for the wages of the archers it
supplied.[9] As the Welsh rebellion faded and the lands of the
principality were brought under control and made to yield
revenue, a new generation of officials, with local knowledge

---

[9] Griffiths, 'Henry, Prince of Wales', pp. 56–82; A. Curry, 'Cheshire and the
Royal Demesne, 1399–1422', *Transactions of the Historic Society of Lancashire
and Cheshire*, 128 (1978), 115–26; John Hatcher, *Rural Economy and Society
in the Duchy of Cornwall, 1300–1500* (Cambridge, 1970), pp. 148–56.

and connections, was given the task of repairing its finances. Large compositions were levied on communities which had been in revolt and after Henry became king war taxes were introduced. The receipts from the chamberlains of North and South Wales rose spectacularly between 1409 and 1420.[10] This pattern of rigorous inquisition into seigneurial rights and regular conciliar scrutiny was likewise applied in the estates of the duchy of Lancaster. Within three months of Henry's accession commissions had been issued to inquire into the misdeeds and frauds of local officials of the duchy, some of whom were removed, while in the higher offices a clean sweep was made and men known and trusted by the king were appointed. In 1414 local receivers were summoned to come before the king at the Leicester parliament with their receipts and accounts. This general shake-up of the administration culminated in a special meeting of the duchy council in the king's presence in the Tower of London during February 1417, in which the fruit of these investigations was embodied in ordinances aimed at preventing fraud and waste, ensuring honest stewardship, and increasing the revenues. Even when he was abroad the king kept in constant touch with the duchy council which repeatedly made inquiry into the concealments of ducal rights and profits. A systematic reduction of the annuities paid from the duchy was achieved, from £9,000 under Henry IV to £5,000 in 1418-19, despite the fact that Henry recruited extensively from the duchy for his expeditions. Annuities were now paid only to those who actually accompanied the king or were engaged in the defence of the north. The result of these efforts was to increase the gross revenue of the duchy from an average of £14,600 p.a. under Henry IV to over £15,800 in the years 1418-19, while its clear yield rose from £2,500 p.a. under Henry IV to over £6,000 in

---

[10] R. A. Griffiths, 'Patronage, Politics and the Principality of Wales, 1413-61', in *British Government and Administration*, ed. H. Hearder and H. R. Loyn (Cardiff, 1974), p. 76. The chamberlains' accounts show a rise from some £500 p.a. each at the beginning of Henry IV's reign to an average over £1,800 p.a. in S. Wales and £1,300 p.a. in N. Wales over 1409-20. PRO, SC 6/1216/2, 3; SC 6/1222/10-13, 1223/1-4. The principality itself yielded only some £250 p.a. PRO, E 364/50, 64.

1418-19, as a result of the reduction in annuities.[11]

When Henry became king this pattern of investigation and resumption of royal rights, the systematic increase of revenues, and reduction of outgoings, was extended to most areas of crown revenue. Adam of Usk reports a series of measures which Henry took at the very beginning of his reign. 'He got large sums from the general pardon; in confirming annuities granted by his father he reserved the first year's yield to himself; the fees for patents of grants reissued at the beginning of the new reign were doubled; and all the Welsh and Irish were ordered home unless they bought permission to remain.'[12] This can be confirmed from the records. In his first parliament the king issued a general pardon to all who sued for it before Christmas, and further general pardons were granted in the parliaments of November 1414 and November 1416 in consideration of generous grants of taxes. Individuals could purchase the pardon, which covered a wide range of criminal offences and liabilities arising from the crown's fiscal prerogatives, for a standard fee of 16*s*. 4*d*. In 1413 pardons were purchased by some eight hundred subjects, in 1415 by almost five thousand, and these included Queen Joan, the Earl Marshal, and other nobility, churchmen and religious houses, urban and rural communities, and all manner of other individuals. Only a very small minority were hardened criminals, and though in a sense Henry can be accused of trading due punishment for financial gain, when combined with a vigorous policy of law enforcement a general pardon could contribute effectively both to the social peace and to royal revenue.[13] Already in his father's reign the prince had increased the revenue of the hanaper, the sealing office, from £470 to £1,200 p.a. by cancelling all exemptions from its fees and by reducing the annuities paid from it. Now, as King, he was determined to profit from the confirmation of his father's patents for

[11] Somerville, *Duchy of Lancaster*, i, 176-7, 183-9. The important ordinances of 1417 are in PRO, DL 42/17 fos. 174^V-175. For the exploitation of the Welsh estates of the duchy see R. R. Davies, 'Baronial Accounts, Incomes and Arrears in the Later Middle Ages', *Ec HR*, 2nd ser. xxi (1968), 211-29.

[12] Usk, *Chronicon*, p. 299.

[13] PRO, C 67/36, 37. See Dr Powell's discussion in chapter iii. Further pardons are in *CPR, 1416-22*, pp. 282-94 and *CCR, 1413-19*, pp. 278-80.

offices and annuities, and of charters to individuals and corporations. These are recorded on twenty-five closely written membranes of the Fine Roll for the first year of the reign. For some the charge was only 6*s*. 8*d*. or 13*s*. 4*d*., but others were set at much higher rates. The burgesses representing King's Lynn in this parliament reported that, whereas the ratification of borough charters used to be granted for ten marks or £10, now one hundred marks or £100 was asked, which they thought excessive.[14]

Parallel efforts to enlarge the revenue from the old crown lands had greater symbolic than fiscal significance. From the beginning of the reign increments were added to all farms of the ulnage, farms of alien priories, and leases of crown lands when these fell in for renewal. On the ulnage little more than a five per cent increase was achieved, raising the yield by only £200 p.a.; on farms of crown lands there was a ten per cent increase, even the smallest having a shilling or two added, though here again the total increase was trifling.[15]

More potentially profitable were the king's feudal prerogatives, for these were more flexible and larger sums were involved. Throughout the reign commissions were issued in different shires into concealments of the king's rights and dues, which doubtless provided an inducement for the purchase of pardons, since attempts to defraud the crown were heavily penalized. Composition for the king's rights over his greater tenants-in-chief had to be made personally with Henry V. In a previous chapter I mentioned the 10,000 marks which the Earl of March paid for his right of marriage and which nearly drove him into rebellion, and how the Countess of Oxford's lands were seized when she illegally married a young squire. With Joyce, daughter of Edward, lord of Powys, the king was taking no chances: she was bound by recognizance of 4,000 marks in 1421 not to marry without his licence. Death in battle brought many lands into

[14] N. Pronay, 'The Hanaper under the Lancastrian Kings', *Proceedings of the Leeds Philosophical and Literary Society*, xii (1967), 80; PRO, C 66/220; M. McKisack, *The Parliamentary Representation of English Boroughs during the Middle Ages* (Oxford, 1932), pp. 140–1.

[15] Calculations from the *Calendar of Fine Rolls*, vol. xiv. The farms of ulnage were raised from £758 p.a. to £958 p.a., those of alien priories from £1,431 p.a. to £1,630 p.a.

the king's hands and some of the larger were directly managed by royal officials. More often the marriages of royal wards and the custody of their lands were sold at realistic sums. This applied even to Henry's near relations: his sister-in-law, the Duchess of Clarence, yielded a whole year's income from Holderness to the king in order to retain it at farm after her husband's death, and Sir John Cornewaill, married to the king's aunt, paid 2,000 marks for the marriage of the heir of Sir John Arundell.[16] Vacancies in episcopal and abbatial sees likewise gave the temporalities into the king's hands. Henry was too conscientious a churchman to prolong these for the crown's profit—though for at least half the reign the papal schism gave him ample opportunity—but neither did he waive his rights. Chichester was vacant four times in the reign and on each occasion was farmed at the rate of 650 marks p.a., while Archbishop Chichele compounded for £400 when the temporalities of Canterbury were restored to him after a vacancy of three and a half months. St Mary's abbey in York yielded 100 marks for a two-month vacancy, and Westminster abbey was farmed at 800 marks.[17] These rates were not excessive and Henry conformed to the precepts of 'bone governance' in assigning the profits from reliefs, wardships, marriages, and temporalities to the expenses of his household. Through strict attention to royal rights and the steady exaction of royal dues the ancient revenues of the crown and the feudal profits rose from about £10,260 in 1406-7 to £15,210 in 1420-1.[18] That was not spectacular, but it was useful, and was important in showing that the king was making the best use of his 'own'. A more spectacular increase might have reflected a grasping and 'tyrannical' kingship, and that was not his model.

Far more lucrative than the hereditary crown revenues

[16] For commissions into concealments, see *CPR, 1413-16*, p. 224, *CPR, 1416-22*, pp. 296-315, 320, 328, 384, 422-3, 444; for Joyce, see *CCR, 1419-22*, pp. 207, 219-20; for Clarence and Cornewaill, see *Proc. PC*, ii, 334 and *CFR, 1413-22*, p. 420. For other sales of wardships and marriages, see *CFR, 1413-22*, pp. 288, 293, 325-6, 341, 355, 391, 393, 413, 435-7; *CPR, 1416-22*, pp. 215, 217-18, 249, 260, 296, 315, 340, 360, 375, 412, 443; *Cal. Signet Letters*, no. 864.

[17] *CFR, 1413-22*, pp. 12, 139, 173, 247, 354-5, 439; *CPR, 1416-22*, p. 403; PRO, E 28/30, 26 Jan.

[18] These figures represent the total of all receipts from these revenues on the receipt rolls, in cash and uncancelled assignments.

were the customs and subsidies on exports, notably of wool; indeed these were the bedrock of royal finance and upon their maintenance at a high level depended the prosecution of the war. The crown could seek to ensure this in two ways: it could take administrative measures to improve collection, and it could endeavour to maintain the flow of trade by controlling piracy and securing protection for traders by treaties. Within days of his accession Henry V ordered the provision of customs houses in every port where all wool had to be packed and all exports and imports assessed for payment. Hitherto this had too often been done in the merchants' own houses. Searchers in all ports were appointed regularly. He also notified the mayor and aldermen of London of his great desire to ensure free and safe passage of merchandise. The key to this was the Burgundian alliance. As Prince, Henry had cultivated this, and even in the period when he and John the Fearless were pursuing parallel but potentially competitive campaigns in France, from 1417 to 1419, the truces with the Four Members of Flanders were carefully maintained. In 1414 the Statute of Truces imposed severe penalties for piracy and though it was in a measure relaxed after 1416, the war against privateering continued, and the king insisted on the restitution of seizures from Flemish goods and shipping.[19] Wool exports were undoubtedly affected by the war, falling to below 10,000 sacks in 1419-20, their lowest hitherto; but before and after this the level averaged some 15,000 sacks, giving a gross yield of about £49,000 p.a., compared with £47,000 in the latter years of Henry IV.[20] Since the period saw an overall decline in wool exports, this was a significant achievement.

The efforts to increase crown revenues were matched by measures to reduce the charges upon them. By 1401 annuities from royal revenues had risen to £24,000 as Henry IV bought support right across the board in an effort to consolidate

[19] *CCR, 1413-19*, pp. 4, 6; *Proc. PC*, ii, 131, 186, 250-61; *CFR, 1413-22*, p. 245.
[20] E. M. Carus Wilson and O. Coleman, *England's Export Trade, 1275-1547* (Oxford, 1963), pp. 56-7; Sir J. H. Ramsay, *Lancaster and York* (Oxford, 1892), i, 151, 313.

the new dynasty. It was now safe to make a reduction in this total and be more selective about whom the crown retained. Henry's first parliament authorized the king to make a cut of £10,000 in annuities and apply this sum to the expenses of his household. It was a shrewd move, just what the Commons had been asking for ten years earlier; but it was not window-dressing as Henry IV's proposal in 1404 for a year's restraint on annuities had largely been. Orders were at once sent to all local revenue collectors to pay no annuities and to bring all their receipts to the exchequer where payment could be made on such annuities as the king sanctioned. Future pay-ment of an annuity was only to be had by a special writ, dispensing from the general preference given to the king's £10,000, which was available only to those who rendered service to the crown. For each royal expedition all who wished to retain their annuities were required to accompany the king.[21] Even stricter limitations were placed on annuities from the customs and subsidies. When they granted Henry the wool subsidies for life, in 1415, the Commons stipulated that no annuities should be paid from these, and the king appears to have respected this. Payment from the ancient customs had often to be authorized by the king's letters. As a result of these measures annuities had, by 1421, been reduced to £12,000 p.a., half the figure under Henry IV. At the same time a careful watch had been kept on the accumulation of grants by individuals, and anyone who petitioned for a grant of land or revenue was required to list all those he already enjoyed.[22]

The king's attempts to cut the perpetual seepage of revenue in the crown's overseas dependencies were less successful. Calais, Gascony, and Ireland should each have contributed to their own upkeep, though they would never be self-financing. An act in Henry V's first parliament deplored the wasteful disposal of revenues and offices at Calais under previous kings, and abolished these grants. A new treasurer of Calais,

---

[21] *Proc. PC*, i, 154; *Rot. Parl.* iv, 5 (10). Numerous warrants and dispensations will be found in *CCR, 1413–19 Cal. Signet Letters*, E 404/29–32, and E 28/34–6. See also *Proc. PC*, ii, 215, 308, 334.

[22] *Rot. Parl.* iv, 63; E 404/37/105; *Proc. PC*, ii, 313–14; E 28/30 18 Jan. 1415, E 28/31, 5 and 23 May 1415.

Roger Salvayn, was appointed, and next year the Earl of Arundel went in person to pay the garrison's £11,000 arrears and to conduct an inquiry into tenures and embezzlement by the victualler. Whatever abuses this uncovered, it resulted in no permanent increase in local revenues, and when Salvayn died in 1420 the garrison's arrears stood at £28,718. A deputation to the parliament of December 1421 warned of the danger of mutiny, and in February 1422 the council, having examined the treasurer's accounts, allocated 16s. 8d. of the wool subsidy for the next two years to discharge the debt. With the threat of war removed, trade with Flanders improving, and a mint established in the town to enforce payment in bullion, a further commission was sent to Calais to inquire into the usurpation of royal rights and revenues and fresh regulations drawn up vesting the grant of lands and offices in Calais solely in the treasurer. But Henry V's death followed within a matter of months, and in April 1423 the garrison, despairing of payment, came out in revolt.[23] Henry initially took the same line over Gascon revenues. In June 1413 he ordered an inquiry into the excessive gifts and concessions made by his predecessors from the revenues of the duchy, and the constable of Bordeaux was ordered to resume all these into the king's hands and apply them to the costs of defence. But such grants proved necessary to retain Gascon loyalties and the revenues of the duchy continued to decline throughout the reign.[24] In Ireland, the replacement of the Duke of Clarence by Sir John Stanley at the beginning of the reign enabled Henry V to fulfil his long-standing purpose of reducing the charge upon the English exchequer. Before 1406 this had been running at £6,000 p.a. and more, and in 1408 it had been cut to 7,000 marks. Now, in 1413, a further reduction was proposed, to a mere £2,000, and this took effect during the lieutenancy of Stanley's successor John Talbot (1414-20). It was intended to match this with a resumption and exploitation of Irish revenues, but Talbot's

[23] *Rot. Parl.* iv, 13, 159; for the commissions of inquiry, see PRO, acquisition 30/26/184-5, E 101/187/3, 4, and *Proc. PC*, ii, 310, 317, 363-7. A previous attempt to clear arrears and make provision for Calais was made in February 1417. See *Proc. PC*, ii, 212, 214, 217 and in general Kirby, 'Financing of Calais'.

[24] M. G. Vale, *English Gascony, 1399-1453* (Oxford, 1970), pp. 204-5 and table 5 on p. 236.

vigorous military campaigns and lack of personal resources in the lordship led him to incur debts, make unpopular exactions, and alienate crown lands to buy support. It is doubtful if Irish revenues were effectively increased. When the Earl of Ormond succeeded Talbot in February 1420 the policy was carried a stage further. Not only was his salary further reduced, to 2,500 marks, but after one initial English payment of 1,250 marks this was to be a charge on the Irish exchequer, only to be supplemented from England on certification of the insufficiency of Irish resources. Ormond undertook a systematic review of these and did for the two years 1420-2, succeed in raising Irish revenue to a level where it was sufficient to sustain him without recourse to England. Henry V came nearer to making Ireland pay for itself than any king for the past sixty years.[25]

The picture that has emerged of Henry V's financial administration is of an ubiquitous and vigorous attempt to improve the collection of crown revenue, increase its yield, and ensure that it was spent effectively. Not all these measures were successful. In some cases the increases in revenue were hardly commensurate with the effort, and in others fiscal reforms were frustrated by the needs of politics and war. But much was achieved, and in a short space the tempo of government was changed. We are so accustomed to the idea that late medieval kings, and the Lancastrians in particular, were too weak or too negligent to collect their fiscal dues, that the similarity with the methods of the 'New Monarchy' comes as something of a surprise. Henry VII's meticulous attention to detail and personal interest in his finances has been seen as unaccustomed, even unprecedented, for a medieval king, and his examination of the chamber accounts, which he annotated and signed in his own hand, has elicited much admiring comment. Chamber accounts do not exist for Henry V's reign, though as the treasurer of the chamber

---

[25] I am indebted to Mrs Elizabeth Matthew for permission to draw on her paper, given at a symposium at Reading in 1983, on 'The Financing of the Lordship of Ireland under Henry V and Henry VI', to be published in *Property and Politics: Essays in Late Medieval History*, ed. A. Pollard (forthcoming). See also J. Otway-Ruthven, *A History of Medieval Ireland* (London, 1968), pp. 347-61; J. F. Lydon, *The Lordship of Ireland in the Middle Ages* (London and Dublin, 1972), pp. 191-4, 217-29, 246-50.

was directly and solely accountable to the king it is all too likely that Henry VII's practice was traditional. Certainly Henry V regularly inspected the duchy of Lancaster valors. But more than that, we know from the chance jotting by the clerk of the council that on his return to France in 1421—and remember that he was returning to repair the catastrophe of Baugé, with his mind set on stabilizing and enlarging the conquest—the king found time to examine the accounts of the keeper of the great wardrobe, John Spencer, who had died four years earlier. Now these were not the king's personal finances, as was the chamber, and such accounts were habitually audited at the exchequer. Nevertheless, the king had totted and signed them with his own hand, instructing the auditors to make diligent inquiry and report on those matters against which the king had set in the margin the words 'ad inquirendum', and others which he had marked with a black dot.[26] If I had to choose one illustration of Henry V's practice of kingship, this would be it. Nothing escaped him; he maintained a continuous and personal control over the details of government, at one moment giving his fullest attention to such, and at the next to the unfolding and realization of his most ambitious schemes. No moments were wasted, all could be filled to good effect, and he probably sought little relaxation from the business of kingship because he found fulfilment in it.

Undoubtedly he was as business-like as Henry VII, but there the comparison ends. For he was not just a man of business. He had no pleasure in money, in accumulating or hoarding it. It gave him no sense of safety or power, for his security and authority were based on his relations with his subjects. He gathered money in order to spend it. How much he had in his chamber we do not know, though a tantalizingly undated letter from his officers in Harfleur reveals that there alone he had stored £30,000 in gold coins, and £2,000 in silver, with blocks of silver weighing half a 'ton-tight', while at his death his personal accoutrements—

---

[26] *Proc. PC*, ii, 290; Steel, *Exchequer*, p. 164. Spenser's enrolled account is in PRO, E 361/1 m. 11ᵛ.

not money—were valued at £18,400.[27] His style of life was neither parsimonious nor prodigal. The chroniclers repeatedly note that his immediate entourage was small, but also insist that he could appear royally apparisoned and with commanding dignity when the occasion demanded. His diplomatic meetings did not have the ostentatious extravagance of the Field of the Cloth of Gold, which outraged even Henry VIII's contemporaries, but at different times the Emperor Sigismund and Charles VI and his queen were royally entertained at his expense. Even for the reception of the French and Burgundian ambassadors at the Leicester parliament a sum of £2,600 was provided. Such expenses were mainly borne by the king's chamber, into which were paid the revenues from the duchy of Lancaster and probably the king's own profits of war. But this personal wealth was devoted to his political and military aims. We are told that after the Treaty of Troyes he paid the wages of the Burgundian administration in Paris from his own coffers and the accounts of the treasurer of war for the king's final year record £21,000 received from the chamber.[28]

That suggests a final comparison with the practices of the Yorkist and Tudor kings. Although Henry V used his chamber as a spending department under his personal control, he never relegated the exchequer to a subordinate role. The confusion into which royal finance had sunk under Henry IV might have given ground for a change. Henry V made none, not because he was indolently conservative but because he knew that the existing system could be made to work. He retained the financial system evolved in the preceding century in which the exchequer was the central agency for national finance. By budgeting and a strict control of priorities, by reducing assignments and ensuring that they were made upon actual revenue, by increasing the hereditary revenues and reserving taxes for the payment of wages of war, Henry V showed that the financial machinery of the late medieval

[27] I have been unable to trace the original letter printed in *Original Letters Illustrative of English History*, ed. Sir H. Ellis, ser. ii (London, 1827), p. 83; *Rot. Parl.* iv, 242.

[28] *Gesta*, p. 113; E 28/30 12 Dec. 1414 (costs of the ambassadors); *First English Life*, p. 174; Wylie and Waugh, *Henry the Fifth*, iii. 390–1.

State could furnish the means to fight a major war without plunging royal finances into confusion, as had happened in the reigns of Edward I and III and of his own father. He did indeed die leaving debts, but not outrageous ones; nor is there any indication that his plans were at any juncture delayed or inhibited by lack of money.

That brings me back to the point I made at the start of this chapter: that money is the instrument of policy. Both as Prince and King, Henry's revenues were spent mainly on war. To us that may seem immoral or irresponsible, a betrayal rather than a fulfilment of statecraft. The medieval view was quite the reverse. Although a king should not fight to gain wealth, he was bound to fight to defend the rights of his crown, and the safety and property of his people. Henry's just rights, as Prince of Wales, Duke of Normandy, and Heir of France were only to be obtained at the point of the sword. For this purpose he could with justice and rigour exact the crown's lawful dues from his subjects and his claim upon their wealth through taxation was the more compelling for his readiness to contribute so largely of his own. His financial policy was thus of a piece with the rest of his practice of kingship; he could give his people 'bone governance', because he himself was a 'prince bien governé'.

IX

Diplomacy

MAURICE KEEN

Although the title given to this chapter is 'diplomacy', what I am really going to talk about are treaties—which traditionally are the diplomatically negotiated alternative to war in international affairs and confrontations. The Hundred Years War produced many minor treaties, and two great ones, the Treaty of Brétigny of 1360 and the Treaty of Troyes of 1420.[1] Each, as it happened, marked a moment of flood-tide in English success in the wars. Each equally represented an important effort to put an end to the confrontation between England and France, which had caused the Hundred Years War and was older than it was, by a settlement which, it was hoped, would allow reasonably for the aspirations of both English and French. The two treaties represent respectively two different approaches to the problems at issue between the two kingdoms. Brétigny proposed a substantial dismemberment of the territories that formed the kingdom of France, ceding to the English in full sovereignty, independent of the French crown, wide territories in the south-western provinces that had traditionally been subject, in some degree or other, to that crown, so leaving to the Valois French kings a diminished inheritance. Troyes, Henry V's treaty, made a clean different approach: the crown of France was not to be dismembered and the bounds of the kingdom would remain much as they had traditionally been; but the Valois heir would be disinherited in favour of a Plantagenet who would marry a Valois princess and secure the inheritance to a Plantagenet-Valois line. In both cases the central problem was the same: would the settlement—could the settlement—be made acceptable to the French? Did it allow for their

---

[1] *Foedera*, vi, 219–228 (Brétigny); ix, 895–904 (Troyes).

aspirations sufficiently reasonably to put a stop to the fighting, at least semi-permanently?

I am going to commence by discussing the first of these treaties, Edward III's Treaty of Brétigny. This may seem irrelevant to a student of Henry V; but I shall have to mention Henry V many times, and for good reason. The Treaty of Brétigny was a settlement with a good deal more importance, and a wider potential frame of relevance, than those of the immediate circumstances in which it was agreed in 1360. Indeed it was still highly relevant to the diplomacy of the early years of Henry V's reign.

Before examining this treaty, I would like to say an introductory word about the nature of diplomacy, as I conceive it. Diplomacy is an art inevitably related to the circumstances of a particular moment. If one uses the Aristotelian definition of an art as a capacity of doing something well, it is the art of *realpolitik*, and artistry in it must be in conformity with the limits of its material, which are the exigencies of the immediate situation, available force, possible combinations, and so on. But diplomacy demands artistry in *realpolitik* in another way too, for it is—or at least it was by the fourteenth century and has been ever since—a professional business. What I mean to say is that its solutions must not only conform to the *realpolitik* exigencies of a situation, but must also be *presentable* (I think that is the best word) in terms of the ideas of international law, natural justice, and international custom prevalent at the time. It is not just a matter of calculating in the arithmetic of power, but more like moves on a chess-board. The moves, and especially the taking of pieces, must follow the rules: they must be made to *look* right, and whether justifiable or not must be made to look justifiable to reasonably independent onlookers, who in the game of diplomacy are always about. That is where it calls most sharply for professional expertise.

About the Treaty of Brétigny I want initially to make two points, both of which arise out of the fact that, as a settlement, it proved abortive. Part of the reason for this was a matter of *realpolitik*, and this is my first point. The treaty was made at a moment when French fortunes were at a terrible ebb, in the aftermath of Poitiers, when the French king had been made prisoner and his kingdom had been distraught by the *Jacquerie* and the revolt of the 'children of Navarre'. These were short-term conditions, whose effect was to give the French very little alternative to agreeing to the terms of the treaty: but the central element in the settlement, the cession to the English of an enlarged Aquitaine as a sovereign principality, was not in the long run acceptable to the French kings, nor was it sufficiently clearly in the interest of all the inhabitants of the new principality (though it was very acceptable to some of them, notably the citizens of Bordeaux and Bayonne). The other part of the reason why the treaty proved abortive—and this is my second point and the one that I want to stress for a moment—is that the treaty was not juridically watertight: that is to say, it was not only inadequately conceived in terms of *realpolitik*, but also insufficiently well drafted. The result was that the French were able to claim, at the first moment that suited them, that it was not binding.

The facts here have now become familiar. At a late stage in negotiations an essential part of the treaty, the formal and final renunciations, by the English and French respectively of the claim to the crown of France on the one hand and the sovereignty over Aquitaine on the other, were cut out of the main treaty, and postponed (so as to ensure that all the territorial adjustments agreed had actually taken place before the renunciations were made).[2] In the event, and as a consequence of their being taken out of the main treaty, the renunciations were never made (whether through the fault of the French or the English remains a matter of debate). As a result, Charles V was able to claim in 1369 that, since he had never renounced sovereignty in Aquitaine, he was entitled to hear in his court the complaints of the Gascon lords against their *seigneur*, the Black Prince. Because it was a fact that, since the sealing of the treaty, Edward III had ceased to use the title of King of France and also that the

---

[2] R. Delachenal, *Histoire de Charles V*, (Paris, 1909-31), ii, 242-50; P. Chaplais, Some Documents regarding the Fulfilment of the Treaty of Brétigny', in *Camden Miscellany XIX* (1952), pp. 5-8; and see J. Le Patourel, 'The Treaty of Brétigny, 1360', *TRHS*, 5th Series, 10 (1960), 19-39, especially 37-9.

French king had ceased to exercise sovereign rights in Aquitaine, there was a delicate legal question in issue here, and Charles did not make his claim without taking professional advice. Christine de Pisan, in her biography of the king, tells us that he consulted carefully, before taking the final step, with the jurists of Bologna, that famous centre of jurisprudential learning.[3] Charles was not the only one to consult lawyers, either. Pierre Chaplais has printed the advice that was offered by two Bolognese jurists, John of Legnano and Richard of Saliceto, to the consuls of Millau and Rodez, who were concerned because their cities lay in the Black Prince's territories, over which now both he and Charles were simultaneously claiming sovereignty.[4] With a wealth of legal reasoning and due citation of key passages from the Digest and its glosses, the two professors (who were almost certainly those who had advised Charles also) concluded that the King of France was entitled to claim sovereignty, in spite of the Treaty of Brétigny. It followed that that treaty was abortive, because unfulfilled, and that legally the status quo ante was in force, and that Gascony was dependent on the French crown in the way that had been made clear in the terms of the Treaty of Paris of 1259. The opinions of John and Richard were copied out and served up, with their implications clarified, as erudite propaganda in that great royalist text of Charles V's court circle, the *Songe du Verger*.[5] Of course these were only opinions; the English view was quite different. Nevertheless, the whole incident indicates and illustrates the importance of professionalism in diplomacy in the period. It also helps to explain why every English embassy, of Henry V's time and before, included among its named personnel experts in civil law, such as Honyngham, Ware, Kemp, and Philip Morgan—the last of whom we see in Henry V's reign leading the negotiations for the English at Alençon, and rising to be chancellor of Normandy and Bishop of Worcester. Diplomatic professionalism was already part of an established career structure.

[3] C. de Pisan, *Le Livre des fais et bonnes moeurs du sage Roy Charles V*, ed. S. Solente (Paris, 1936–40), ii, 119.
[4] Chaplais, *Camden Miscellany XIX*, pp. 58–78.
[5] See Chaplais, pp. 56–7.

I hope that the moral of the events that I have been rehearsing is clear. They illustrate just how important it was, in the late middle ages, that treaties should be well drafted, so that their terms should have a chance of *sticking*; so that it should be as hard as possible to find, as circumstances changed (and circumstances always do) loopholes that would justify discarding solemnly sealed rolls of parchment as 'scraps of paper'. *Realpolitik*, in other words, if it was to reach its end, had to be reinforced with all the skill of professionalism to protect its settlements against the new *realpolitik* of changed circumstances. The propaganda purposes to which the French put the learned opinions of John of Legnano and Richard of Saliceto, professors of Bologna, is a useful illustration of the respect in which juridical professionalism, in the context of treaties, was held in the period.

There is one further point that must be made about the Treaty of Brétigny. It may have been abortive: that does not mean that it was unimportant, or that the main treaty was particularly ill drafted. It represented a real effort to find a settlement, and it gave France and England nine years of peace with one another. In doing just that, it came nearer to providing a lasting settlement than any other treaty that the war threw up, the Treaty of Troyes included. In consequence, it remained important, even after it was abrogated unilaterally by the French, and especially after it became clear (after 1374) that they would not be able to carry that abrogation the whole way through—that they would not be able to re-establish the legal status quo ante, and force the English to accept that Gascony was a fief of the French crown. Because the English and French remained formally at war, and because it remained the nearest thing to a settlement that had been achieved in the great confrontation of Plantagenet and Valois, the shape of its terms continued to dominate Anglo-French diplomatic exchanges from the end of Edward III's reign to the end of Henry IV's, and to a substantial degree into the reign of Henry V. From the time of the discussions in the presence of the papal mediators at Bruges in 1374–5, through Richard II's reign, down to the 'Treaty' of Bourges in 1412 and into Henry V's reign, the great diplomatic query remained the same: what would the

French be willing to offer in Aquitaine, and could the English accept it.[6] Boundaries, and terms of tenure of lands to be ceded to the English in the south-west, remained the crucial issues. The French, after 1369, remained consistently unwilling to offer lands in full sovereignty: the English, equally, were never prepared to accept less as the basis of a final settlement. Various expedients were explored: the grant of Aquitaine as a fief to a cadet of the Plantagenet line (John of Gaunt became duke in the 1390s, and the question of whether he might hold the duchy by liege homage of the French king was explored, but fell foul of Gascon resistance): a long truce, perhaps combined with a dynastic marriage (this was the solution attempted in 1396, when Richard and Charles VI were drawing closer, and Richard took the infant Isabella of France as his second bride);[7] a smaller sovereign Aquitaine (which is what the French princes who had joined the Duke of Orléans in league against the Duke of Burgundy were prepared for in 1412).[8] This last offer was the best, from an English point of view, that the French made over the whole period, and they would not have made it but for the civil war that had broken out in France after Duke John of Burgundy had murdered Duke Louis of Orléans in 1407. The fact that in 1412 French princes of the blood were prepared to offer this much was important for Henry V.

* * *

I have said that the terms of Brétigny dominated exchanges over the period from the 1370s to the accession of Henry V; they really did, and that was how it came to be commonly known at the time as 'the great peace'. Aquitaine and the south-west was its focus. The English claim to Normandy as part of the ancestral inheritance of their kings, which had been under review at the time of the (abortive) Treaty of Guînes of 1354 and when the second (abortive) Treaty of

---

[6] On the Bruges negotiations, see E. Perroy, 'The Anglo-French Negotiations at Bruges, 1374-7', in *Camden Miscellany XIX* (1952), Introd., especially pp. xvi-xix; on the Bourges treaty, see M. G. A. Vale, *English Gascony, 1399-1453* (Oxford, 1970), pp. 59-62.

[7] For further discussion of these negotiations see J. J. N. Palmer, *England, France and Christendom* (London, 1972), pp. 142-63, 166-78.

[8] Vale, op. cit., pp. 59-60.

London was drafted in 1359, was not mentioned at Brétigny, and was more or less out of sight thereafter, until 1413.[9] No one in that long interim expected more than the English claims in the south-west to come under discussion. This is what marks a sharp break in diplomatic history at the beginning of Henry V's reign. From the first, or from very early on anyway, Henry in diplomacy is found raising quite new issues—new in the sense that they raised matters not touched on in the 'great peace'. I suppose they might more properly be called old issues, newly raised. The instructions that he gave to his ambassadors in 1414 and 1415 bid them bring into the picture English rights in Normandy, Maine, Anjou, Touraine, parts of Provence, Nogent, and Beaufort, each of which claims had an ancient history of its own (that to Normandy going back to William the Conquerer; Maine, Anjou, and Touraine to Henry II's inheritance from his father Geoffrey; and the Provençal claims to the rights of Henry III's wife, Eleanor of Provence).[10] Having raised these claims initially, Henry V was never afterwards prepared to back away from them toward the limits of what his great-grandfather had gained by the 'great peace', except on two occasions, and then only temporarily: once in 1415, and once in 1416 when he was anxious to demonstrate his moderation to the Council of Constance and to Emperor Sigismund.[11] I do not see any reason to suppose that on either occasion his objective was more than tactical: he consistently wanted more than had been ceded at Brétigny and meant to get it.

Henry V was able to press for more than his father or Richard II or Edward III in his later years could ever dream of obtaining because of a new situation in France. In 1407 retainers of John the Fearless had murdered Louis of Orléans

[9] On the negotiations of 1353-4 see K. Fowler, *The King's Lieutenant: Henry of Grosmont, First Duke of Lancaster* (London, 1969), pp. 113-14, 129-30, 135-8: on the 'second treaty' of London, 1359, see Delachenal, *Charles V*, ii, 80-3, and Le Patourel, *TRHS*, 10 (1960), 28-31.

[10] *Foedera*, ix, 209-15.

[11] *Foedera*, ix, 212 (1415); ix, 786 (recapitulating 1416); and on the manœuvres of 1416 see further Wylie and Waugh, *Henry the Fifth*, iii, 15, and references there cited. I suspect Henry's moderation in 1415 was similarly tactical, to gain time to launch the Agincourt expedition and to impress observers, especially the Fathers of Constance, with his reasonableness.

under cover of dark in the streets of Paris, and by 1410 his party and that of Louis' son, Charles of Orléans, were moving toward armed confrontation, forcing their fellow princes in France to take sides. In the circumstances it was inevitable that both parties should look to England for support, for each knew that if they did not the other would. In 1411, when Prince Henry was effective chief of his father's council, the English and Burgundians were close, and an English force under the Earl of Arundel and Sir John Oldcastle was dispatched to France: they distinguished themselves in the fighting near Paris, at St Cloud. In 1412, after the *putsch* which ousted the prince and the Beauforts from the council, the Armagnacs got the better reception, and their exchanges with the English led to that Treaty of Bourges which I have already mentioned. The French princes leagued against Burgundy agreed to recognize Henry IV's just title to the duchy of Aquitaine, without any mention of French sovereignty: in return, they were promised military support, and an expeditionary force larger than that of 1411 was mustered under the Duke of Clarence. Clarence sailed for France and might have achieved something substantial there, but for the cessation of hostilities agreed by the French princes at the 'pacification' of Auxerre. The cessation was only temporary, however, and all through Henry V's reign the struggle between the parties in France continued, intermittently. Through the first six years of his reign, down to 1419, whichever side was in greater difficulties could be relied on to bid importantly for his support.

In 1414, when the civil wars reached a new peak of ferocity and Charles VI unfurled the *Oriflamme* against John of Burgundy, the duke was ready to go a long way to secure military aid, until the peace of Arras relieved the pressure on him.[12] In 1416 again, when it was imperative for him to forestall any possibility of an alliance of Henry, Sigismund, and Charles VI against him, he was anxious at the great summit meeting at Calais to give the impression of being complaisant towards the English, who seem even to have entertained hopes that he might recognize Henry as King of

---

[12] See R. Vaughan, *John the Fearless* (London, 1966), pp. 205-7.

France.[13] In 1418, when John had secured Paris, his enemies the Armagnacs were ready to discuss a possible alliance with Henry, on the basis of a division of the spoils to be won in Burgundian territory.[14] Every twist and turn of fortune in the French civil wars was an opportunity for Henry, and he exploited the opportunities with skill, and to the full.

Essentially, what Henry needed to do, during the period when his army was overrunning Normandy, was to keep the French parties in a situation where they preferred to look to him in the hope of triumph over their rivals, rather than fall back on their natural alliance, as Frenchmen, against the 'ancient adversary' of France. So successful was he, that in the summer of 1419 he was near a new measure of victory. John the Fearless and Queen Isabella came in June of that year to Meulan to discuss in earnest terms much more generous than those Edward III had won at the 'great peace', which would give England Normandy in full sovereignty as well as Aquitaine, the settlement to be sealed by a dynastic marriage alliance between Henry and the Valois princess Catherine of France.[15] Just how serious the French were is revealed in a letter written by Queen Isabella to Henry in September, when the situation had changed, which also explains why a settlement was not reached. 'Although the offers that you then made were agreeable enough to us, there was nevertheless great difficulty in the way of accepting them and concluding with you, for at the time all were advising that we should incline to our son (the Dauphin, who was with the Armagnacs); and if we and our own said cousin (Duke John) had accepted the terms and concluded on them, all the lords, knights, cities and good towns would have abandoned us and joined with our said son; whence even greater war would have arisen.'[16] The French parties were more concerned with their position *vis-à-vis* one another than with the English threat.

All through the period down to September 1419, while

---

[13] See Vaughan, pp. 213–15, and references there cited.
[14] *Proc. PC*, ii, 350–8; *Foedera*, ix, 628–31, 632–45.
[15] *Foedera*, ix, 761–4, 775–6, 788–90; and see Wylie and Waugh, *Henry the Fifth*, iii, 160–70.
[16] G. Du Fresne de Beaucourt, *Histoire de Charles VII* (Paris, 1881), i, 187.

Henry was seeking (or was at least assumed by most men to be seeking) a settlement on the Brétigny lines that would grant him territories (preferably a good deal more extensive than those ceded in 1360) in full sovereignty, the records show repeatedly how important the professional and technical aspects of negotiations were. Henry was demonstrably aware of their significance. English negotiators were always armed with carefully referenced arguments about the 'great peace' and what it had given the English, and about other claims arising out of it, for example the unpaid arrears of King John the Good's ransom. The 'great peace', buttressed by the Treaty of Bourges of 1412, provided a splendid basis for diplomatic propaganda; and in 1415, on the eve of sailing on the Agincourt expedition, Henry dispatched copies of the Bourges agreement to the emperor and to the Council of Constance, 'so that all Christendom should know of the injuries that the duplicity of the French had inflicted on him'.[17] In his personal letter to Tiptoft at Constance, written on 25 January 1417 to explain the proposals for a settlement mooted to him by his prisoner, the Duke of Bourbon, Henry showed he had the documents to hand: 'and Tiptoft, ye shall understand that the lands [to be ceded] been named by him also, much as is comprehended within the Great Peace, in the form as they be therein comprehended; and Harfleur with as much of Normandy that lieth next to it as I will agree me; and all holden in the form as the Peace maketh mention'.[18] Henry and his advisers knew the texts, knew their technical implications, and understood the rules of the game. The council's *aide-mémoire* of 1418, preparatory to instructing the embassy that would meet the Armagnacs at Alençon, perhaps best illustrates their professionalism. It opens by rehearsing the *realpolitik* grounds for treating: unless agreement could be reached there was no foreseeable end to war; holding Normandy with paid forces was already proving an excessive expense, which fell principally on England; and so on; and 'for all these causes . . . it were as well to take the shortest way, stinting of war and shedding of Christian

---

[17] *Gesta*, p. 16.
[18] *Foedera*, ix, 428.

blood'.[19] But the difficulties of making an alliance with the Dauphin and the Armagnacs had to be considered. Was the Dauphin of sufficient age to make an alliance? What security could be obtained that an alliance with him would be ratified in due course by the King of France? Would an alliance with him compromise Henry's claim to the crown of France? What would the legal situation be if, after an alliance had been agreed, John the Fearless should offer to do homage to Henry: would the king be entitled to receive his homage? The French showed the same concern with legal technicalities, as witness the debate in Burgundy's council, before the meeting at Meulan in 1419, with Rapiout and Rolin putting the arguments as technical experts: could the cession of Normandy be legally justified, they asked?[20] Since sovereignty would be alienated, it would dismember the crown of France: had Duke John, as the king's lieutenant, the right to alienate in such a degree? Concern with expert and technical points was common ground to English and French alike.

Henry V did succeed in keeping the warring factions in France apart, and did, in consequence, come close to achieving a settlement on the lines of Brétigny but still more generous to the English. John the Fearless and Queen Isabella would not have come to Meulan in person in June 1419 and they would not have brought Princess Catherine with them if they had not intended to do business in earnest with Henry, and they cannot have expected that he would be satisfied with anything less than Aquitaine 'in the form as it is comprehended in the great peace' and Normandy in full sovereignty. The fact remains that Henry did not achieve such a settlement. When it came to the point, John and Isabella found not that *Henry* could not accept the terms proposed (though his lack of moderation in his demands was unhelpful), but that *they* could not accept them themselves, as the queen's subsequent letter explained. Desperate as the military situation was from the point of view of the Burgundian party in the summer of 1419, it was not desperate enough for its leaders to hope that they could maintain their credit if they allowed themselves

[19] *Proc. PC*, ii, 351.
[20] P. Bonenfant, *Du meutre de Montereau au traité de Troyes*, (Brussels, 1958), p. 14 n. 1.

to acquiesce in such a dismemberment of the territories of the crown of France as was proposed, even with their own followers. It seemed better to turn to the only possible alternative, to seek an alliance to resist the English with the Dauphin and the Armagnacs, even though the blood of the leaders of that party and of their kinsmen and colleagues cried so loud for vengeance on John of Burgundy as to render such an accommodation wholly unnatural.

The Burgundians' temporary success in forging this alliance with the Armagnacs (by the Treaty of Pouilly) put Henry's achievement in greater peril than it had been at any earlier point, for it threatened·to present him with an enduring commitment to war in France that would strain and almost inevitably overstrain his English resources—which were all he could count on to maintain the struggle, now that his French enemies were united. 'Fair cousin, we wish you to know that we will have the daughter of your King, and all that we have asked,' he said in his last words to John the Fearless; 'or we will drive him and you out of his kingdom.' 'Sire, you may be pleased to say so,' John replied, 'but before you can drive my lord and me out of his kingdom, I make no doubt that you will be heartily tired.'[21] John was right; Henry was on the point of having overreached himself, of being unable to force a peace on his terms, and unable equally to sustain indefinite war.

He was saved from this dilemma not by his own skill, but because the alliance of Burgundy and Armagnac really was too unnatural, and because the blood of Louis of Orléans, Bernard of Armagnac, Henri de Marle, and countless others did cry too loud for vengeance. When on 10 September Duke John was murdered by the Dauphin's men on the bridge of Montereau, whither he had gone to solemnly meet his new allies, the whole situation, military and diplomatic, was changed overnight. The murder precipitated a situation in which the Burgundians under their new duke Philip had no real alternative to allying with the English, since if they did not they were effectively bound to lose Paris to Henry and likely to lose control of the court to the Dauphin, and further

[21] Monstrelet, *Chronique*, iii, 321-2.

to run the risk of being isolated between two enemies who could not be relied upon not to make common cause. The terms on which they had to do so were however entirely outside the Brétigny tradition, which had conceived of settlement in terms of the cession of French lands to the English king in full sovereignty, and which had dominated diplomacy in the Anglo-French confrontation for over sixty years. Henry had now come into the open with a new set of *realpolitik* objectives, which would set his draughtsmen new problems in the art of Anglo-French treaty-making.

* * *

The Treaty of Troyes, of 1420, made a clean break with the old tradition. Argument over the cession of lands was abandoned, and a settlement was sought by completely different means, by an attempt to divert the line of succession to the French throne to the English descendants of the French royal line. The treaty was the direct product of the quite exceptional circumstances following the murder of John the Fearless, and in any other conditions could not have stood any hope of being rendered acceptable to French opinion. Creation that it was of a particular moment and an unforeseeable outrage, its terms nevertheless bear testimony to Henry V's skill as a negotiator, and to his grasp of what it was essential to strive for: to make the terms legally watertight (as those of Brétigny had proved disastrously not to be), and to draft them in such a way as to render them acceptable to as wide a body of opinion in France as possible.[22]

The essential purpose of the Treaty of Troyes was to settle the succession to the French throne on Henry V, who should marry Catherine of France, and on their heirs, as legitimate successors to Charles VI. There were a number of difficulties to be overcome here, but two principal ones: the now established 'Salic Law' that the crown of France could not pass to a female or through the female line, and the existence, in the person of the Dauphin, of a legitimate son of Charles VI. The last was not really tackled in the treaty itself, but was

[22] For what follows, I am much indebted to the ideas of my former pupil, Miss Ruth Thomas of Somerville College, set out by her in a paper read to the Oxford undergraduate seminar on Henry V, several years ago.

dealt with outside it: the Dauphin had already been declared guilty of lese-majesty, which would render him incapable of succession, and this was confirmed by the sentence delivered at a formal *lit de justice* in 1421.[23] Great care was taken however to get round the other difficulty of the law of succession, in as satisfactory a way as was feasible. Charles VI's own authority, as King regnant of France, was invoked, first and foremost, to validate Henry's succession, which meant leaving him on his throne for his lifetime and dropping altogether from the treaty all references to the Plantagenet claim to the crown of France. So the treaty opened with the statement that King Charles, in consideration of the marriage of Henry to his daughter Catherine, had taken Henry to him as his son, and Henry had taken him and his Queen Isabella to him and would honour them as father and mother. It went on to explain that King Charles had agreed that on his death, 'the crown and kingdom of France with all its rights and appurtenances shall pass to and perpetually abide with the said Henry our son and his heirs'.[24] The formal terms further stressed the continuity of the succession by the title 'Heir of France', which Henry was to assume at once, and by the stipulation that in Charles's lifetime all official acts of regality should be in Charles's name, and under his seal. This continuity was later to become a staple element in English propaganda, deployed effectively in iconographic depictions of Henry VI showing his descent from the two royal houses of Valois and Plantagenet, which both carried the blood of St Louis in their veins.[25]

The legality of the treaty was not however to depend solely on the authority of Charles VI (who was mad; and in any case, had any king on his own authority the right to alienate his crown from the true line of succession as if it were private property?). Its terms expressly provided that they must be ratified by the estates of both realms, as they in fact were. In current juristic theory, the most secure

---

[23] Bonenfant, op. cit., pp. 128-9, 177-9; *Ordonnances des Rois de France*, xii (Paris, 1777), 273-7.

[24] *Foedera*, ix, 897.

[25] See J. W. McKenna, 'Henry VI and the Dual Monarchy: Aspects of Royal Political Propaganda, 1422-32', *Journal of the Warburg and Courtauld Institutes*, xxviii (1965), 145-62.

manner in which the fundamental laws of a country could be changed was by the incorporated authority of the whole people and their sovereign (personal or collective): was not that the manner in which the authority of the Roman Republic had been legally transferred to the emperors in antique days? Given that awesome precedent, this was a way of altering the fundamental law of succession that civilians could understand, and defend. In an effort to buttress still further the legally binding force of the treaty, oaths were sought individually from the lords, the communities, and personally from the subjects of the King of France to adhere to it (which rendered them perjured and traitors if they were found in breach of their oaths). Duke Philip's concern at Arras in 1435 to have his oath to the Treaty of Troyes declared invalid before completing his break with the English is witness to the importance and effectiveness of this device. He needed the authority of a papal legate to enable him to do it: the architects of Troyes had shown skill in their efforts to make its authority watertight.

By dropping the Plantagenet claim and presenting himself as the heir of Charles, married to his daughter, Henry made what was from an English point of view a very major concession, and at the same time made an important commencement on the task of making sure that the terms of Troyes were not only lawful but could be made acceptable to a sufficient body of Frenchmen. A series of further detailed clauses were drafted with this object clearly in mind. Henry was to be a French king, in due course, to his French subjects. The kingdoms and customs of France and England were to be kept entirely separate and independent, the union of their crowns to be purely personal. To all lords, cities, towns, universities, and churches of France Henry promised that he would maintain them in their ancient and due rights and privileges. He would maintain the authority of the *parlement* and would exercise his powers of government with the advice of the 'noble and wise men of France', and appoint to office with their counsel persons 'able and agreeable' to French custom—Frenchmen, that is to say. There would be no attempt at anglicization. Further, he promised that no taxes would be levied except in grave necessity, and that he would abide always by the laws and customs of France. He would not dismember the crown: Normandy, on his accession, would revert to its status of a dependency of the crown of France. All lands recovered from the adherents of the Dauphin (with whom Henry promised to make no peace without the assent of both the king and the new Duke of Burgundy) would revert immediately to the French crown. As an inducement to those Burgundians who had lost lands in Normandy in the course of the war so far, Henry promised to find them recompense from these conquered lands (he could not, naturally, disinherit now the Englishmen to whom their Norman fiefs had been granted). The Duke of Burgundy himself had secured his cut already, having been promised back at Christmas 1419 that wide lands in northern France would be added to his territories once peace was made.[26] To Frenchmen at large the greatest inducement of all, of course, was the prospect of peace, which, as the text laboured, was the principal object of the treaty—peace, free commercial intercourse with England, and hopes of returning prosperity for a harried kingdom and a desperate people. Peace was indeed the most important thing that Henry suggested he could deliver—and the most difficult of delivery.

Altogether, one may say of the terms of the Treaty of Troyes, given that it was the product of a quite sudden and unforeseen twist in the course of events, that they were remarkably skilfully drafted. By that I mean no more than I say. Whether they could really be made to stick depended on other factors; the reaction of great waverers, like the Duke of Brittany and the Count of Foix, neither of whom were parties to the agreements of May 1420; on the success of the English and Burgundians in pressing the war further against the discredited Armagnacs; on whether the inducements and assurances that the terms offered would prove sufficient to hold together at least the Burgundian party in France. In 1420-2, the key years when Henry was still alive and looked set fair to enter on his French inheritance, there were signs that might justify cautious optimism in these regards (though there were others too, whose implications

[26] *Foedera*, ix, 826.

were rather alarming). Henry's military advances were less rapid, but he continued to advance his conquests. At the time that he died, negotiations were well advanced which looked like bringing both the Duke of Brittany and the Count of Foix into the treaty. On the whole, the old Burgundian party in France accepted it. There were some notable hesitations and some defections: Louis d'Orange refused to take the oath to Troyes, as initially did the city of Tournai, and the powerful Count of Tanquarville went over to the Armagnacs. But in Paris Burgundian councillors and civil servants remained at their posts in the parlement and the *chambre des comptes*: there was no mass exodus from the university: and the chapter of Notre Dame, after a show of reluctance, accepted the situation. Such an observer as the 'Bourgeois de Paris' was not very enthusiastic for the new dispensation, but he thought the English were much preferable to the Armagnacs.[27] As things began to settle, men who had left their homes in Normandy and in the Paris basin, when the theatre of active hostilities seemed to be approaching their homelands, started to trickle back. Henry himself was personally highly regarded by many Frenchmen. Had he lived it seems just possible that he might have made the Troyes settlement durable—just possible, though for myself I cannot see it as very likely.

The real trouble with the Treaty of Troyes was that the Anglo-Burgundian alliance, which was the cornerstone of the whole settlement, was at root thoroughly unnatural. It had been precipitated by the act of naked assassination which ended John the Fearless's life at the bridge of Montereau. When in November 1419 the Burgundian council concluded that 'de deux maulx le moins pire est a eslire'[28] and that that meant allying with Henry, they were accepting the *realpolitik* implications of an emergency: they had no real long-term interest in a Plantagenet succession in France, even if diplomatic skill could present it as something less than that, as a kind of quasi-adoptive Valois succession. It would not gain their duke any influence in Paris. It bound the French Burgundians, who had prided themselves on their patriotism as Frenchmen, to the leader of a people who

[27] *Bourgeois*, p. 139.
[28] Bonenfant, op. cit., p. 218.

were traditional enemies of the French. Unless the Dauphin's support were to collapse totally and quickly, it would not bring peace. And if the Dauphin's support did not collapse quickly, the Burgundian French—the duke included—were bound to find that they had closer and more important national ties and associations with the lords and people of his party than they had with King Henry and his English captains. That is indeed what they did discover, or rather rediscover, after Henry was dead. Once they did so, it did not take long before experts began to look for legal loopholes in the Treaty of Troyes, which cumulatively would provide justification for its abrogation by the Burgundian French.[29]

However, it took the Burgundians fifteen years from 1420 to come round finally to that point. That in itself is witness to the skill with which the Treaty of Troyes had been drafted. Altogether its terms testify to the outstanding talent of King Henry in what I called at the beginning of this chapter the art of diplomacy. He was certainly a master of *realpolitik*, skilled in calculating the arithmetic of power, and a bold one. In 1419 he could without any difficulty have achieved a settlement on the Brétigny lines, but more generous; he preferred to go for the larger prize, because he saw he had a chance of getting it, and that if he got it, the problems of maintaining a Brétigny-type settlement, of defending English Gascony and English Normandy, would disappear. He would not need to fear the recovery of France because he would be King of France. In the detail of the settlement which brought him his prize, he showed that he fully appreciated the importance of the technical side of treaty-making, that arrangements must be made as far as possible juridically watertight, and must look presentable. A question must nevertheless remain with regard to his diplomatic talents, brilliant, knowledgeable, and hard-working as he undoubtedly was in this field. It is whether his skill was not at the tactical rather than the strategic level, in diplomacy if not in war. What is most open to criticism is his sense of the limits of the possible. The

[29] On the legal arguments that were finally presented in criticism of the treaty, at Arras in 1435, see J. G. Dickinson, *The Congress of Arras, 1435* (Oxford, 1955), pp. 66–75, 173–7; and J. Ferguson, *English Diplomacy, 1422–61* (Oxford, 1972), pp. 169–74.

murder of John the Fearless, and the great opportunity that it opened, saved him in 1419 from having to maintain his conquest with English resources that were almost certainly inadequate. Instead he obtained the triumph of being recognized as Heir of France; but the settlement embodying this triumph was intrinsically unstable. It did not cater sufficiently for the long-term interests of any substantial party, and was too much the product of temporary circumstance. He had high ambitions and great gifts; it is not quite so clear that he was the kind of man who could think through to the end where these were leading him.

X

Conclusion

G. L. HARRISS

The simple record of Henry V's achievement is sufficient to establish him as a great king. He inherited a contentious title and a kingdom recently afflicted by magnate revolt, subversive heresy, nationalist separatism, and social unrest. His father's authority had been eroded by his failure to cope with insolvency, local disorder, and parliamentary opposition, while satire and criticism of political and ecclesiastical institutions reflected a mood of widespread disillusionment. All this Henry V's reign reversed. He left to his infant son a secure throne, a united political class, an efficient administration, and a people orthodox in belief, with a new pride in their achievement and destiny. The reputation of English arms stood at its highest for centuries, and English influence in Europe was greater than at any time since the reign of Henry II. Even before he came to the throne Henry had embarked on this programme of recovery and renewal. He had masterminded the suppression of the Welsh revolt, restored order to royal finance, brought new drive and authority to the council, and started to win the confidence and co-operation of parliament. Calais and the sea had been made secure, and English troops had again demonstrated their worth in France. Expectations of the new king were thus set high, for men looked to a monarch not merely to rule them wisely and lead them bravely but to mediate God's favour to his people. Henry V approached this awesome task with dedication. He came to the throne more deeply experienced in the problems of English government than any previous king, and with a proclaimed and definite programme of 'good governance' to fulfil.

The failure of the two overt challenges to Henry V at the beginning of his reign, from Oldcastle's rising and the Earl of Cambridge's plot, showed that he had already captured the initiative with the promise of a new order. His own sincere piety and attested orthodoxy, and his demand for revitalized public worship and a clergy responive to lay needs, gave him a moral authority over the English church greater than any other post-conquest king. Papal authority was in abeyance, while Lollardy had been not merely defeated and rendered leaderless but discredited among the political nation. Similarly, although the plot to assassinate Henry in 1415 had deep roots in past feuds, it also confirmed that these had been finally laid to rest. The king's policy of reconciliation had drawn their sting. Henry had demonstrated his detachment from these old quarrels and offered a fresh start, in which the traditional interests of magnate families would be respected and they could earn fresh rewards by service to the crown. In both spheres Henry pointed the way from dissension and made the crown the focus of new hope and unity.

Swift justice meted out to rebels, coupled with a long-term policy of healing the breaches in political society, were likewise characteristic of Henry V's campaign to restore law and order. Lacking the coercive power to police and punish on a wide scale, the crown necessarily depended on the nobility and gentry not only to enforce the law but to respect it in their own quarrels. The king's action had to be exemplary, in personifying justice himself and in enforcing it on recalcitrant subjects—if need be, even the greatest. Thus it was the prompt despatch of the king's bench to the western midlands in 1414, to suppress disorder and maintenance by the nobility, that reasserted royal authority and affirmed the king's concern for law and order. Henry's reputation for justice became a byword, and its effect was preventative. Moreover, like the defeat of Lollardy and treachery, law enforcement helped to repair the social peace. To discipline law-breakers was merely the first step in requiring them to act with self-discipline in office or in arms. Henry's arbitration of quarrels among all grades of the nobility, like his calling them to service in the field, underlined the immediate and personal responsibility which they owed to the king. Their awareness of this was the key to

Henry's hold over the political nation.

A similar sense of direct answerability to the king was probably present in the royal administration, though it is less easy to document. Here the results are more evident than the measures which produced them. The speed with which the superior eyre of 1414 handled its work, the searching inquisitions into administrative efficiency on the crown's patrimonial estates, the estimating of revenue and expenditure, and the tight control maintained over exchequer assignment which prevented the collapse of exchequer credit under the strain of war, and finally—above and beyond this—the detailed planning on a vast scale which ensured the dispatch of three major expeditionary forces and the continued supply of *matériel* for a prolonged war of conquest across the Channel: all these are proof that the royal administration was working at a new tempo and with a degree of smoothness that was rare in the medieval period. Both on the royal estates and in the national administration any king drew on long traditions of expertise and well-tried routines, but Henry V continuously scrutinized and tightened up the machinery, replaced and chose officials, and communicated a new sense of urgency and driving purpose. His diplomats, too, worked under pressure, to anticipate the changing contingencies of Henry's diplomacy and secure the permanence of the settlement which his military operations had gained.

It was in parliament that this new-found harmony in political society, and the king's insistence on justice, order, and economical administration, bore fruit in a renewed spirit of co-operation. The legacy of mistrust was not dispelled overnight, and confidence in the king had to be carefully fostered by the servants of the crown in both houses. Soon the quickened pace of parliamentary proceedings and the sense of participation in an unfolding programme of good government, together with the king's instinct for tactical concessions which yet left the substance of royal policies and plans intact, ensured that throughout virtually every parliament royal policy was endorsed with the support of the realm. That was most strikingly manifested in the readiness of the Commons to grant taxation at an unprecedented rate for the five years of war, without mistrust, recrimination, or complaint, or even such traditional safeguards as war treasurers. A half century of friction between king and parliament came to an end, and Henry's relations with parliament mirrored very closely his standing in the realm.

Yet though his subjects desired the establishment of good government as an end in itself, for Henry V it formed the prologue to the renewal of war in France, for which he already began to make preparations in 1414. Must we, then, set against the record of a king devoted to his subjects' welfare the picture of an adventurer who wasted their wealth on his unrealistic ambitions? For both Henry V and his subjects such a dichotomy would have been largely incomprehensible. The vindication of the crown's traditional rights in France was the logical complement to the restoration of true kingship in England. In so amply fulfilling his subjects' expectations of kingship at home Henry bound them to support his vision of kingship in France. For Henry V is better seen as a visionary than as an adventurer, and one of some originality. In 1411 and 1412 the divisions of the French nobility into warring factions had presented opportunities for adventure and profit, while on neither occasion had English military intervention yielded effective recognition of the English crown's claims. Nevertheless from the first Henry V saw war as an instrument of policy rather than profit. He went beyond the Treaty of Brétigny, not merely in reviving the French title, but in demanding all the territories over which, since the Norman conquest, the kings of England had held sway. The sweeping historical perspective, the tireless insistence on the recovery of his legitimate inheritance, and the unreadiness at any point to renounce unequivocally his claims to the French throne in exchange for territories suggest that Henry saw his role in France as the extension of that in England. The feuds of Burgundy and Orléans which opened the door attested a fundamental disorder in the French body politic which only the restoration of true kingship could cure. It was easy to believe that England and its king had been chosen not merely to punish but to redeem France, and restore good government there as in England.

There are sufficient indications that this attitude informed Henry's operations in Normandy. He insistently proclaimed that he came to recover his inheritance, not to despoil it, and the keynote of his government was to be the restoration of traditional rights and institutions (including the Norman estates), the conciliation of all native Normans who would accept his rule, and the re-establishment of order, justice, trade, and a sound coinage. The same themes are embodied in the Treaty of Troyes, where Henry is both true heir and rejuvenator of the French monarchy, not its conqueror, and where the validation of the traditional rights of all subjects is underwritten by their individual and communal assent to the treaty. French and English are guaranteed equality at law and perpetual peace through a common kingship. We can be fairly certain that the concept of the dual monarchy was Henry's own, though when it was conceived we do not know. It had certainly been formulated before the unforeseeable murder of John the Fearless put the crown within his grasp, for whereas the parties of both the perpetrators and victims appeared stunned and irresolute in the aftermath of the crime, Henry immediately grasped the logic of its consequences which he remorselessly pressed until he had secured his ends.

But the task he set himself in France was far more difficult and lengthy than that in England. He had exploited and deepened the divisions which he now had to heal; neither did he possess the intuitive understanding of his new subjects, or their natural loyalty, which underlay his leadership of the English nation. If he commanded the respect of some Frenchmen and met their longing for peace, others would always hate and repudiate him as a usurper. To judge whether his vision was practicable is a difficult and complex matter and would divert us from our theme. One thing is clear. The principal obstacle to Henry V's acceptance as King of France was the existence of the Dauphin. His removal by death, capture, papal verdict of disinheritance, or negotiation—and all these were possibilities—would have decapitated the opposition and created a wholly different situation. The Treaty of Troyes thus marked a half-way stage; it was the blueprint for a different order, not one that had been achieved.

It is tempting to say that its fulfilment was impossible, except that the achievement of 1420 would itself have been reckoned so in 1415. Nor can we presume to measure as shrewdly or realistically as Henry himself the obstacles and opportunities which he ceaselessly turned over in his mind.

Such, in brief, was Henry V's achievement as King; what does it tell us of his qualities as a ruler, and of the requirements of late medieval kingship? Every aspect of his rule attested his great mental and physical energy. As we follow him presiding over the proceedings of the 1414 eyre or those of successive parliaments, abbreviating his wedding celebrations to press the siege of Sens, and revitalizing English government in his four-month visit in 1421, we are tempted to say that the pace he set was killing. There is no indication of relaxation, in hunting, tournament, or courtly diversions. The note of urgency is unmistakeable, as if he were haunted by the disparity between the size of his ambitions and the time available to accomplish them. Certainly he was conscious of the limits of his resources, and his mind was constantly busy with how these could be used to best advantage. It was indicative of this that, to offset the cost of the enlarged navy, the royal ships were for the first time used for trading. To the collection and employment of all forms of revenue he gave ceaseless attention; his distribution of honours and rewards was carefully regulated in terms of the service yielded; ceremonial served political ends, and prayer itself was measured by its effectiveness. Nor was the king's initiative confined to administration. He yearned for practical knowledge and commissioned books on war and kingship, on Normandy and Scotland, setting a fashion which his nobility followed. He was constantly concerned with the meaningfulness of liturgy and attempted to reorder the daily life of the Benedictines. This ubiquitous insistence on efficiency made him a rigid disciplinarian, requiring from both his civil and military officers a punctilious performance of their duties. The discipline which curtailed plunder on the march to Agincourt, enforced the slaughter of the prisoners in the battle, and held the army together during winter sieges had its counterpart in his government of the duchy of Lancaster and the swift punishment of corrupt or oppressive officials like Thomas Barnby.

His mind was not only given to these daily concerns. It is evident that he found time to think and reflect. We have precious evidence of his mental processes in the memorandum of 1418 which wrestled with the question of alliance with the Dauphin and its consequences. Even though it was a fairly remote possibility, all aspects were probed. Equally searching consideration must have been given to the more serious negotiations at Meulan and those that led up to the Treaty of Troyes. It was foresight and the anticipation of problems that enabled Henry to seize the initiative in diplomacy as in dealing with domestic discord. Both his nervous energy and his political insight were nourished by a sense of mission, though since he viewed himself as an instrument of divine will, he neither displayed nor took pride in his victories. Undoubtedly he drew on deep spiritual resources, but his piety took a puritanical rather than a mystical form.

Yet a king's own drive and energy could achieve little without the backing of his subjects. To win this a ruler had to show himself responsive to their particular interests, for it was in respecting individual rights, eschewing arbitrariness and favouritism, and exercising royal power beneficially that he commanded confidence. In general Henry's reputation stood high, though on occasion he did press his advantage unduly. Those who took liberties with him, or sought to upstage him, felt the full weight of royal displeasure; but he was not vindictive and tempered justice with mercy, permitting criminals, corrupt officials, and even the overweening Beaufort to redeem themselves by service. On a wider scale this reconciliation of individuals was subsumed in the sense of identity of the king and his realm. Henry believed that the nation, as well as he himself, had a mission, and he took sober pride in its greatness. The remnant at Agincourt were surrogates for all Englishmen; their victory was England's victory. Henry sought to convey this through the propaganda of the written word, the recited poem, and the symbolic entries into London in 1415 and 1421. At the commencement of the reign his first proclamation had spoken of the banners of peace stilling the whirlwinds of discord, and his solemn reinterment of Richard II at Westminster signalled his hope for reconciliation and unity. This knitting together of the political nation under the crown and calling it to a high destiny was at the root of Henry's achievements.

Nevertheless the obsessive character of his kingship had great dangers. He strained every resource, human and material, driving his kingdom and his subjects to the limit. A ruler can only do that safely and effectively while his subjects share his vision and objectives; otherwise he becomes an isolated and embittered figure, believing himself betrayed by his subjects and perceived by them as a threat to their welfare. John, Edward I, and Richard II were all, in different ways, victims of the delusion that the pursuit of royal power and the rights of the crown constituted an imperative which brooked no refusal or limitation. Although at the time of his death Henry V was far from such a position, there were signs that the war had produced exhaustion and reaction, and that his own ambitions had outrun those of his subjects. The tensions in the parliaments of 1420 and 1421, the accumulating debts, harsher financial expedients, and dwindling military reserves were all indicative of this. One can only speculate about how Henry would have responded to growing detachment and resentment in England, and whether the demands of his new role would have accentuated the imperiousness and harshness that in right measure became majesty, but in excess might beget tyranny. For Henry had always been determined to have his own way, nor was he hesitant about twisting the arms of those whom he saw as his tools: Emperor Sigismund, Queen Isabella, the Duke of Bourbon, and the Duke of Brittany. Indeed so convinced was he of his own purposes that he was inclined to underrate opposition and to overlook that others would seek to use him for their own ends. More than once he apparently expected or assumed that John the Fearless would acknowledge his title; he probably expected Martin V to prove amenable to English interests; and there are signs that he was unprepared for the extent of Norman and French resistance and reluctance to accept his rule. If he had been faced with coherent opposition in England to the war he might have become, like Edward I, intransigent and embattled.

*   *   *

As King of England Henry fulfilled, to near perfection, a traditional role. He had no new concept of kingship and made no radical innovations in government or administration. His importance here lies in showing that traditional kingship and the perfected system of late medieval government could work effectively to give the realm order, economy, unity, and respect for the crown. The principal charge against Henry V is that in France he attempted the impossible: that his ambitions led to unjustifiable aggrandizement which was beyond English resources to sustain and which would, ultimately, face England with the crisis of its failure. That was not how Henry saw it. For his ambitions in France were inspired by a new vision and new methods. He saw the vindication of his rights as a sacred duty, not an opportunity for chivalric prowess or profitable freebooting. Therefore his systematic conquest and occupation of Normandy demanded a new type of warfare, a new standard of discipline, new military organization, and eventually a new concept of the subordination of military to civil rule. It demanded a policy of conciliation of native sentiment by word and deed and the imposition of obligations on English soldiers and colonizers. In five short years from 1417 to 1422 Henry set himself to educate the English in a new European role and by his death, though his schemes were half complete, those with him in France had come to understand his objectives. Bedford and others strove, to their more limited abilities, to continue his policies. In England there was less comprehension and less sympathy for Henry's aims. Normandy was valued as a colony, but the Treaty of Troyes was suspect. But, as Henry had grasped after the failure of the Meulan negotiations in 1419, only the possession of the crown itself could guarantee the safety of Normandy; and the crown could only be securely held by one whom the French people accepted as King in the same measure as Englishmen did. That, too, was the only way in which the age-old enmity of the two peoples could be brought to an end. Kingship alone could bring reconciliation out of hate, unity out of conflict, justice out of wrongdoing, legitimacy out of usurpation; it alone could mediate God's will for both nations. That was Henry's vision, and it was neither unworthy nor wholly impossible. Given the years, energy, and luck, he might have reshaped the development of both nations just as, in brief space, he had restored the fortunes of England. In the event it was the very grandeur of his aims which proved fatal for Lancastrian kingship and for the good governance which had become its justification.

Further Reading

Full references to most of the following are to be found in the list of Abbreviations.

The best short surveys of the reign are E. F. Jacob's *Henry V and the Invasion of France* (1947) and chapters iv and v in *The Fifteenth Century* (Oxford History of England, 1961). A more detailed narrative is that of J. H. Wylie and W. T. Waugh, *The Reign of Henry the Fifth*, 3 vols. (1914–29). Good character studies of Henry V have been made by C. T. Allmand, *Henry V* (Historical Association, 1968) and K. B. McFarlane, *Lancastrian Kings and Lollard Knights* (1972). Contemporaries' views of the king can be gained from the *Gesta Henrici Quinti*, ed. F. Taylor and J. S. Roskell (1975) and from the *First English Life of King Henry the Fifth*, ed. C. L. Kingsford (1911). Henry's military campaigns are discussed in K. Fowler, ed., *The Hundred Years War* (1971), A. H. Burne, *The Agincourt War* (1956), and R. A. Newhall, *The Conquest of Normandy* (1924), and his policy in Normandy by C. T. Allmand, *Lancastrian Normandy* (1983). Diplomatic relations figure in *John the Fearless* by R. Vaughan (1966) and in the detailed study by P. Bonenfant, *Du meutre de Montereau au traité de Troyes* (1958). Lollardy and Oldcastle's rising are treated by K. B. McFarlane in *John Wyclif and the Beginnings of English Nonconformity* (1952), while E. F. Jacob's *Archbishop Henry Chichele* (1967) presents one of Henry V's leading churchmen and two articles on Henry Beaufort in K. B. McFarlane, *England in the Fifteenth Century* (1981) another. The parliaments of Henry V's reign are reviewed chronologically in J. S. Roskell, *The Commons and their Speakers in English Parliaments* (1965) and in their late medieval context by A. L. Brown in *The English Parliament in the Middle Ages*, ed. R. G. Davies and J. H. Denton (1981). A survey of exchequer finance in the period has been made by A. Steel, *The Receipt of the Exchequer* (1954) and a detailed examination of war finance by R. A. Newhall, 'The War Finances of Henry V and the Duke of Bedford', *EHR*, xxxvi (1921). Crime and disorder is discussed by J. G. Bellamy, *Crime and Public Order in England in the Later Middle Ages* (1972), and a useful introduction to the legal system in A. Harding, *The Law Courts of Medieval England* (1973). The major study of the late medieval nobility is by K. B. McFarlane, *The Nobility of Later Medieval England* (1973) and the literature of the age is surveyed by V. J. Scattergood, *Politics and Poetry in the Fifteenth Century* (1971).

Index